DAY HIKES IN

Grand Teton

NATIONAL PARK

89 GREAT HIKES

Robert Stone

5th EDITION

Day Hike Books, Inc.

RED LODGE, MONTANA

Published by Day Hike Books, Inc.
P.O. Box 865 · Red Lodge, Montana 59068
www.dayhikebooks.com

Distributed by The Globe Pequot Press
246 Goose Lane · P.O. Box 480
Guilford, CT 06437-0480
800-243-0495 (direct order) · 800-820-2329 (fax order)
www.globe-pequot.com

Cover photograph by Derek DiLuzio
Back cover photograph by John Slaughter
Layout/maps by Paula Doherty

The author has made every attempt to provide accurate information in this book. However, trail routes and features may change— please use common sense and forethought, and be mindful of your own capabilities. Let this book guide you, but be aware that each hiker assumes responsibility for their own safety. The author and publisher do not assume any responsibility for loss, damage, or injury caused through the use of this book.

Library of Congress Control Number: 2012954094

Cover photo:
The Tetons at sunset from Schwabacher's Landing, Hike 59

Back cover photo:
At the head of Death Canyon, approaching
the Death Canyon Shelf, Hike 8

Table of Contents

Grand Tetons National Park overview 10

MAP OF THE HIKES. 12

THE HIKES

Moose Junction area

PHELPS LAKE TO JACKSON LAKE MAP (Hikes 1—30). 14

1. Blacktail Butte
   Southeast Access from Gros Ventre Road. 16

2. Blacktail Butte
   North Access from Highway 89. 19

3. Menor's Ferry • Noble Cabin. 22

4. Sawmill Ponds 24

Phelps Lake area:
Death Canyon Trailhead

PHELPS LAKE AREA MAP: LOWER GRAND TETON (Hikes 5—15) 26

5. Phelps Lake Overlook to Phelps Lake. 28

6. Death Canyon to Patrol Cabin. 31

7. Death Canyon to Static Peak Divide 34

8. Death Canyon to Fox Creek Pass 37

9. Open Canyon to the Open Canyon Creek Bridge. 41

10. Open Canyon to Mount Hunt Divide 44

Phelps Lake area:
Laurance S. Rockefeller Preserve

11. Lake Creek—Woodland Loop. 48

12. Phelps Lake Loop 51

13. Lake Creek—Aspen Ridge Loop. 54

14. Woodland—Boulder Ridge Loop. 57

15. Granite Canyon Trail: Granite Canyon Trailhead 60

Bradley and Taggart Lakes
Lupine Meadows

16. Taggart Lake Loop: Taggart Lake Trailhead. 64

17. Taggart and Bradley Lakes Loop: Taggart Lake Trailhead 66

18. Cottonwood Creek. 68

19. Surprise and Amphitheater Lakes
    Lupine Meadows Trailhead. 70

20. Garnet Canyon to Spalding Falls
    Lupine Meadows Trailhead. 73

Jenny Lake:
South Jenny Lake Trailhead

JENNY LAKE · LEIGH LAKE MAP:
CENTRAL GRAND TETON (Hikes 21—30) 76

21. Jenny Lake Loop from South Jenny Lake Trailhead 78

22. Hidden Falls and Inspiration Point
    South Jenny Lake Trailhead to Cascade Canyon 81

23. Cascade Canyon to the Canyon Fork 84

24. South Fork Cascade Canyon to Hurricane Pass 88

25. North Fork Cascade Canyon to Lake Solitude 92

26. Moose Ponds 96

String Lake · Leigh Lake

27. String Lake Loop: String Lake Trailhead. .98

28. Leigh Lake to Bearpaw Lake: Leigh Lake Trailhead 100

29. Paintbrush Canyon Trail to Holly Lake: Leigh Lake Trailhead. . .102

30. Paintbrush Canyon Trail to Paintbrush Divide
    Leigh Lake Trailhead 106

Lower Jackson Lake area:
Jackson Lake Lodge · Colter Bay

LOWER JACKSON LAKE MAP (Hikes 31—47) 108

31. Snake River Fisherman's Trail 110

32. South Landing: Jackson Lake 112

33. Signal Mountain: Jackson Point Overlook 114

34. Oxbow Bend: Snake River 117

35. Emma Matilda Lake 119

36. Two Ocean Lake 123

37. Pacific Creek Trail 124

38. Christian Pond Trail: Jackson Lake Lodge 128

39. Lookout Rock: Jackson Lake Lodge 130

40. Grand View Point: Jackson Lake Lodge area 132

41. Lunch Tree Hill Loop: Jackson Lake Lodge 134

42. Willow Flats to Second Creek: Jackson Lake Lodge 136

43. Willow Flats Loop: Colter Bay · Jackson Lake 138

44. Lakeshore Trail at Colter Bay: Colter Bay · Jackson Lake 140

45. Swan Lake and Heron Pond: Colter Bay · Jackson Lake 142

46. Hermitage Point: Colter Bay · Jackson Lake 144

47. Sargents Bay: Jackson Lake 146

John D. Rockefeller Jr. Memorial Parkway
Flagg Ranch area

ROCKEFELLER JR. MEMORIAL PARKWAY MAP (Hikes 48—56) 148

48. Flagg Canyon Trail along the Snake River 150

49. Polecate Creek Loop from Flagg Ranch 152

50. Huckleberry Hot Springs 154

51. Glade Creek Trail 156

52. South Boundary Lake from the east
    South Boundary Trail from Yellowstone South Entrance 158

53. South Boundary Lake from the west
    South Boundary Trail from Grassy Lake 161

54. Buela Lake 164

55. Mountain Ash Creek—Cascade Creek Loop 166

56. Cascade Creek Trail to Terraced Falls 169

Moran Junction to Moose Junction
East side of Jackson Hole

57. Cunningham Cabin 173

58. Toppings Lakes Trail 174

59. Schwabacher's Landing 177

60. Shadow Mountain Trail to Antelope Peak 179

Gros Ventre Range

61. Lower Slide Lake: Gros Ventre Slide Interpretive Trail 182

62. Horsetail Creek Trail: Gros Ventre Wilderness 184

63. Grizzly Lake: Gros Ventre Wilderness .187

64. Lower Sheep Creek Canyon to Curtis Canyon Viewpoint . . . 190

65. Curtis Canyon Trail from Curtis Canyon Viewpoint 193

66. Goodwin Lake: Gros Ventre Wilderness 195

67. Upper Sheep Creek Canyon 198

Around the town of Jackson
Snow King Mountain • Gros Ventre Range

Snow King Trail Network map (Hikes 68—73) 200

68. Cache Creek Canyon Loop: Cache Creek Trailhead 202

69. Woods Canyon: Cache Creek Trailhead 205

70. Hagen Loop: Cache Creek Trailhead 207

71. Cache Creek Canyon to Snow King Summit
Cache Creek Trailhead 209

72. Wilson Canyon to Five-Way Meadow 212

73. Game Creek Loop 215

74. South Park 218

South of Jackson
Bridger Tetons to Gros Ventre Range

75. Dog Creek Trail 220

76. Granite Falls and Hot Springs 222

Teton Village • Jackson Hole Ski Resort

JACKSON HOLE SKI AREA MAP (Hikes 77—78) .224

77. Rock Springs Loop—Rendezvous Mountain 226

78. Rendezvous Mountain—Granite Canyon Loop 228

West of Jackson:
Jackson to Victor, Idaho • Teton Pass Trail Network

79. Snake River Northeast Dike 232

TETON PASS TRAIL NETWORK MAP (Hikes 80—88) 234

80. Phillips Canyon Trail to Phillips Pass 236

81. Big Rocks—Lower Black Canyon Loop 239

82. Trail Creek to Crater Lake Loop
    Crater Trail—Teton Pass Trail (Old Pass Road) 241

83. Trail Creek to Teton Pass Loop
    Crater Trail—History Trail—Teton Pass Trail (Old Pass Road) . . .244

84. Black Canyon Loop
    Crater—History—Pass Ridge—Black Canyon Trails 248

85. Pass Ridge Trail to Mount Elly Overlook .252

86. Phillips Ridge 254

87. Phillips Pass Trail to Ski Lake 256

88. Coal Creek Trail 258

89. Moose Creek Trail to Moose Meadows
    Jedediah Smith Wilderness 260

Companion Guides 266

Index 267

Grand Teton National Park

Grand Teton National Park is one of the most beautiful parks in the Rocky Mountains. The craggy Teton peaks reach as high as 13,770 feet, forming a bony ridge through Wyoming along the Continental Divide. Fronting the Teton Range lies the twisting and curving Snake River, winding its way down the Jackson Hole valley. The reflections of the Tetons gently ripple across the river's serene water.

The 96,000-acre Grand Teton National Park lies just south of Yellowstone National Park, their borders connected by the John D. Rockefeller Jr. Memorial Parkway. The Snake River's headwaters originate in Yellowstone, then the river runs the length of Grand Teton Park. En route, the river forms the 25,000-acre Jackson Lake. Tributaries of the Snake cascade down the Teton Range and form a string of large morainal lakes along the front range. The river continues down the expansive Jackson Hole valley and past the town of Jackson. The Snake River watershed and the valley create a natural corridor teeming with wildlife.

Grand Teton National Park was officially established in 1929. Prior to this, however, people occupied the area for 12,000 years. Native American tribes, including the Blackfeet, Crow, Gros Ventre, and Shoshone, used this high valley for habitation and hunting during the warmer seasons. Mountain men, trappers, and settlers followed in the 1800s. Through the establishment of the park, the Teton Range received protection from development and overuse of its resources. Parts of the Jackson Hole area were added in 1950.

Jackson Hole is a 60-mile-long valley running north and south along the Teton Range. This 10-mile-wide valley runs through Grand Teton National Park and south past the town of Jackson. The valley is surrounded by rugged mountain ranges and forested wilderness areas.

The majestic Teton Range lies to the west of Jackson Hole. This range of jagged, snowcapped mountains boasts 30 peaks rising above 11,000 feet, including ten peaks above 12,000 feet. The three peaks of Grand Teton, Teewinot, and Mount Owen—known collectively as the Cathedral Group—are the centerpiece of the park. These peaks were first called "Les Trois Tetons" by French Canadian trappers in the early 1800s. (Ask a French-speaking person the literal translation.) The Teton peaks rise 3,000 to 7,000 feet from the valley floor to a high of 13,770 feet at the summit of Grand Teton.

Day Hikes In Grand Teton National Park includes a thorough cross-section of 89 day hikes throughout this park and around its perimeter. The hikes are located along the meandering Snake River and its tributaries, Jackson Lake's shoreline, up into the valleys and canyons of the Teton Range, and across the peaks straddling the Continental Divide. The trails have been chosen for their scenery, variety, and ability to be hiked within a day. All levels of hiking experience are accommodated, with hikes ranging from easy lakeshore paths to rugged canyon hikes that gain several thousand feet in elevation. Highlights include panoramic vistas, glacier-carved canyons, tumbling creeks and waterfalls, several large lakes, old-growth forests, meadows, hot springs, historical sites, prime wildlife habitats, North America's largest landslide, and two hikes atop the Jackson Hole Ski Resort.

A quick glance at the hikes' summaries will allow you to choose a hike that is appropriate to your ability and desire. An overall map on the next page identifies the locations of the hikes. Several other regional maps, as well as maps for each hike, provide the essential details. Many commercial maps are available for further hiking. Suggestions are listed with each hike.

Even though these trails are described as day hikes, many of the trails involve serious backcountry hiking. Reference the hiking statistics listed at the top of each page for an approximation of difficulty, and match the hikes to your ability. Hiking times are calculated for continuous hiking. Allow extra time for exploration. Feel free to hike farther than these day hike suggestions, but be sure to carry additional trail and topographic maps. Use good judgement about your capabilities, and be prepared with adequate clothing and supplies.

Because many of the hikes are located in high altitude terrain, be aware that the increased elevation will affect your stamina. Weather conditions undoubtedly change throughout the day and seasons. It is imperative to wear warm, layered clothing. Snacks, water, and a basic first aid kit are a must. Both black and grizzly bears inhabit the region, so wear a bear bell and hike in a group whenever possible. Ranger stations—located throughout the park— have the latest information on weather, trail conditions, and bear activity. Some preparation and forethought will help ensure a safe, enjoyable, and memorable hike.

Hiking in and around this national park will give you a deep appreciation of the area's beauty. You are sure to take home great memories of your hikes in the shadows of the Tetons and around Jackson Hole.

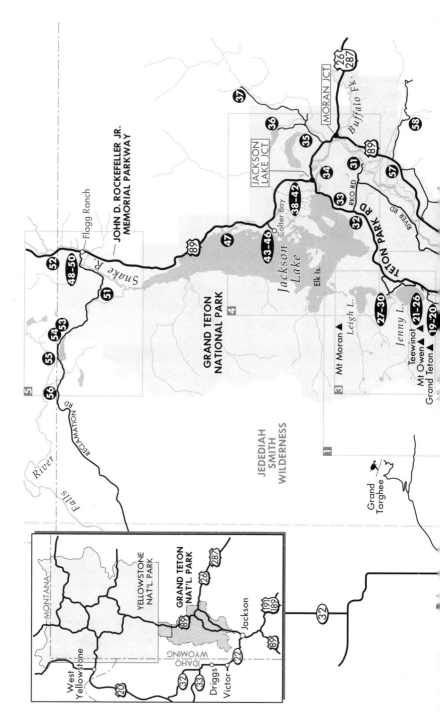

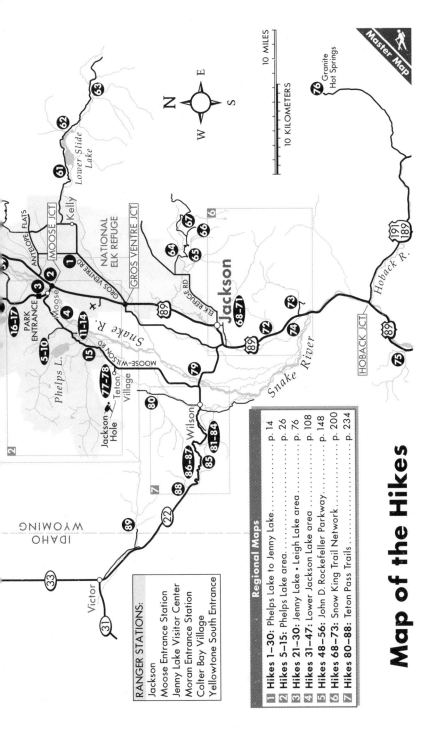

Master Map

10 MILES

10 KILOMETERS

Granite
Hot Springs

Lower Slide
Lake

MOOSE JCT

Kelly

NATIONAL
ELK REFUGE

GROS VENTRE JCT

Jackson

PARK
ENTRANCE

Moose

Snake R.

Phelps L.

MOOSE-WILSON RD

Teton
Village

Jackson
Hole

Wilson

Snake River

Hoback R.

HOBACK JCT

IDAHO
WYOMING

Victor

RANGER STATIONS:

Jackson
Moose Entrance Station
Jenny Lake Visitor Center
Moran Entrance Station
Colter Bay Village
Yellowtone South Entrance

Regional Maps

1 **Hikes 1–30:** Phelps Lake to Jenny Lake .... p. 14
2 **Hikes 5–15:** Phelps Lake area .... p. 26
3 **Hikes 21–30:** Jenny Lake • Leigh Lake area .... p. 76
4 **Hikes 31–47:** Lower Jackson Lake area .... p. 108
5 **Hikes 48–56:** John D. Rockefeller Parkway .... p. 148
6 **Hikes 68–73:** Snow King Trail Network .... p. 200
7 **Hikes 80–88:** Teton Pass Trails .... p. 234

Map of the Hikes

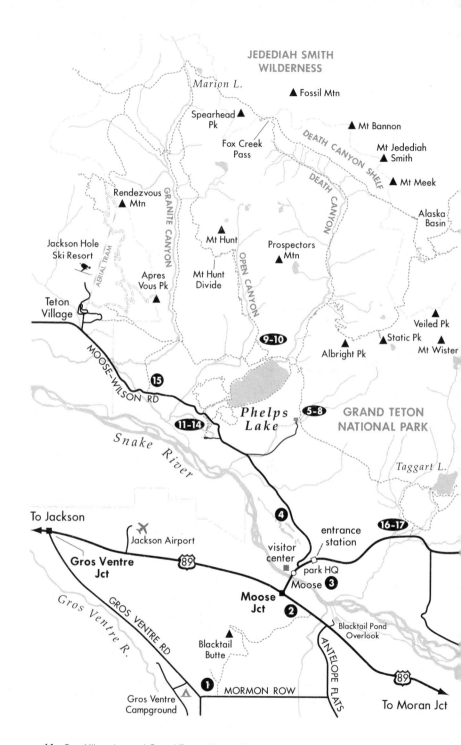

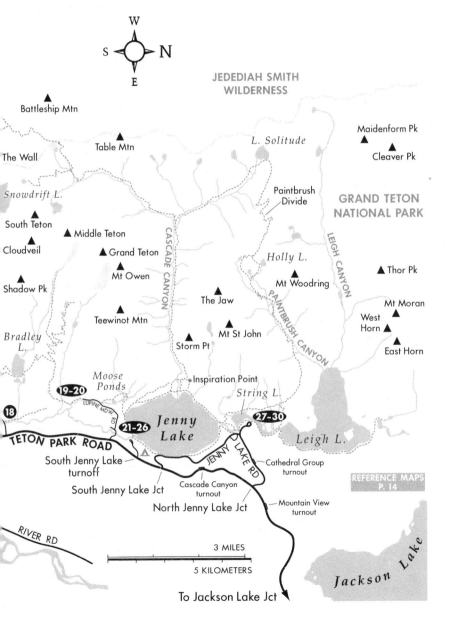

Phelps Lake to Jackson Lake
CENTRAL GRAND TETON

W
S ✦ N
E

JEDEDIAH SMITH
WILDERNESS

▲ Battleship Mtn

Maidenform Pk
▲

▲ Table Mtn

L. *Solitude*

Cleaver Pk
▲

The Wall

Paintbrush
Divide

GRAND TETON
NATIONAL PARK

Snowdrift L.

▲ South Teton

▲ Middle Teton

CASCADE CANYON

LEIGH CANYON

Holly L.

▲ Thor Pk

▲ Cloudveil

▲ Grand Teton
▲ Mt Owen

▲ Mt Woodring

▲ Shadow Pk

▲ The Jaw

PAINTBRUSH CANYON

Mt Moran
▲

West
Horn ▲

▲ Teewinot Mtn

▲ Mt St John

East Horn
▲

*Bradley
L.*

▲ Storm Pt

*Moose
Ponds*

• Inspiration Point

String L.

19-20

27-30

18

LUPINE MDW RD

21-26

*Jenny
Lake*

Leigh L.

TETON PARK ROAD

South Jenny Lake
turnoff

JENNY LAKE RD

Cathedral Group
turnout

South Jenny Lake Jct

Cascade Canyon
turnout

North Jenny Lake Jct

Mountain View
turnout

REFERENCE MAPS
P. 14

RIVER RD

3 MILES

5 KILOMETERS

To Jackson Lake Jct ↘

Jackson Lake

1. Blacktail Butte—Southeast Access
from GROS VENTRE ROAD

Hiking distance: 5.6 miles round trip
Hiking time: 3 hours
Configuration: out-and-back
Elevation gain: 1,100 feet
Difficulty: moderate
Exposure: mostly exposed hillside with shaded pockets
Dogs: not allowed
Maps: U.S.G.S. Gros Ventre Junction and Moose
National Geographic Trails Illustrated: Grand Teton Nat'l. Park

Blacktail Butte is an imposing landmass that rises up from Antelope Flats near the middle of the Jackson Hole valley just east of Moose Junction. The 7,688-foot isolated butte is easily visible after driving a few miles north of Jackson on Highway 89. The butte rises 1,100 feet from the valley floor, extending approximately three miles long and two miles across. Glaciers moving through the valley originally sculpted the oval-shaped form from Madison limestone.

Blacktail Butte has trailheads at both the north end (Hike 2) and the southeast side near Gros Ventre Road—this hike. Both trails connect at the summit. This route from the south climbs up the butte through its more exposed side through sagebrush and wildflowers, passing stunning rock outcrops, where rock climbers are known to scale up the massive walls. From atop the butte are panoramic views that stretch for miles across the park. Herds of grazing bison and elk may be seen moving across the valley to and from their winter feeding grounds in the National Elk Refuge to the southeast.

The paths from both trailheads connect at the summit. Hikes 1 and 2 can be combined for a 4.8-mile, one-way shuttle hike.

To the trailhead

From the town square in downtown Jackson, drive 7 miles north on Highway 89 to the posted Gros Ventre Junction. Turn right on Gros Ventre Road, and continue 5 miles to Mormon Row, a wide, unsigned road on the left. The road is located 0.4 miles past the

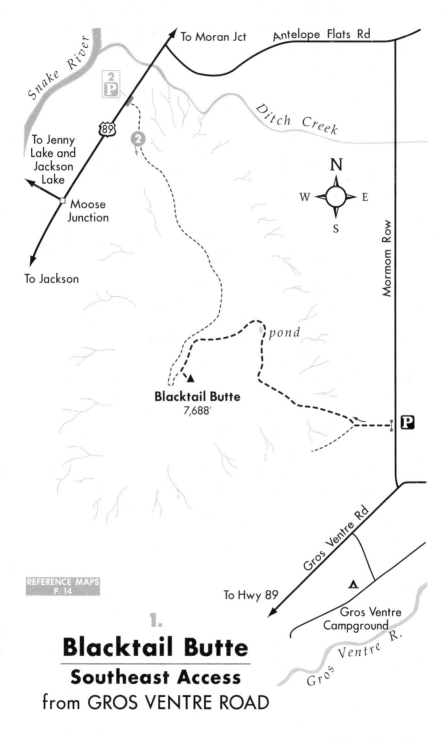

To Moran Jct

Antelope Flats Rd

Snake River

Ditch Creek

P 2

89

To Jenny
Lake and
Jackson
Lake

N

W—E

S

Moose
Junction

Mormom Row

To Jackson

pond

Blacktail Butte
7,688'

P

Gros Ventre Rd

To Hwy 89

Gros Ventre
Campground

Gros Ventre R.

1.

Blacktail Butte

Southeast Access

from GROS VENTRE ROAD

Gros Ventre Campground. Turn left and drive 0.4 miles on the unpaved road to the metal gate on the left. Park off road without blocking the gate.

From Moose Junction, the Gros Ventre Junction is 5.5 miles south on Highway 89.

The hike

Walk west on the vehicle-restricted dirt road, heading across the sage-covered flat to the base of Blacktail Butte. Climb a small rise dotted with aspens. Just before reaching the top of the slope, a narrow footpath veers off to the right. Take this path and steeply climb the 500-foot ridge of the barren, east-facing slope. At the ridgetop are sweeping vistas from the Jackson Hole valley to the town of Jackson. Traverse the rolling ridge between the forested north slope and the sage-covered south slope. Cross a saddle and curve to the right, passing through a small pocket of fir trees. Continue climbing on the open slope, traversing the hillside to a saddle at the head of the draw. Walk through a meadow with a round, crater-shaped pond, then wind through Douglas fir and lodgepole pine groves while looping around to the left. Ascend the open slope as the trail fades. Just before reaching the top of the knoll, an unsigned path bears left. Take this path a short distance to a ridge with a spur trail on the left. Head up this path 25 yards to the 7,688-foot summit. This is the turn-around spot. After enjoying the views, return on the same trail.

This hike can be combined with Hike 2 for a 4.8-mile, one-way shuttle hike. ▦

2. Blacktail Butte—North Access
from HIGHWAY 89

Hiking distance: 4 miles round trip
Hiking time: 2.5 hours
Configuration: out-and-back
Elevation gain: 1,100 feet
Difficulty: moderate
Exposure: a mix of exposed hillside and forest pockets
Dogs: not allowed
Maps: U.S.G.S. Moose

map
page 21

Blacktail Butte is a large, isolated land form rising 1,100 feet from the Jackson Hole valley floor. The 7,688-foot butte lies just to the east of the Moose entrance station. From the summit are amazing 360-degree views. To the north and west are wide vistas across the expansive valley to the Teton Range. To the south and east, the views span across the National Elk Refuge to the Gros Ventre Range. In contrast to the more populated pullouts along the main park roads, the hike offers a quiet view of the beautiful scenery.

The summit of Blacktail Butte can be accessed from two trailheads. This hike begins from the north end by Moose Junction. The trail steadily gains elevation up the partially forested, northwest slope of the butte, wooded with lodgepole pine, Douglas fir, Engelmann spruce, and a few aspens. From atop the butte are sweeping vistas of the surrounding landscape. Much of the wide Jackson Hole valley is visible, as well as great views of the Tetons and the Snake River meandering through the valley.

The paths from both trailheads—Hikes 1 and 2—connect at the summit. The hikes can be combined for a 4.8-mile, one-way shuttle.

To the trailhead

From the intersection of Highway 89 and Teton Park Road at Moose Junction (located 12 miles north of Jackson), drive 0.9 miles north on Highway 89 to the Blacktail Butte parking lot on the right.

The hike

Take the path on the right, and head south along the base of Blacktail Butte through a mix of pines, aspens, and sagebrush. At 0.3 miles, the trail curves left, following the contour of the mountain. Walk through open grasslands and aspen groves to the mouth of the wooded canyon. Enter the canyon and hop over to the east side of the stream. Cross a talus slope and walk beneath an overhanging rock wall and huge outcroppings. Steadily climb the wooded drainage on the west-facing hillside to an open, sloping meadow with colorful wildflowers. At the top (south) end of the meadow, enter the forest again. Wind through the trees on a gentle grade. After a short, steep ascent, the path emerges from the forest to a sage-covered slope. Climb the slope to incredible views of the majestic Teton Range to the northwest. Make a sharp left bend, and head 40 yards uphill to a junction at the ridge. Take the spur trail 25 yards to the right to the 7,688-foot summit. This is the turn-around spot. ◼

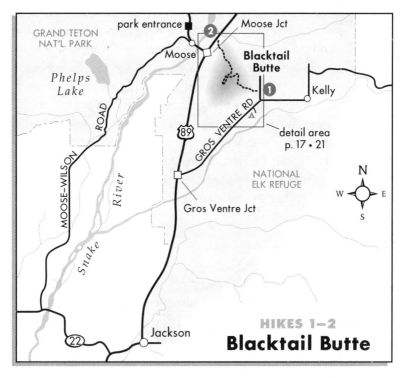

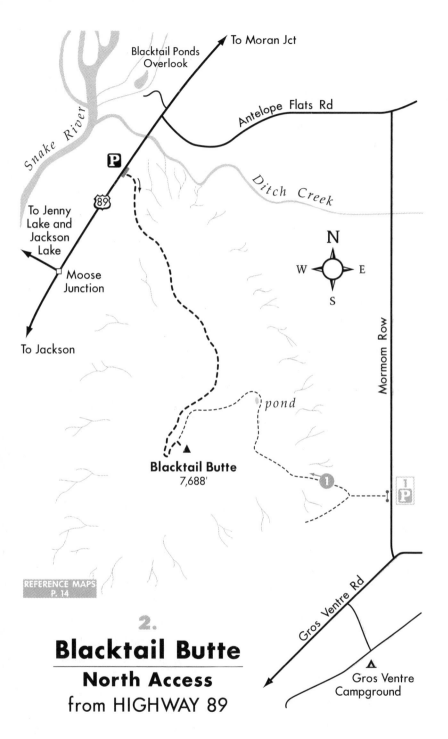

To Moran Jct

Blacktail Ponds
Overlook

Antelope Flats Rd

Snake River

P

Ditch Creek

89

To Jenny
Lake and
Jackson
Lake

N

W —◇— E

S

Moose
Junction

Mormom Row

To Jackson

pond

Blacktail Butte
7,688'

①

P

REFERENCE MAPS
P. 14

2.
Blacktail Butte
North Access
from HIGHWAY 89

Gros Ventre Rd

▲
Gros Ventre
Campground

3. Menor's Ferry • Noble Cabin

Hiking distance: 0.6-mile loop
Hiking time: 30 minutes
Configuration: loop
Elevation gain: level
Difficulty: very easy
Exposure: a mix of exposed and shaded streamside habitat
Dogs: not allowed
Maps: U.S.G.S. Moose
Menor's Ferry Historic District Guide and Map

Menor's Ferry and the Noble Cabin are near the park headquarters in Moose. The historical site was home to Bill Menor in the late 1800s, one of the area's first settlers. His original homestead cabin and country store, built in 1892, face the river. Adjacent to the cabin is Menor's Ferry, an in-use replica of the original ferry that was used as a vital crossing of the Snake River. The vessel consisted of a platform set on two pontoons. Pulleys were attached to the fixed cables on each shore. The river's current propelled the ferry, moving sideways across the river.

The Noble Cabin was moved from Cottonwood Creek in 1918 when Maude Noble purchased Menor's Ferry. The cabin is currently a small natural history museum with an exhibit of historical photographs and a look at the life of early settlers and pioneers in Jackson Hole.

To the trailhead

From the intersection of Highway 89 and Teton Park Road at Moose Junction (located 12 miles north of Jackson), drive one mile on Teton Park Road to the national park entrance. Continue 0.2 miles past the entrance station, and turn right at the first turn. Drive 0.4 miles to the parking area on the left, just past the Chapel of the Transfiguration.

The trail can also be accessed from the Craig Thomas Discovery and Visitor Center, just after crossing over the Snake River but before entering the park entrance station. Parking is available along both sides of Teton Park Road.

The hike

From the Chapel of the Transfiguration (a log chapel built in 1925), follow the paved path towards the Snake River. Begin the loop to the left. Head northeast to Menor's Cabin at the Snake River. Curve right and follow the river downstream, across from Dornan's. Pass the reconstructed ferry and cable-works to a collection of covered wagons, coaches, and carriages in a log shelter. Continue downstream through a cottonwood stand to Maude Noble's cabin. Complete the loop to the right.

From the Noble Cabin, a trail continues along the Snake River toward the Teton Park Road and visitor center. A road also leads through the park employee residences. ▪

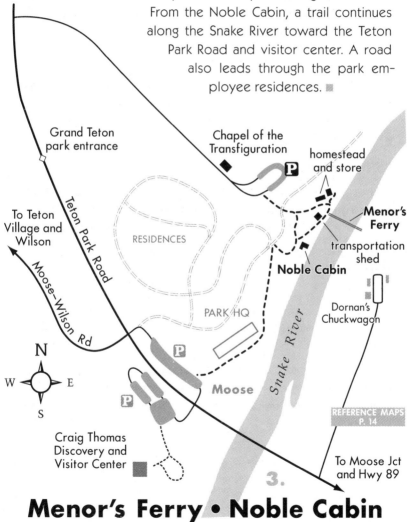

Menor's Ferry • Noble Cabin

4. Sawmill Ponds

Hiking distance: 1.4 miles round trip
Hiking time: 45 minutes
Configuration: out-and-back with short side paths
Elevation gain: level
Difficulty: easy
Exposure: mostly exposed with shaded pockets
Dogs: not allowed
Maps: U.S.G.S. Moose

The Sawmill Ponds are a series of spring-fed ponds in a wetland below the Moose-Wilson Road. The wetland provides a year-around habitat for moose and other wildlife. Beavers have dammed the stream, forming the ponds. The hike parallels the cliffs above the wetlands. From the sagebrush-covered terrace, there are bird's-eye views of the streams and ponds below, offering a great opportunity for viewing wildlife. The Teton peaks rise high above the trail to the north.

To the trailhead

From the intersection of Highway 89 and Teton Park Road at Moose Junction (located 12 miles north of Jackson), drive a half mile ahead on Teton Park Road to the Moose-Wilson Road on the left. Turn left and continue 1.2 miles to the parking area on the left with the "Moose Habitat" information sign.

The hike

Follow the wide, unsigned path at the south end of the parking area. The trail, an unpaved road that is closed to vehicles, follows the flat terrace above the Sawmill Ponds and wetlands. Side footpaths lead to overlooks and hug the edge of the cliffs that run parallel to the road. Continue past stands of aspens and pines. The trail ends on the sagebrush plain at an old landing strip. Return along the same route back to the trailhead. ▪

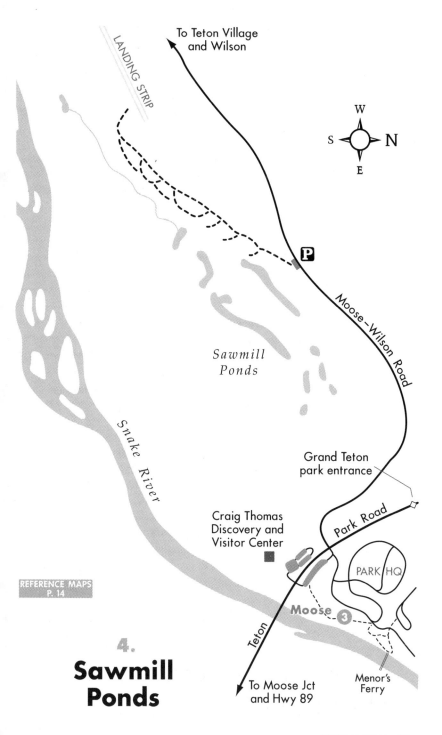

To Teton Village and Wilson

LANDING STRIP

W
S N
E

P

Moose–Wilson Road

Sawmill Ponds

Snake River

Grand Teton park entrance

Park Road

Craig Thomas Discovery and Visitor Center

PARK HQ

REFERENCE MAPS P. 14

Moose 3

Teton

Menor's Ferry

4.
Sawmill Ponds

To Moose Jct and Hwy 89

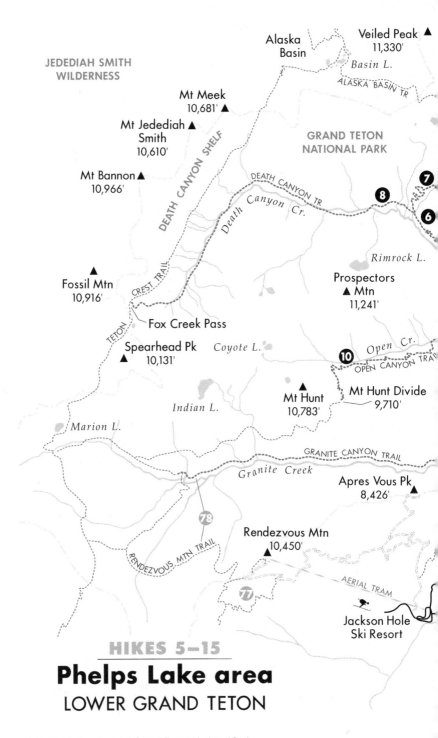

Alaska Basin

Veiled Peak ▲
11,330'

JEDEDIAH SMITH
WILDERNESS

Basin L.

ALASKA BASIN TR

Mt Meek
10,681' ▲

Mt Jedediah ▲
Smith
10,610'

GRAND TETON
NATIONAL PARK

Mt Bannon ▲
10,966'

DEATH CANYON TR

DEATH CANYON SHELF

Death Canyon Cr.

8

7

6

Rimrock L.

Fossil Mtn
10,916'

CREST TRAIL

Prospectors
▲ Mtn
11,241'

Fox Creek Pass

TETON

Spearhead Pk
10,131'

Coyote L.

10

Open Cr.

OPEN CANYON TRAIL

Indian L.

Mt Hunt
10,783'

Mt Hunt Divide
9,710'

Marion L.

GRANITE CANYON TRAIL

Granite Creek

Apres Vous Pk
8,426' ▲

78

RENDEZVOUS MTN TRAIL

Rendezvous Mtn
10,450'

AERIAL TRAM

77

Jackson Hole
Ski Resort

HIKES 5–15
Phelps Lake area
LOWER GRAND TETON

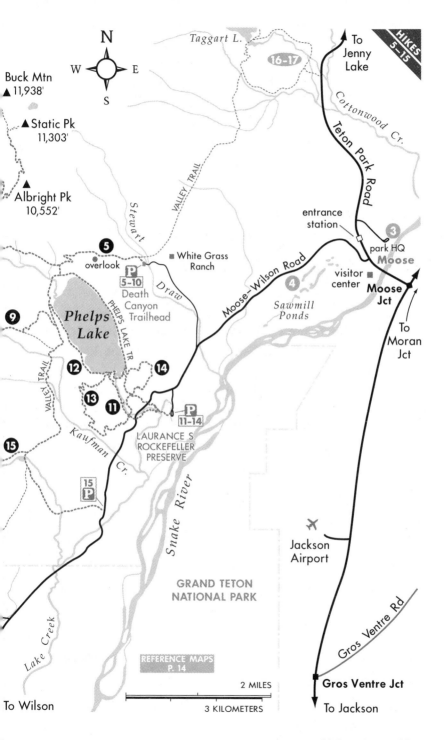

N
W   E
S

Taggart L.

16-17

To Jenny Lake

Buck Mtn
▲ 11,938'

▲ Static Pk
11,303'

▲ Albright Pk
10,552'

Cottonwood Cr.

Teton Park Road

Stewart Draw

VALLEY TRAIL

entrance station

3

park HQ
Moose

5
overlook

P
5-10
Death Canyon Trailhead

■ White Grass Ranch

PHELPS LAKE TR

Phelps Lake

Moose-Wilson Road

visitor center ■

Moose Jct

Sawmill Ponds

4

9

To Moran Jct

12

14

VALLEY TRAIL

13

11

P
11-14

Kaufman Cr.

LAURANCE S. ROCKEFELLER PRESERVE

15

15
P

Snake River

Jackson Airport

GRAND TETON NATIONAL PARK

Gros Ventre Rd

REFERENCE MAPS
P. 14

2 MILES

3 KILOMETERS

Lake Creek

To Wilson

Gros Ventre Jct

To Jackson

5. Phelps Lake Overlook to Phelps Lake

DEATH CANYON TRAILHEAD

Hiking distance: Phelps Lake Overlook: 2 miles round trip
Phelps Lake: 4 miles round trip
Hiking time: 1 to 2 hours
Configuration: out-and-back
Elevation gain: 400 feet
Difficulty: easy
Exposure: shaded forest and open meadows
Dogs: not allowed
Maps: U.S.G.S. Grand Teton · Adventure Maps: Jackson Hole
Beartooth Publishing: Grand Teton National Park map
National Geographic Trails Illustrated: Grand Teton Nat'l. Park

The Death Canyon trailhead is located at Phelps Lake at the south end of Grand Teton National Park. The trailhead offers access into deep and remote canyons that lead west to Static Peak, the Alaska Basin, and the dramatic Death Canyon Shelf. The canyon trails connect to the Teton Crest Trail and south to Jackson Hole Ski Resort. While the trail to Phelps Lake is fairly easy and quite popular, the routes into the canyons become increasingly more strenuous and less traveled. Hikes 5–10 lead to various points

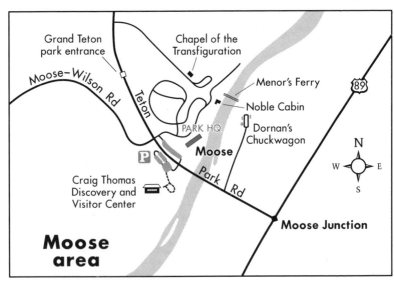

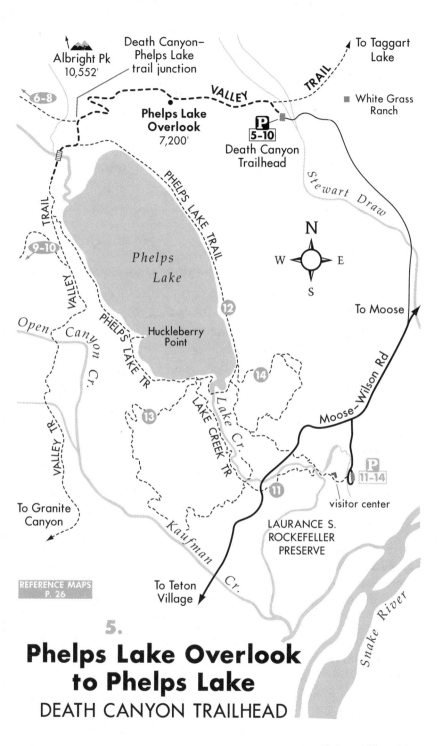

Albright Pk
10,552'

Death Canyon–
Phelps Lake
trail junction

6-8

VALLEY TRAIL

To Taggart
Lake

White Grass
Ranch

Phelps Lake
Overlook
7,200'

P
5-10

Death Canyon
Trailhead

Stewart Draw

PHELPS LAKE TRAIL

TRAIL

9-10

Phelps
Lake

N
W   E
S

12

To Moose

VALLEY TR

Open Canyon Cr.

PHELPS LAKE TR

Huckleberry
Point

14

Lake Cr.

Moose-Wilson Rd

13

LAKE CREEK TR

VALLEY TR

11

P
11-14

visitor center

To Granite
Canyon

Kaufman Cr.

LAURANCE S.
ROCKEFELLER
PRESERVE

Snake River

REFERENCE MAPS
P. 26

To Teton
Village

5.

Phelps Lake Overlook
to Phelps Lake
DEATH CANYON TRAILHEAD

along Death Canyon and Open Canyon, ranging from easy to very strenuous. From the trails are fantastic views of the alpine landscape.

This hike follows a beautifully forested trail to Phelps Lake Overlook, a 7,200-foot viewing area of the 525-acre Phelps Lake. The large, glacier-formed lake sits along the base of the Teton Range at the entrance to Death Canyon. The vertical walls of Death Canyon dominate the landscape to the north. Along the way to Phelps Lake are frequent springs and abundant wildflowers. From the overlook, the trail descends 600 feet to the lake's shoreline.

To the trailhead

From the intersection of Highway 89 and Teton Park Road at Moose Junction (located 12 miles north of Jackson), drive a half mile ahead on Teton Park Road to the Moose-Wilson Road on the left. Turn left and continue 3 miles to the Death Canyon Trailhead turnoff on the right—turn right. Drive 1.6 miles to the end of the road, and park in the trailhead parking area.

From Teton Village, drive 5 miles north to the trailhead (3.9 miles past the national park entrance kiosk).

The hike

Walk 0.1 mile west to a junction with the Valley Trail. The right fork heads northeast to the Beaver Creek Trail and Taggart Lake. Take the left fork towards the west. Wind through a lodgepole pine, subalpine fir, and Engelmann spruce forest, crossing small streams. Leave the forest and steadily climb the moraine through a meadow to the 7,200-foot Phelps Lake Overlook at one mile.

After savoring the views of the lake, the valley floor, the Gros Ventre Range, and the mouth of Death Canyon, continue down the glacial moraine via switchbacks to a junction at 1.6 miles. The Death Canyon Trail heads to the right (west)—Hikes 6—8. Stay on the Valley Trail (left fork) to explore the west side of Phelps Lake, passing the Phelps Lake Trail and crossing the bridge over Death Canyon Creek. After the bridge, return along the same trail.

For a longer hike, the next five hikes lead to various points in Death Canyon and Open Canyon. ▧

6. Death Canyon to Patrol Cabin
DEATH CANYON TRAILHEAD

Hiking distance: 7.5 miles round trip
Hiking time: 4 hours
Configuration: out-and-back
Elevation gain: 1,500 feet
Difficulty: moderate to somewhat strenuous
Exposure: shaded forest and open meadows
Dogs: not allowed
Maps: U.S.G.S. Grand Teton · Adventure Maps: Jackson Hole
     Beartooth Publishing: Grand Teton National Park map
     National Geographic Trails Illustrated: Grand Teton Nat'l. Park

**map
page 33**

Death Canyon is a magnificent vertical-walled canyon with some of the oldest rock in the Teton Range, dating back 2.5 billion years. The canyon is a wide, glacier-carved canyon with a broad floor, a gorgeous cascading creek, and jagged mountain peaks. Death Canyon Creek flows more than 2,000 feet down the canyon, from just below Fox Creek Pass into Phelps Lake.

This hike leads to the Death Canyon patrol cabin, a small log structure built in the 1930s. It is occupied by crews patrolling and maintaining the trails. The trail climbs through the narrow rock portals at the mouth of the canyon and traverses the north flank of the canyon to the patrol cabin, where an adjoining trail splits off to Static Peak.

To the trailhead

From the intersection of Highway 89 and Teton Park Road at Moose Junction (located 12 miles north of Jackson), drive a half mile ahead on Teton Park Road to the Moose-Wilson Road on the left. Turn left and continue 3 miles to the Death Canyon Trailhead turnoff on the right—turn right. Drive 1.6 miles to the end of the road, and park in the trailhead parking area.

From Teton Village, drive 5 miles north to the trailhead (3.9 miles past the national park entrance kiosk).

The hike

Walk 0.1 mile west to a junction with the Valley Trail. The right fork heads northeast to the Beaver Creek Trail and Taggart Lake. Take the left fork towards the south. Wind through a lodgepole pine, subalpine fir, and Engelmann spruce forest, crossing small streams. Leave the forest and steadily climb the moraine through a meadow to the 7,200-foot Phelps Lake Overlook at one mile. After savoring the views of Phelps Lake, the valley floor, the Gros Ventre Range, and the mouth of Death Canyon, continue down the glacial moraine via switchbacks to a junction at 1.6 miles.

From the posted junction, the Valley Trail (left fork) continues on the west side of Phelps Lake. Take the right fork and head west through the sloping, sage-covered meadow with large groves of spruce and cottonwoods. Continue towards the dramatic rock portals guarding the mouth of Death Canyon. Enter the narrow canyon, steadily gaining elevation up the north side. Stay to the right of cascading Death Canyon Creek, and pass gorgeous rock formations beneath the towering rock walls. At 2.7 miles, climb a series of switchbacks while viewing the tumbling cascades and magnificent vistas of Phelps Lake, the Jackson Hole valley, and the Gros Ventre Range. Atop the switchbacks, the narrow, steep-walled canyon levels out and opens up into a classic U-shaped, glaciated canyon with giant slabs of granite. Follow the meandering, grass-lined stream through meadows and forest on the flat canyon floor. Keep an eye out for moose, which inhabit the area. The trail reaches the Death Canyon patrol cabin at 3.7 miles. It is located on the left near a posted trail split. This is the turnaround spot.

To hike farther, the Alaska Basin Trail branches to the right, leading to Static Peak Divide (Hike 7) and Alaska Basin. The left fork continues west in Death Canyon to Fox Creek Pass, the Teton Crest Trail, and Death Canyon Shelf (Hike 8). ∎

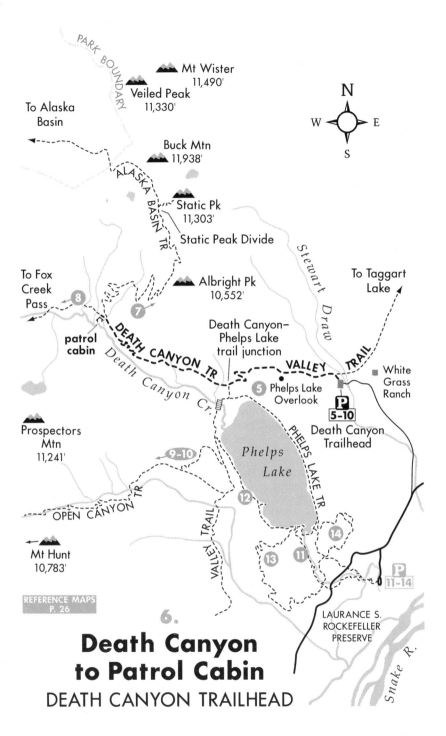

To Alaska Basin

PARK BOUNDARY

Mt Wister
11,490'

Veiled Peak
11,330'

Buck Mtn
11,938'

ALASKA BASIN TR

Static Pk
11,303'

Static Peak Divide

To Fox Creek Pass

8

7

Albright Pk
10,552'

Stewart Draw

To Taggart Lake

patrol cabin

DEATH CANYON TR

Death Canyon Cr.

Death Canyon–
Phelps Lake
trail junction

VALLEY TRAIL

White Grass Ranch

5

Phelps Lake Overlook

P
5-10

Death Canyon Trailhead

Prospectors Mtn
11,241'

9-10

Phelps Lake

PHELPS LAKE TR

OPEN CANYON TR

VALLEY TRAIL

12

14

Mt Hunt
10,783'

13

11

P
11-14

REFERENCE MAPS
P. 26

6.

LAURANCE S.
ROCKEFELLER
PRESERVE

Snake R.

Death Canyon
to Patrol Cabin
DEATH CANYON TRAILHEAD

7. Death Canyon to Static Peak Divide
DEATH CANYON TRAILHEAD

Hiking distance: 15.4 miles round trip
Hiking time: 8 hours
Configuration: out-and-back
Elevation gain: 4,000 feet
Difficulty: very strenuous
Exposure: shaded forest and canyon with open meadows
Dogs: not allowed
Maps: U.S.G.S. Grand Teton · Adventure Maps: Jackson Hole
Beartooth Publishing: Grand Teton National Park map
National Geographic Trails Illustrated: Grand Teton Nat'l. Park

**map
page 36**

The 10,790-foot Static Peak Divide, near the national park boundary, is a high-alpine divide that lies between Death Canyon and
Avalanche Canyon. This hike climbs up Death Canyon to the patrol cabin (Hike 6), then veers north to Static Peak Divide on the
Alaska Basin Trail. Nestled beneath the sheer, jagged cliffs of the
Teton Range, the strenuous Alaska Basin Trail gains 3,000 feet in
four miles up to the divide. From the divide are sweeping panoramic vistas of Jackson Hole, the Snake River, and the Gros
Ventre Range. Beyond the divide, the trail drops into Alaska Basin
in the Jedediah Smith Wilderness.

To the trailhead

From the intersection of Highway 89 and Teton Park Road at
Moose Junction (located 12 miles north of Jackson), drive a half
mile ahead on Teton Park Road to the Moose-Wilson Road on the
left. Turn left and continue 3 miles to the Death Canyon Trailhead
turnoff on the right—turn right. Drive 1.6 miles to the end of the
road, and park in the trailhead parking area.

From Teton Village, drive 5 miles north to the trailhead (3.9
miles past the national park entrance kiosk).

The hike

Walk 0.1 mile west to a junction with the Valley Trail. The right
fork heads northeast to the Beaver Creek Trail and Taggart Lake.
Take the left fork towards the west. Wind through a lodgepole
pine, subalpine fir, and Engelmann spruce forest, crossing small

streams. Leave the forest and steadily climb the moraine through a meadow to the 7,200-foot Phelps Lake Overlook at one mile. After savoring the views of Phelps Lake, the valley floor, the Gros Ventre Range, and the mouth of Death Canyon, continue down the glacial moraine via switchbacks to a junction at 1.6 miles.

From the posted junction, the Valley Trail (left fork) continues on the west side of Phelps Lake. Take the right fork and head west through the sloping, sage-covered meadow with large groves of spruce and cottonwoods. Continue towards the dramatic rock portals guarding the mouth of Death Canyon. Enter the narrow canyon, steadily gaining elevation up the north side. Stay to the right of cascading Death Canyon Creek, and pass gorgeous rock formations beneath the towering rock walls. At 2.7 miles, climb a series of switchbacks while viewing the tumbling cascades and magnificent vistas of Phelps Lake, the Jackson Hole valley, and the Gros Ventre Range. Atop the switchbacks, the narrow, steep-walled canyon levels out and opens up into a classic U-shaped, glaciated canyon with giant slabs of granite. Follow the meandering, grass-lined stream through meadows and forest on the flat canyon floor. Keep an eye out for moose, which inhabit the area. The trail reaches the Death Canyon patrol cabin at 3.7 miles—on the left near a posted trail split.

The left fork continues up Death Canyon, leading to Death Canyon Shelf and Fox Creek Pass (Hike 8). Take the right fork—leaving Death Canyon—on the Alaska Basin Trail towards Static Peak Divide. At just over 4 miles, the path begins steep switchbacks. Climb the open, then wooded, slope through groves of subalpine fir, Engelmann spruce, and whitebark pine, staying to the west side of the drainage. Cross the stream at 5.3 miles and continue uphill. At 6.8 miles, the trail reaches a 10,200-foot saddle between Static Peak and Albright Peak. Side paths scramble up to the summit, with vistas of the canyon and the Jackson Hole valley. The main trail curves north (left) and follows the rocky ridge across loose talus for nearly a mile to 10,790-foot Static Peak Divide at 7.7 miles. An unofficial quarter-mile side path scrambles 500 feet up the southern slope of Static Peak to the 11,303-foot summit. This is the turn-around spot.

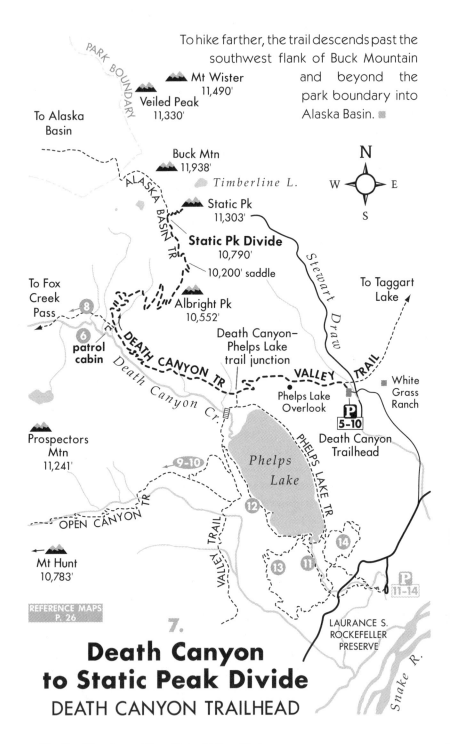

To hike farther, the trail descends past the southwest flank of Buck Mountain and beyond the park boundary into Alaska Basin. ■

To Alaska Basin

PARK BOUNDARY

▲ Mt Wister
11,490'

▲ Veiled Peak
11,330'

▲ Buck Mtn
11,938'

Timberline L.

ALASKA BASIN TR

▲ Static Pk
11,303'

Static Pk Divide
10,790'

10,200' saddle

Stewart Draw

To Fox Creek Pass

⑧

⑥
patrol cabin

DEATH CANYON TR

Death Canyon Cr.

▲ Albright Pk
10,552'

Death Canyon–
Phelps Lake
trail junction

VALLEY TRAIL

To Taggart Lake

■ White Grass Ranch

● Phelps Lake
Overlook

P
5–10

Death Canyon
Trailhead

N
W — E
S

▲ Prospectors Mtn
11,241'

⑨–⑩

OPEN CANYON TR

Phelps Lake

PHELPS LAKE TR

⑫

VALLEY TRAIL

◄ ▲ Mt Hunt
10,783'

⑬ ⑪

⑭

P
11–14

REFERENCE MAPS
P. 26

LAURANCE S.
ROCKEFELLER
PRESERVE

Snake R.

7.

Death Canyon
to Static Peak Divide
DEATH CANYON TRAILHEAD

8. Death Canyon to Fox Creek Pass
DEATH CANYON TRAILHEAD

Hiking distance: 18.4 miles round trip
Hiking time: 9 hours
Configuration: out-and-back

map
page 38

Elevation gain: 3,100 feet
Difficulty: very strenuous
Exposure: shaded canyon and high, exposed slopes
Dogs: not allowed
Maps: U.S.G.S. Grand Teton and Mount Bannon
       Adventure Maps: Jackson Hole
       Beartooth Publishing: Grand Teton National Park map
       National Geographic Trails Illustrated: Grand Teton Nat'l. Park

The hike up Death Canyon to Fox Creek Pass is the longest in this book. It requires much physical stamina and an early departure (or plan the hike as an overnight trek). The 9,560-foot Fox Creek Pass is at the boundary of Grand Teton National Park and the Jedediah Smith Wilderness on the crest of the Teton Range, where the trail joins the Teton Crest Trail. The trail steadily climbs up Death Canyon to the headwaters of the creek and Fox Creek Pass. The views throughout the canyon and from atop the pass are fantastic. As the trail nears the pass, it follows below the expansive Death Canyon Shelf at the head of the canyon (back cover photo). The rock shelf formation forms a towering wall along the upper canyon, surrounded by jagged 10,000-foot peaks. The shelf is an impressive limestone wall with thick horizontal stripes that stretches for three miles, from Fox Creek Pass to Mount Meek.

To the trailhead

From the intersection of Highway 89 and Teton Park Road at Moose Junction (located 12 miles north of Jackson), drive a half mile ahead on Teton Park Road to the Moose-Wilson Road on the left. Turn left and continue 3 miles to the Death Canyon Trailhead turnoff on the right—turn right. Drive 1.6 miles to the end of the road, and park in the trailhead parking area.

From Teton Village, drive 5 miles north to the trailhead (3.9 miles past the national park entrance kiosk).

The hike

Walk 0.1 mile west to a junction with the Valley Trail. The right fork heads northeast to the Beaver Creek Trail and Taggart Lake. Take the left fork towards the west. Wind through a lodge-pole pine, subalpine fir, and Engelmann spruce forest, crossing small streams. Leave the forest and steadily climb the moraine through a meadow to the 7,200-foot Phelps Lake Overlook at one mile. After

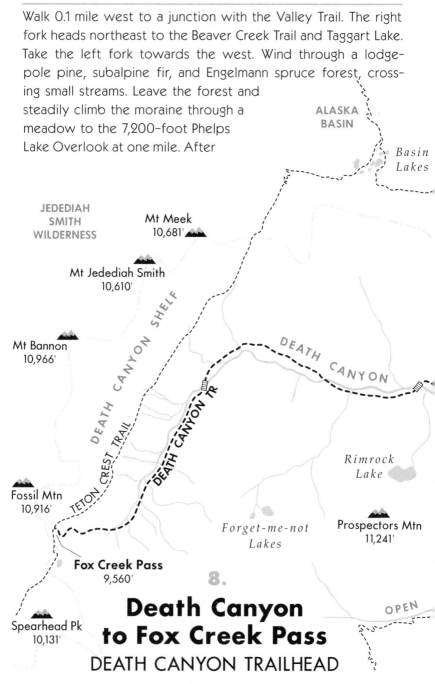

ALASKA
BASIN

Basin Lakes

JEDEDIAH
SMITH
WILDERNESS

Mt Meek
10,681'

Mt Jedediah Smith
10,610'

DEATH CANYON SHELF

Mt Bannon
10,966'

DEATH CANYON

DEATH CANYON TRAIL

TETON CREST TRAIL

DEATH CANYON TR

Rimrock Lake

Fossil Mtn
10,916'

Forget-me-not Lakes

Prospectors Mtn
11,241'

Fox Creek Pass
9,560'

8.

OPEN

Spearhead Pk
10,131'

Death Canyon
to Fox Creek Pass
DEATH CANYON TRAILHEAD

savoring the views of Phelps Lake, the valley floor, the Gros Ventre Range, and the mouth of Death Canyon, continue down the glacial moraine via switchbacks to a junction at 1.6 miles.

From the posted junction, the Valley Trail (left fork) continues on the west side of Phelps Lake. Take the right fork and head west through the sloping, sage-covered meadow with large groves of spruce and cottonwoods. Continue towards the dramatic rock

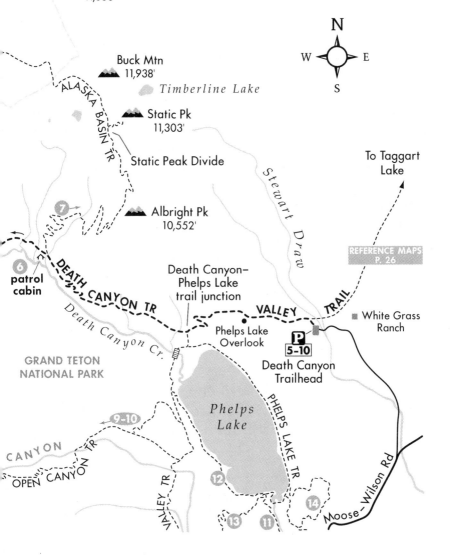

89 Great Hikes – **39**

portals guarding the mouth of Death Canyon. Enter the narrow canyon, steadily gaining elevation up the north side. Stay to the right of cascading Death Canyon Creek, and pass gorgeous rock formations beneath the towering rock walls. At 2.7 miles, climb a series of switchbacks while viewing the tumbling cascades and magnificent vistas of Phelps Lake, the Jackson Hole valley, and the Gros Ventre Range. Atop the switchbacks, the narrow, steep-walled canyon levels out and opens up into a classic U-shaped, glaciated canyon with giant slabs of granite. Follow the meandering, grass-lined stream through meadows and forest on the flat canyon floor. Keep an eye out for moose, which inhabit the area. The trail reaches the Death Canyon patrol cabin at 3.7 miles. It is located on the left near a posted trail split.

The right fork leads up to Static Peak Divide and Alaska Basin (Hike 7). Take the left fork towards Fox Creek Pass, staying in Death Canyon along the creek. Follow the north side of the meandering, willow-lined Death Canyon Creek through the large meadow, a prime habitat for moose. A half mile beyond the cabin, pass a beautiful cascade flowing out of Rimrock Lake 2,000 feet above to the south. Cross two footbridges over the creek, entering the Death Canyon camping zone. For the next mile, climb through a forest of spruce and fir, reaching a flower-covered meadow with huge granite slabs. At 6 miles, the trail curves south to views of the upper canyon. Follow the drainage beneath the awesome Death Canyon Shelf on the north canyon wall. Cross a bridge to the south side of the creek at 6.6 miles, and traverse the open meadows. Cross a few small bridges over tributary streams, and climb out of the camping zone at the headwaters of Death Canyon Creek. Climb the open slopes with the aid of switchbacks, reaching the 9,560-foot Fox Creek Pass on the Teton Crest at the boundary between Grand Teton National Park and the Jedediah Smith Wilderness. Atop the crest is a posted junction with the Teton Crest Trail, the turn-around point for this hike. Return along the same trail.

The 38-mile Teton Crest Trail continues south to Ski Lake (Hike 87) and north to Cascade Canyon (Hike 25) along the spine of the Teton Range. ■

9. Open Canyon to the Open Canyon Creek Bridge

DEATH CANYON TRAILHEAD

Hiking distance: 8.2 miles round trip
Hiking time: 4 hours
Configuration: out-and-back
Elevation gain: 1,200 feet
Difficulty: moderate
Exposure: shaded canyon and high, exposed slopes
Dogs: not allowed
Maps: U.S.G.S. Grand Teton · Adventure Maps: Jackson Hole
　　　　Beartooth Publishing: Grand Teton National Park map
　　　　National Geographic Trails Illustrated: Grand Teton Nat'l. Park

map
page 43

Open Canyon, due west of Phelps Lake, rests between Death Canyon and Granite Canyon along the Teton front range. It is a shallow canyon in relation to the other canyons in the park. Open Canyon is V-shaped, formed by water erosion rather than the typical U-shaped canyons formed by scouring glacial ice.

Hikes 9 and 10 start at the Death Canyon trailhead and head into Open Canyon. The lightly used Open Canyon Trail curves around the north end of Phelps Lake and climbs up the canyon to the Mount Hunt Divide at 9,710 feet. This hike—the easier of the two—leads to the Open Canyon Creek bridge, where the trail crosses to the other side of the canyon. Hike 10 continues from the bridge and strenuously climbs up to the divide between Open Canyon and Granite Canyon, the next drainage to the south.

To the trailhead

From the intersection of Highway 89 and Teton Park Road at Moose Junction (located 12 miles north of Jackson), drive a half mile ahead on Teton Park Road to the Moose-Wilson Road on the left. Turn left and continue 3 miles to the Death Canyon Trailhead turnoff on the right—turn right. Drive 1.6 miles to the end of the road, and park in the trailhead parking area.

From Teton Village, drive 5 miles north to the trailhead (3.9 miles past the national park entrance kiosk).

The hike

Walk 0.1 mile west to a junction with the Valley Trail. The right fork heads northeast to the Beaver Creek Trail and Taggart Lake. Take the left fork towards the south. Wind through a lodgepole pine, subalpine fir, and Engelmann spruce forest, crossing small streams. Leave the forest and steadily climb the moraine through a meadow to the 7,200-foot Phelps Lake Overlook at one mile. After savoring the views of Phelps Lake, the valley floor, the Gros Ventre Range, and the mouth of Death Canyon, continue down the glacial moraine via switchbacks to a junction at 1.6 miles.

From the posted junction, the right fork leads into Death Canyon (Hikes 6–8). Take the Valley Trail to the left, and cross a bridge over Death Canyon Creek. Ascend the wooded moraine above the expansive west side of Phelps Lake, keeping an eye out for moose. Follow the base of the Teton Range to a posted junction at 2.6 miles. Leave the Valley Trail and bear right on the Open Canyon Trail. Climb through the woodland, then cross the open slopes of Prospectors Mountain. Angle left into Open Canyon to a junction. Go to the right (up canyon) and traverse the stream-fed canyon bottom. Pass through a meadow and cross a bridge over Open Canyon Creek at just over 4 miles. The bridge is our turn-around spot.

Hike 10 continues on the Open Canyon Trail up to Mount Hunt Divide. ▩

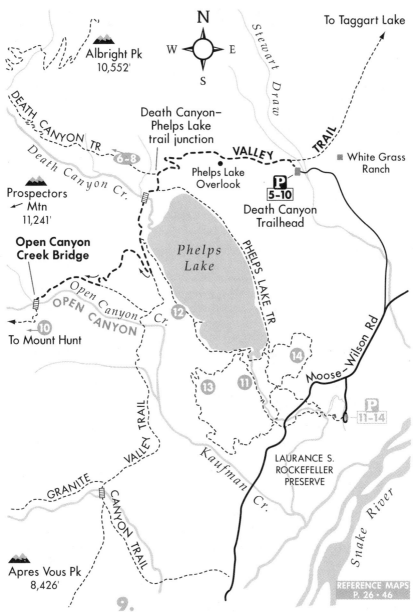

To Taggart Lake

N
W E
S

Albright Pk
10,552'

DEATH CANYON TR

Death Canyon Cr.

Death Canyon–
Phelps Lake
trail junction

6-8

VALLEY   TRAIL

Stewart Draw

White Grass
Ranch

Phelps Lake
Overlook

P
5-10

Death Canyon
Trailhead

Prospectors
Mtn
11,241'

Open Canyon
Creek Bridge

Phelps
Lake

PHELPS LAKE TR

Open Canyon Cr.

OPEN CANYON

10

To Mount Hunt

12

14

13   11

Moose-Wilson Rd

P
11-14

VALLEY TRAIL

Kaufman Cr.

LAURANCE S.
ROCKEFELLER
PRESERVE

Snake River

GRANITE

CANYON TRAIL

Apres Vous Pk
8,426'

REFERENCE MAPS
P. 26 · 46

9.

Open Canyon to the
Open Canyon Creek Bridge
DEATH CANYON TRAILHEAD

10. Open Canyon to Mount Hunt Divide

DEATH CANYON TRAILHEAD

Hiking distance: 14.6 miles round trip
Hiking time: 7.5 hours
Configuration: out-and-back
Elevation gain: 3,000 feet
Difficulty: strenuous
Exposure: shaded canyon and high, exposed slopes
Dogs: not allowed
Maps: U.S.G.S. Grand Teton · Adventure Maps: Jackson Hole
       Beartooth Publishing: Grand Teton National Park map
       National Geographic Trails Illustrated: Grand Teton Nat'l. Park

**map
page 46**

Mount Hunt Divide sits at the base of Mount Hunt between Prospectors Mountain and Apres Vous Peak. From the stark, jagged terrain at the summit are magnificent top-of-the-world views of the southern Teton Range, including the predominant Rendezvous Mountain and Apres Vous Peak to the south (the back side of the Jackson Hole Ski Resort), Prospectors Mountain and the major Teton Peaks to the north, and the Gros Ventre Range far to the east. From the Open Canyon Creek bridge (Hike 9), the trail continues parallel to the creek, then steeply zigzags up the canyon through spruce, fir, and pines to Mount Hunt Divide, a thousand feet below Mount Hunt. The divide lies between Open Canyon and Granite Canyon, the next drainage to the south.

To the trailhead

From the intersection of Highway 89 and Teton Park Road at Moose Junction (located 12 miles north of Jackson), drive a half mile ahead on Teton Park Road to the Moose-Wilson Road on the left. Turn left and continue 3 miles to the Death Canyon Trailhead turnoff on the right—turn right. Drive 1.6 miles to the end of the road, and park in the trailhead parking area.

From Teton Village, drive 5 miles north to the trailhead (3.9 miles past the national park entrance kiosk).

The hike

Walk 0.1 mile west to a junction with the Valley Trail. The right fork heads northeast to the Beaver Creek Trail and Taggart Lake. Take the left fork towards the west. Wind through a lodgepole pine, subalpine fir, and Engelmann spruce forest, crossing small streams. Leave the forest and steadily climb the moraine through a meadow to the 7,200-foot overlook at one mile. After savoring the views of Phelps Lake, the valley floor, the Gros Ventre Range, and the mouth of Death Canyon, continue down the glacial moraine via switchbacks to a junction at 1.6 miles.

From the posted junction, the right fork leads into Death Canyon (Hikes 6—8). Take the Valley Trail to the left, and cross a bridge over Death Canyon Creek. Ascend the wooded moraine above the expansive west side of Phelps Lake, keeping an eye out for moose. Follow the base of the Teton Range to a posted junction at 2.6 miles. Leave the Valley Trail and bear right on the Open Canyon Trail. Climb through the woodland, then cross the open slopes of Prospectors Mountain. Angle left into Open Canyon to a junction. Go to the right (up canyon) and traverse the stream-fed canyon bottom. Pass through a meadow and cross a bridge over Open Canyon Creek at just over 4 miles.

From the Open Canyon Creek bridge, head up the canyon on the north-facing slope. Traverse the hillside above the creek, climbing through Douglas fir, lodgepole pine, and Engelmann spruce, crossing a few avalanche chutes. Emerge from the forest at 6 miles to views of the meadows on the floor of Open Canyon and Phelps Lake far below. Continue up the canyon slope to the northeast flank of Mount Hunt. Turn to the south, and begin the trek from the creek bottom up to the divide. Climb the limestone cliffs on short, steep switchbacks through groves of lodgepole and whitebark pines to the 9,710-foot saddle at Mount Hunt Divide. After enjoying the great views, return on the same trail.

To extend the hike, the Open Canyon Trail continues past Mount Hunt and descends into Granite Canyon to the Granite Canyon Trail (Hike 15). The Open Canyon Trail and the Granite Canyon Trail can be hiked as a 21-mile loop, returning to the Death Canyon trailhead. ▩

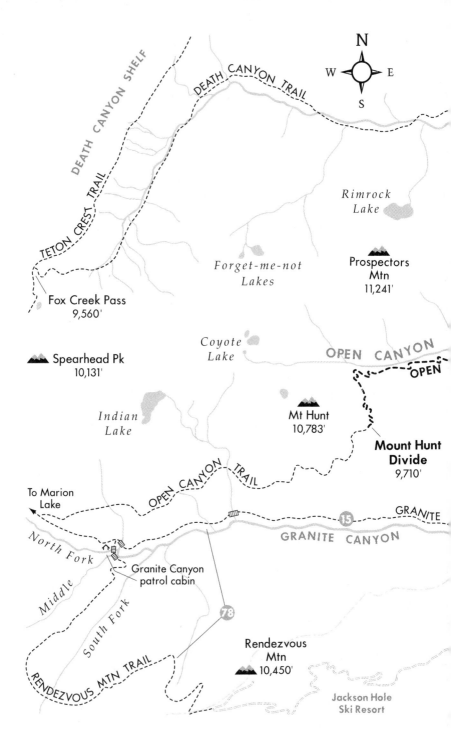

DEATH CANYON SHELF

DEATH CANYON TRAIL

TETON CREST TRAIL

N
W · E
S

Rimrock
Lake

Forget-me-not
Lakes

Prospectors
Mtn
11,241'

Fox Creek Pass
9,560'

Coyote
Lake

OPEN CANYON

OPEN

Spearhead Pk
10,131'

Indian
Lake

Mt Hunt
10,783'

Mount Hunt
Divide
9,710'

To Marion
Lake

OPEN CANYON TRAIL

GRANITE

North Fork

15

GRANITE CANYON

Granite Canyon
patrol cabin

Middle

South Fork

78

RENDEZVOUS MTN TRAIL

Rendezvous
Mtn
10,450'

Jackson Hole
Ski Resort

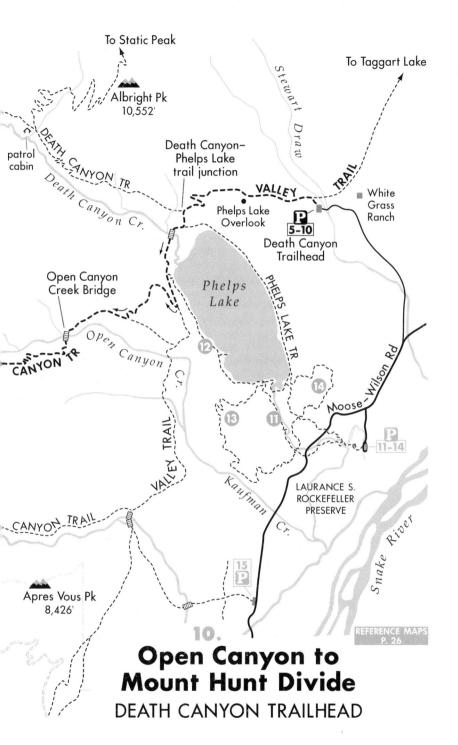

To Static Peak

Albright Pk
10,552'

patrol cabin

DEATH CANYON TR

Death Canyon Cr.

To Taggart Lake

Stewart Draw

VALLEY TRAIL

Death Canyon–
Phelps Lake
trail junction

Phelps Lake
Overlook

White
Grass
Ranch

P
5-10

Death Canyon
Trailhead

Open Canyon
Creek Bridge

*Phelps
Lake*

PHELPS LAKE TR

Open Canyon Cr.

CANYON TR

VALLEY TRAIL

12

14

Moose–Wilson Rd

P
11-14

13

11

CANYON TRAIL

Kaufman Cr.

LAURANCE S.
ROCKEFELLER
PRESERVE

Snake River

Apres Vous Pk
8,426'

15
P

10.

Open Canyon to
Mount Hunt Divide

DEATH CANYON TRAILHEAD

REFERENCE MAPS
P. 26

11. Lake Creek—Woodland Loop
LAURANCE S. ROCKEFELLER PRESERVE

Hiking distance: 2.9-mile loop
Hiking time: 2 hours
Configuration: loop
Elevation gain: 300 feet
Difficulty: easy to slightly moderate
Exposure: a mix of open and shaded forest
Dogs: not allowed
Maps: U.S.G.S. Grand Teton
  Adventure Maps: Jackson Hole
  Laurance S. Rockefeller Preserve Trail Guide (free at trailhead)

The Laurance S. Rockefeller Preserve is a 1,106-acre refuge within Grand Teton National Park at the southern end of Phelps Lake. The preserve, opened to the public in the fall of 2007, was generously donated to the national park by Laurance S. Rockefeller, son of John D. Rockefeller. For nearly 70 years, the site (formerly known as the JY Ranch) served as a summer retreat for the Rockefeller family. Over the course of three years, before public access was open to the preserve, 30 log buildings and other ranch structures were moved off-site or demolished and two roads were removed. The land was returned to its natural state, restoring wetlands, reducing non-native vegetation, and improving the wildlife habitat. Eight miles of hiking trails were developed, forming a series of loops through the 1,106-acre preserve. The trails begin at the Rockefeller Preserve Center, a 7,500-square-foot visitor center. Its green technology includes solar power energy and composting toilets.

The Lake Creek Trail and the Woodland Trail form the central, primary loop within the preserve. The trails connect the visitor center to an overlook on the south shore of Phelps Lake, where there are beautiful views of the Tetons across the wide expanse of water. En route to the overlook, the trail parallels Lake Creek, the outlet stream from Phelps Lake, and returns through a mixed conifer and aspen forest.

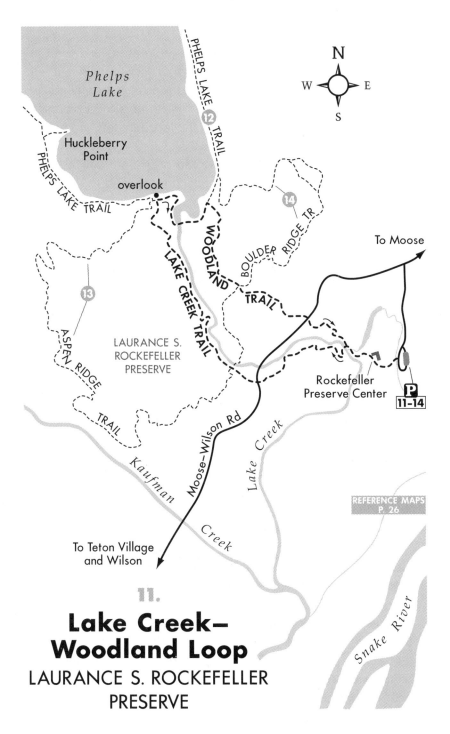

Phelps Lake

Huckleberry Point

overlook

PHELPS LAKE TRAIL

PHELPS LAKE TRAIL

⑫

WOODLAND

LAKE CREEK TRAIL

TRAIL

BOULDER RIDGE TR

⑭

⑬

ASPEN RIDGE

TRAIL

LAURANCE S. ROCKEFELLER PRESERVE

Moose-Wilson Rd

Kaufman

Creek

Lake Creek

To Moose

Rockefeller Preserve Center

P
11-14

To Teton Village and Wilson

REFERENCE MAPS
P. 26

Snake River

N
W   E
S

11.

Lake Creek– Woodland Loop
LAURANCE S. ROCKEFELLER PRESERVE

To the trailhead

From the intersection of Highway 89 and Teton Park Road at Moose Junction (located 12 miles north of Jackson), drive a half mile ahead on Teton Park Road to the Moose-Wilson Road on the left. Turn left and continue 3.7 miles to the signed Laurance S. Rockefeller Preserve entrance on the left. Turn left and go 0.3 miles to the trailhead parking lot.

From Teton Village, the preserve turnoff is on the right at 4.3 miles (3.2 miles past the national park entrance kiosk).

The hike

Pass the trailhead map and head west through the sagebrush meadows towards the Teton Mountains. Stroll through aspen groves to the Laurance S. Rockefeller Preserve Center. Beyond the visitor center, meander along the northeast side of Lake Creek, passing observation decks and a waterfall to a posted junction with the Woodland Trail on the right.

Begin the loop on the Lake Creek Trail straight ahead. Cross the bridge over the creek, and weave through the lodgepole pine and Douglas fir forest. Follow the south side of the cascading creek to the Moose-Wilson Road at 0.6 miles. Cross the paved road to a posted junction with the Aspen Ridge Trail on the left and the Boulder Ridge Trail on the right. Continue straight ahead in the forest, skirting the east edge of a meadow above the creek. At 1.5 miles, the trail crosses the Phelps Lake Trail to an overlook on the south edge of Phelps Lake. From the overlook are views across the lake, with the towering Teton Peaks forming a dramatic backdrop at the mouth of Death Canyon.

After admiring the vistas, go to the right (east) and weave along the lake's south shore. Pass pocket beaches and cross a bridge over a wetland. Cross a bridge over the lake's wide outlet creek to a posted junction at 1.9 miles. Bear right on the Woodland Trail, and wind through the open, forested terrain. At 3.3 miles is a 4-way junction with the Boulder Trail. The right fork cuts across to the Lake Creek Trail. Continue downhill, returning to the Moose-Wilson Road. Cross the road, complete the loop near the bridge, and retrace your steps to the trailhead. ▪

12. Phelps Lake Loop
LAURANCE S. ROCKEFELLER PRESERVE

Hiking distance: 7-mile loop
Hiking time: 4 hours
Configuration: loop
Elevation gain: 400 feet
Difficulty: moderate
Exposure: a mix of open and shaded forest
Dogs: not allowed
Maps: U.S.G.S. Grand Teton and Teton Village
      Adventure Maps: Jackson Hole
      Laurance S. Rockefeller Preserve Trail Guide (free at trailhead)

**map
page 53**

Phelps Lake is a natural lake situated at the southern end of Grand Teton National Park at the mouth of Death Canyon. The scenic, low-elevation lake sits at 6,633 feet. It covers 750 acres with a length of 1.5 miles, making it the fourth largest lake in the park. The stark, vertical walls of Death Canyon add a beautiful background to the lake, with Albright Peak dominating at 10,552 feet.

The trek around Phelps Lake begins at the Laurance S. Rockefeller Preserve Center along the plains of the Snake River. The trail to the lake passes through several diverse habitats that include wetlands with alder thickets, willows, wild mint, mixed forests, sagebrush meadow, and aquatic communities along Lake Creek and Phelps Lake.

To the trailhead

From the intersection of Highway 89 and Teton Park Road at Moose Junction (located 12 miles north of Jackson), drive a half mile ahead on Teton Park Road to the Moose-Wilson Road on the left. Turn left and continue 3.7 miles to the signed Laurance S. Rockefeller Preserve entrance on the left. Turn left and go 0.3 miles to the trailhead parking lot.

From Teton Village, the preserve turnoff is on the right at 4.3 miles (3.2 miles past the national park entrance kiosk).

The hike

Pass the trailhead map and head west through the sagebrush meadows towards the Teton Mountains. Stroll through aspen groves to the Laurance S. Rockefeller Preserve Center. Beyond the visitor center, meander along the northeast side of Lake Creek, passing observation decks and a waterfall to a posted junction with the Woodland Trail on the right.

Begin the loop on the Lake Creek Trail straight ahead. Cross the bridge over the creek, and weave through the lodgepole pine and Douglas fir forest. Follow the south side of the cascading creek to the Moose-Wilson Road at 0.6 miles. Cross the paved road to a posted junction with the Aspen Ridge Trail on the left and the Boulder Ridge Trail on the right. Continue straight ahead in the forest, skirting the east edge of a meadow above the creek. At 1.5 miles, the trail crosses the Phelps Lake Trail to an overlook on the south edge of Phelps Lake. From the overlook are views across the lake, with the towering Teton Peaks forming a dramatic backdrop at the mouth of Death Canyon.

After admiring the vistas, go to the left (west), passing the Aspen Ridge Trail (Hike 13) on the left. Veer right on the Phelps Lake Trail, following the lakeshore path. Cross a grated metal walkway over a wetland to a junction at 2.2 miles. Detour to the right on the short 0.1-mile path to Huckleberry Point, a peninsula jutting out into the lake. Back on the Phelps Lake Trail, traverse the hillside slope along the lake's west side. Near the north end, cross a boardwalk over a spring. Moderately climb to a junction with the Valley Trail at 3 miles, the highest point of the hike. The left fork leads to Open Canyon and on to Granite Canyon.

For this hike, bear right and descend through the forest on the north side of Phelps Lake. Cross a wood bridge over Lake Creek, the lake's inlet stream from Death Canyon. A short distance past the bridge is another trail split. The Valley Trail goes left and climbs up to the Phelps Lake Overlook (Hike 5). Veer right, staying on the Phelps Lake Trail. Descend to a small sandy beach on the northeast shore. The footpath follows the east side of the lake, at times perched on the hillside slope, to the signed Boulder Ridge Trail at the south end of the lake (Hike 14). Descend another 0.1 mile along Phelps Lake's southeast arm to the signed Woodland Trail on the left. The right fork makes a complete loop at the first overlook of Phelps Lake. Instead, go left and wind through the wooded terrain, passing the lower junction with the Boulder Ridge Trail. Continue downhill, returning to the Moose-Wilson Road. Cross the road, complete the loop near the bridge, and retrace your steps to the trailhead. ▪

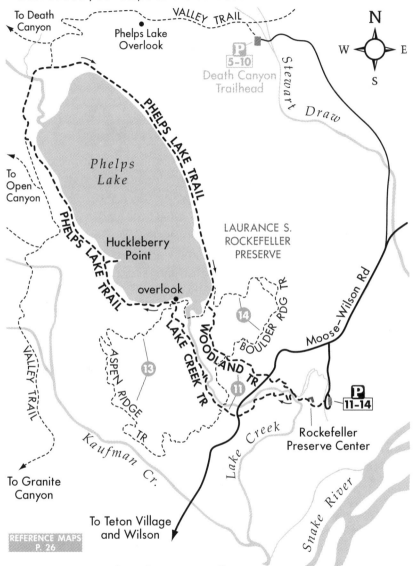

12. Phelps Lake Loop
LAURANCE S. ROCKEFELLER PRESERVE

13. Lake Creek—Aspen Ridge Loop
LAURANCE S. ROCKEFELLER PRESERVE

Hiking distance: 5 miles
Hiking time: 3 hours
Configuration: out-and-back with large loop
Elevation gain: 400 feet
Difficulty: easy to moderate
Exposure: a mix of open and shaded forest
Dogs: not allowed
Maps: U.S.G.S. Grand Teton and Teton Village
Adventure Maps: Jackson Hole
Laurance S. Rockefeller Preserve Trail Guide (free at trailhead)

The land that formed the JY Ranch sits in the southwest corner of Grand Teton National Park on the shore of Phelps Lake. The ranch, used as a summer retreat by the Rockefellers since the early 1930s, was donated to the national park by Laurance Rockefeller and opened to the public in 2007. The year-round trails all depart from the visitor center and lead to Phelps Lake, offering close-up views of the Teton Range and Death Canyon.

This hike loops around the southwest corner of the preserve. The trail begins in dry sagebrush meadows with native grasses, wildflowers, and serene vistas of the forested ridges and jagged Teton Peaks. The trail meanders along the aquatic communities of Lake Creek to an overlook on the shores of Phelps Lake, stretching out from the base of 10,552-foot Albright Peak to the north. The return route climbs up to a series of overlooks on the adjacent glacial ridge. The trail winds through a mixed forest, visits wetlands, and strolls along Kaufman Creek.

To the trailhead

From the intersection of Highway 89 and Teton Park Road at Moose Junction (located 12 miles north of Jackson), drive a half mile ahead on Teton Park Road to the Moose-Wilson Road on the left. Turn left and continue 3.7 miles to the signed Laurance S. Rockefeller Preserve entrance on the left. Turn left and go 0.3 miles to the trailhead parking lot.

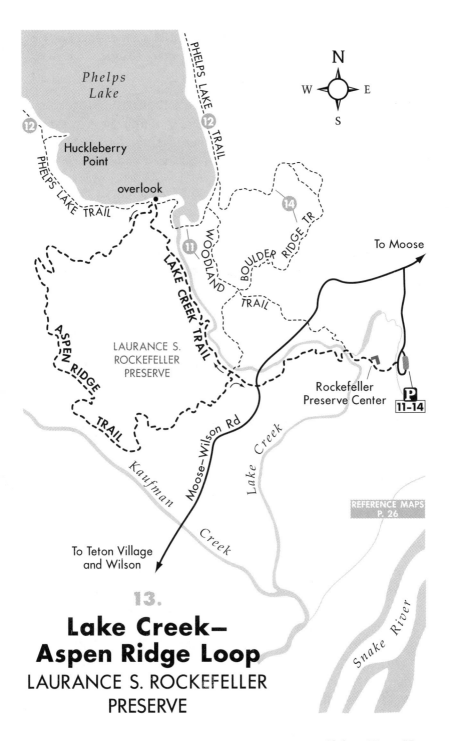

Phelps Lake

Huckleberry Point

overlook

PHELPS LAKE TRAIL

PHELPS LAKE TRAIL

LAKE CREEK TRAIL

WOODLAND TRAIL

BOULDER RIDGE TR.

ASPEN RIDGE TRAIL

LAURANCE S. ROCKEFELLER PRESERVE

To Moose

Rockefeller Preserve Center

Moose-Wilson Rd

Kaufman Creek

Lake Creek

To Teton Village and Wilson

REFERENCE MAPS P. 26

Snake River

13.
Lake Creek–
Aspen Ridge Loop
LAURANCE S. ROCKEFELLER PRESERVE

From Teton Village, the preserve turnoff is on the right at 4.3 miles (3.2 miles past the national park entrance kiosk).

The hike

Pass the trailhead map and head west through the sagebrush meadows towards the Teton Mountains. Stroll through aspen groves to the Laurance S. Rockefeller Preserve Center. Beyond the visitor center, meander along the northeast side of Lake Creek, passing observation decks and a waterfall to a posted junction with the Woodland Trail on the right. Stay on the Lake Creek Trail straight ahead. Cross the bridge over the creek, and weave through the lodgepole pine and Douglas fir forest. Follow the south side of the cascading creek to the Moose-Wilson Road at 0.6 miles. Cross the paved road to a posted junction with the Aspen Ridge Trail on the left and the Boulder Ridge Trail on the right.

Begin the loop straight ahead, staying on the Lake Creek Trail. Skirt the east edge of a meadow above the creek among lodgepole pine and Douglas fir. At 1.5 miles, the trail crosses the Phelps Lake Trail to an overlook on the south edge of Phelps Lake. From the overlook are views across the lake, with the towering Teton Peaks forming a dramatic backdrop at the mouth of Death Canyon.

After admiring the vistas, go to the left (west) for 20 yards to a Y-fork. The Phelps Lake Trail (Hike 12) veers to the right. Take the Aspen Ridge Trail to the left. Descend through the diverse terrain with aspen groves, and pass through a meadow with mountain views. Climb to the ridge and head south, high above the Lake Creek drainage. Zigzag up to the upper ridge at 2.3 miles. Follow the top of the moraine while overlooking forested Granite Canyon, Open Canyon, and 10,783-foot Mount Hunt to the west. Continue down the ridge, then weave down the slope to the banks of Kaufman Creek. Follow the northeast bank of the creek downstream. Curve left, away from the creek, and climb a minor slope. Cross an unpaved service road, staying on the Aspen Ridge Trail. Complete the loop at the junction with the Lake Creek Trail. Bear right on the Lake Creek Trail, returning to Moose-Wilson Road. Cross the road and head back to the trailhead. ▦

14. Woodland—Boulder Ridge Loop
LAURANCE S. ROCKEFELLER PRESERVE

Hiking distance: 3.6 miles
Hiking time: 2 hours
Configuration: out-and-back with loop
Elevation gain: 400 feet
Difficulty: easy to slightly moderate
Exposure: a mix of open and shaded forest
Dogs: not allowed
Maps: U.S.G.S. Grand Teton
      Adventure Maps: Jackson Hole
      Laurance S. Rockefeller Preserve Trail Guide (free at trailhead)

**map
page 59**

The Laurance S. Rockefeller Preserve, lying between the base of the Tetons and the Snake River, features a variety of natural habitats. The wildlife-rich area includes sagebrush meadows; fir, spruce, lodgepole pine, cottonwood and aspen forests; streamside riparian vegetation; glacial ridges; and wetlands that provide food and shelter for migrating birds. The trails begin at the Rockefeller Preserve Center, an ecologically-friendly facility with exhibits about the geology, geography, and diverse plant and wildlife habitats. The exhibits include nature videos, huge landscape photography, and maps.

The Boulder Ridge Trail traverses a minor ridge and winds through a mix of fir, spruce, lodgepole pine, and stands of aspen with an understory of huckleberry and Rocky Mountain maple. The hike visits a series of overlooks atop the adjacent glacial ridge that offer close-up vistas of Phelps Lake and the jagged Teton Range. The trail descends to the south shore of Phelps Lake and returns through wooded terrain on the east side of Lake Creek, the outlet stream of Phelps Lake. The trail passes erratics, randomly strewn boulders left behind by retreating glaciers.

To the trailhead

From the intersection of Highway 89 and Teton Park Road at Moose Junction (located 12 miles north of Jackson), drive a half mile ahead on Teton Park Road to the Moose-Wilson Road on the left. Turn left and continue 3.7 miles to the signed Laurance

S. Rockefeller Preserve entrance on the left. Turn left and go 0.3 miles to the trailhead parking lot.

From Teton Village, the preserve turnoff is on the right at 4.3 miles (3.2 miles past the national park entrance kiosk).

The hike

Pass the trailhead map and head west through the sagebrush meadows towards the Teton Mountains. Stroll through aspen groves to the Laurance S. Rockefeller Preserve Center. Beyond the visitor center, meander along the northeast side of Lake Creek. Pass observation decks and a waterfall to a posted junction with the Woodland Trail on the right at the bridge crossing over Lake Creek. Instead of crossing the creek, go to the right on the Woodland Trail. Wind through the open forest to the Moose-Wilson Road at a half mile. Cross the paved road and continue up among lodgepole pines and Douglas firs to a posted 4-way junction with the Boulder Ridge Trail on the right. The left fork connects with the Lake Creek Trail and Aspen Ridge Trail.

Begin the loop to the right on the Boulder Ridge Trail. Follow the ridge northeast through aspens and evergreens while views of the Teton Peaks emerge through the trees. Wind down into a deep forest, then climb to the head of the minor drainage to the ridge. Walk atop the ridge above a forested canyon to the right. Pass a group of large erratics, boulders that were transported down canyon during the glacial ice-melts. Weave down the mountain to a T-junction with the Phelps Lake Trail. Go to the left along the southeast corner of Phelps Lake 0.1 mile to the Woodland Trail on the left. Go left and wind through the wooded terrain, completing the loop at the junction with the Boulder Ridge Trail. Continue downhill, straight ahead to the Moose-Wilson Road. Cross the road and return to the trailhead. ■

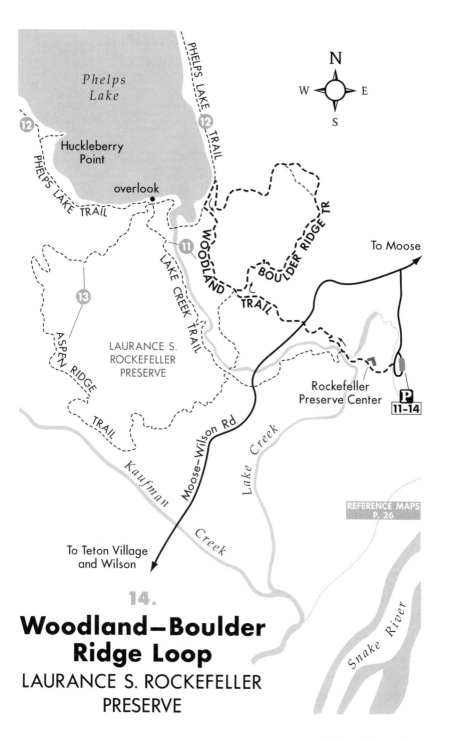

Phelps
Lake

Huckleberry
Point

overlook

PHELPS LAKE TRAIL

PHELPS LAKE TRAIL

PHELPS LAKE TRAIL

WOODLAND TRAIL

BOULDER RIDGE TR

LAKE CREEK TRAIL

ASPEN RIDGE TRAIL

LAURANCE S.
ROCKEFELLER
PRESERVE

To Moose

Rockefeller
Preserve Center

P
11-14

Moose–Wilson Rd

Lake Creek

Kaufman Creek

To Teton Village
and Wilson

REFERENCE MAPS
P. 26

Snake River

N
W   E
S

14.
Woodland–Boulder Ridge Loop
LAURANCE S. ROCKEFELLER PRESERVE

15. Granite Canyon Trail
GRANITE CANYON TRAILHEAD

Hiking distance: 4–12.6 miles round trip
Hiking time: 2–6 hours
Configuration: out-and-back
Elevation gain: 600–1,600 feet
Difficulty: moderate to strenuous
Exposure: open meadows and forested canyon
Dogs: not allowed
Maps: U.S.G.S. Teton Village and Rendezvous Peak
Adventure Maps: Jackson Hole
Beartooth Publishing: Grand Teton National Park map
National Geographic Trails Illustrated: Grand Teton Nat'l. Park

**map
page 62**

Granite Canyon is a U-shaped, glacier-carved canyon near the south end of the Teton Range. The Granite Canyon Trail, which follows the length of the canyon to its headwaters, connects with the Teton Crest Trail near Marion Lake and also with the summit of Rendezvous Mountain at the top of the Teton Village aerial tram (to the canyon's south). The hike can be as short or long as you choose, as entering the canyon for even a short distance is a rewarding hike. The hike begins at the mouth of Granite Canyon and climbs moderately along the cascading watercourse to the upper canyon and high mountain meadows. Near the meadows, the creek branches into three forks by the upper Granite Canyon patrol cabin, a rustic log cabin used primarily by work crews maintaining the trails and by patrolling rangers. From here are great views down the canyon.

The Granite Canyon Trail can be combined with the Open Canyon Trail (Hike 10) for a 21-mile loop or with Rendezvous Mountain (Hike 78) for a 12.4-mile loop (utilizing the ski resort's tram).

To the trailhead

From the intersection of Highway 89 and Teton Park Road at Moose Junction (located 12 miles north of Jackson), drive a half mile ahead on Teton Park Road to the Moose-Wilson Road on the left. Turn left and continue 5.9 miles to the signed Granite Canyon parking area on the right.

From Teton Village, drive 2.1 miles north to the trailhead (one mile past the national park entrance kiosk).

The hike

Take the signed Granite Canyon Trail west through rolling sagebrush meadows and aspen groves. Cross a wooden bridge over Granite Creek and curve north, following the base of the mountains. Pass several overlooks of Granite Creek to a posted Y-fork at 1.5 miles. The left fork (the Valley Trail) leads 2.4 miles to Teton Village. Take the right fork 0.1 mile to a trail split, crossing a bridge over cascading Granite Creek and a second bridge over a creek channel. To the right, the Valley Trail continues to Phelps Lake.

Bear left and curve up Granite Canyon on the north side of the cascading creek, passing large granite boulders. Steadily climb under the towering canyon walls through the forested creek bottom with thick vegetation and talus slopes. Continue climbing the canyon past cascades, with views of avalanche chutes across the canyon, up to a bridge crossing. As you near the upper meadow at 6.2 miles, cross another bridge over a tributary stream to a posted junction by the Granite Canyon patrol cabin. Bear left on the Rendezvous Mountain Trail, and cross bridges over the North Fork, then Middle Fork of Granite Creek. This is the turn-around spot.

To hike farther, there are three options. Option 1: From the patrol cabin, the Granite Canyon Trail continues up the north fork of the canyon 0.8 miles to the Open Canyon Trail on the right. The Open Canyon Trail climbs over Mount Hunt Divide and into Open Canyon, the next drainage to the north, for a 21-mile loop hike (see Hike 10).

Option 2: Continuing straight on the Granite Canyon Trail along the North Fork leads to the Teton Crest Trail near Marion Lake, a high-alpine lake at the base of Housetop Mountain.

Option 3: To the south, the Rendezvous Mountain Trail heads up to the top of the aerial tram from Teton Village at a 10,450-foot summit. Take the ski resort's tram down to Teton Village, and return on the Valley Trail for a 12.4-mile loop (see Hike 77). ■

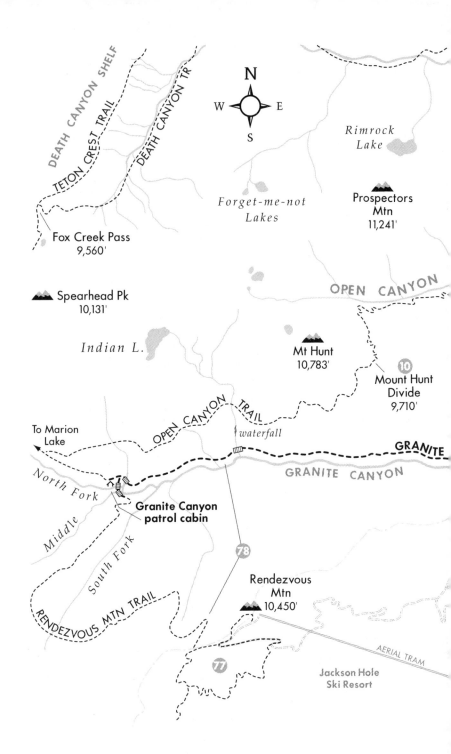

N
W   E
S

DEATH CANYON SHELF

TETON CREST TRAIL

DEATH CANYON TR

Rimrock Lake

Fox Creek Pass
9,560'

Forget-me-not Lakes

▲▲ **Prospectors Mtn**
11,241'

▲▲ **Spearhead Pk**
10,131'

OPEN CANYON

Indian L.

▲▲ **Mt Hunt**
10,783'

(10)

Mount Hunt Divide
9,710'

OPEN CANYON TRAIL

To Marion Lake ◀

↯ *waterfall*

GRANITE

GRANITE CANYON

North Fork

Middle

Granite Canyon patrol cabin

South Fork

(78)

RENDEZVOUS MTN TRAIL

Rendezvous Mtn
▲▲ 10,450'

AERIAL TRAM

(77)

Jackson Hole Ski Resort

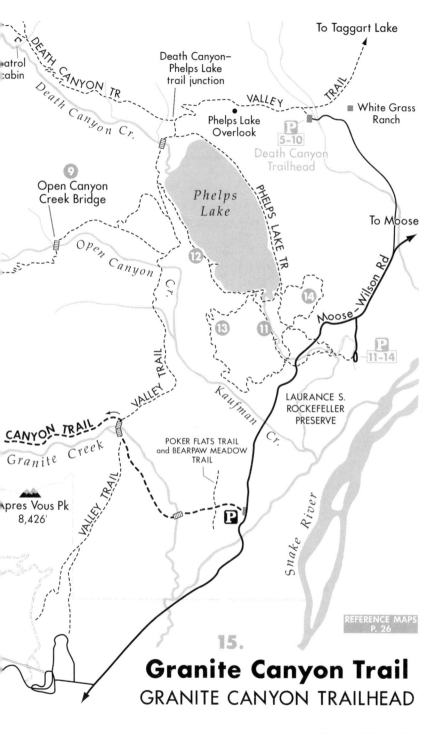

To Taggart Lake

DEATH CANYON TR

Death Canyon–
Phelps Lake
trail junction

VALLEY TRAIL

White Grass
Ranch

Patrol
cabin

Death Canyon Cr.

Phelps Lake
Overlook

P
5-10

Death Canyon
Trailhead

⑨ Open Canyon
Creek Bridge

*Phelps
Lake*

PHELPS LAKE TR

To Moose

Open Canyon Cr.

⑫

Moose-Wilson Rd

⑭

⑬   ⑪

Kaufman Cr.

P
11-14

LAURANCE S.
ROCKEFELLER
PRESERVE

VALLEY TRAIL

CANYON TRAIL

Granite Creek

POKER FLATS TRAIL
and BEARPAW MEADOW
TRAIL

Snake River

Apres Vous Pk
8,426'

VALLEY TRAIL

P

REFERENCE MAPS
P. 26

15.
Granite Canyon Trail
GRANITE CANYON TRAILHEAD

16. Taggart Lake Loop
TAGGART LAKE TRAILHEAD

Hiking distance: 4.4 miles round trip
Hiking time: 2 hours
Configuration: loop
Elevation gain: 300 feet
Difficulty: easy
Exposure: mostly exposed meadows with forested pockets
Dogs: not allowed
Maps: U.S.G.S. Moose and Grand Teton · Adventure Maps: Jackson Hole
Beartooth Publishing: Grand Teton National Park map
National Geographic Trails Illustrated: Grand Teton Nat'l. Park

The Taggart Lake Loop is a leisurely, accessible, and scenic hike at the base of the Tetons. Taggart Lake sits below the towering peaks, formed by a glacier flow from Avalanche Canyon directly to the lake's west. This hike circles the moraine that encloses the lake along the Beaver Creek drainage. The trail climbs over the glacial moraine to an overlook of forest-lined Taggart Lake while the Teton peaks rise in the background. The hike passes through the area burned in the 1985 Beaver Creek Fire. The forest has since renewed itself with lodgepole pines and aspens.

To the trailhead

From the national park entrance at Moose, drive 2.5 miles on Teton Park Road to the Taggart Lake Trailhead on the left. Turn left into the pullout and park.

The trailhead is 4.5 miles south of the South Jenny Lake turnoff.

The hike

Head west across the rolling sagebrush meadow for 0.2 miles to a signed trail fork. The right fork leads to Bradley Lake and is the return route for this loop hike. Take the Beaver Creek Trail to the left. In 100 yards bear left again at a second junction. The trail follows the watercourse of Beaver Creek along its north bank. Continue to a signed junction with the Valley Trail to Phelps Lake, which crosses over the creek at 1.6 miles. Head uphill to the right (north), with great views of the Teton Range. At the morainal ridge is an overlook of Taggart Lake. Descend to the lakeshore and cross a long wooden bridge over Taggart Creek, the outlet stream. Follow the shoreline to a signed junction. The left fork leads to Bradley Lake (Hike 17). Bear right, away from the lake, on the Taggart Lake Trail. Reach another junction a half mile ahead. Bear right again and follow the cascading Taggart Creek downhill. Cross two bridges over the creek, and complete the loop in the meadow. Return to the left. ■

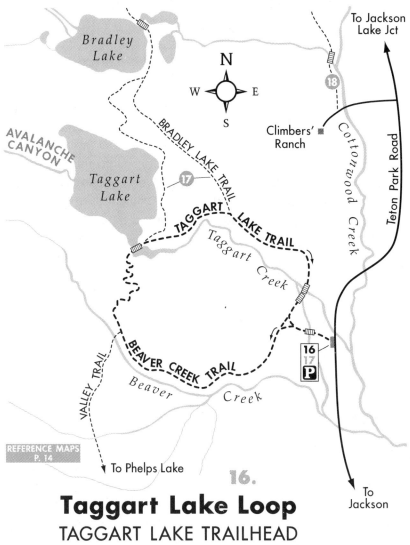

16.

Taggart Lake Loop
TAGGART LAKE TRAILHEAD

17. Taggart and Bradley Lakes Loop
TAGGART LAKE TRAILHEAD

Hiking distance: 4.8 miles round trip
Hiking time: 3 hours
Configuration: out-and-back with loop
Elevation gain: 520 feet
Difficulty: easy to slightly moderate
Exposure: mostly exposed meadows and forested pockets
Dogs: not allowed
Maps: U.S.G.S. Moose and Grand Teton · Adventure Maps: Jackson Hole
Beartooth Publishing: Grand Teton National Park map
National Geographic Trails Illustrated: Grand Teton Nat'l. Park

This pleasant, gentle hike includes a cascading creek and serene lakes at the base of the Tetons. The trail follows tumbling Taggart Creek to Taggart Lake, then makes a loop along the east shore of the lake en route to Bradley Lake. Bradley Lake was formed by a glacier flow from Garnet Canyon, emptying into the lake from the peaks to the west. The trail climbs over a glacial moraine to the lake at the mouth of Garnet Canyon. On the return, there is an excellent overview of the area as the elevated trail perches over Taggart Lake, traversing an area burned in the 1985 Beaver Creek Fire. The new forest has thrived, blanketing the area in lodgepole pines and aspens.

To the trailhead

From the national park entrance at Moose, drive 2.5 miles on Teton Park Road to the Taggart Lake Trailhead on the left. Turn left into the pullout and park.

The trailhead is 4.5 miles south of the South Jenny Lake turnoff.

The hike

From the parking lot, walk west towards the Tetons across the sagebrush flat to a signed junction at 0.2 miles. The left fork parallels Beaver Creek to Taggart Lake (Hike 16). Take the right fork and head uphill, crossing the cascading Taggart Creek via two footbridges. At 1.1 mile is another well-marked trail junction. This is the start of the loop. Go left on the Taggart Lake Trail 0.5 miles to Taggart Lake. From here the trail continues to the right along the eastern shore of the lake. Head over the moraine and through the forest towards Bradley Lake, 1.1 mile ahead. After exploring Bradley Lake along its northeast side, return to the trail junction at the south end of Bradley Lake. Take the Bradley Lake Trail, now to the left, and head back 2.1 miles to the parking lot. ■

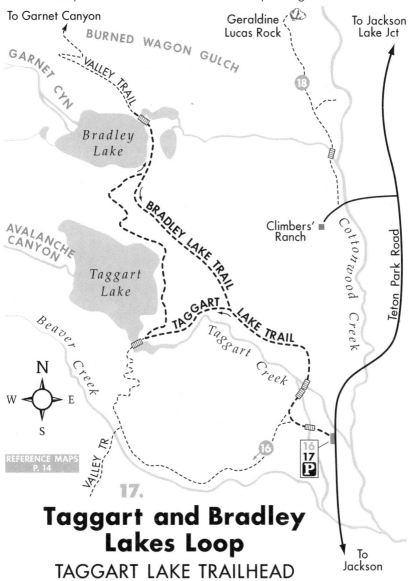

To Garnet Canyon

Geraldine
Lucas Rock

To Jackson
Lake Jct

BURNED WAGON GULCH

GARNET CYN

VALLEY TRAIL

18

Bradley
Lake

BRADLEY LAKE TRAIL

Climbers'
Ranch

Cottonwood Creek

AVALANCHE CANYON

Taggart
Lake

Teton Park Road

TAGGART LAKE TRAIL

Taggart Creek

Beaver Creek

N
W ● E
S

16

16
17
P

REFERENCE MAPS
P. 14

VALLEY TR

17.

Taggart and Bradley Lakes Loop
TAGGART LAKE TRAILHEAD

To
Jackson

18. Cottonwood Creek

Hiking distance: 2 miles round trip
Hiking time: 1 hour
Configuration: out-and-back
Elevation gain: level
Difficulty: easy
Exposure: a mix of open meadows and shaded forest
Dogs: not allowed
Maps: U.S.G.S. Moose

This easy and well-defined trail parallels Cottonwood Creek into two wildflower-covered meadows along the base of the Teton Range. In the first meadow is an abandoned, government-owned log structure from the old Lucas Ranch. Geraldine Lucas, who once owned the ranch, died in 1938. In the second meadow is a large rock. Her ashes are buried beneath the rock, designated by a plaque. The views of the Tetons from both meadows are striking.

The Climbers' Ranch, at the end of the road at the trailhead, offers lodging for rock climbers and hikers.

To the trailhead

From the national park entrance at Moose, continue 3.7 miles on Teton Park Road to the Grand Teton Climbers' Ranch turnoff—turn left. Drive 0.3 miles to a bridge crossing Cottonwood Creek. After crossing, park in the pullout on the right.

The hike

From the parking pullout, the unmarked trail heads to the north through the cottonwood trees along the west side of Cottonwood Creek. The trail crosses two small streams and a bridge over a larger outlet stream from Bradley Lake, 400 feet above. After crossing the stream, enter a meadow, where the historic Lucas Ranch building resides. Leave the trail and head east to get a closer look at the log structure. After returning, continue along the trail through the forest to a second meadow, where the trail fades out. The Geraldine Lucas rock sits in the middle of the meadow. Return along the same route. ■

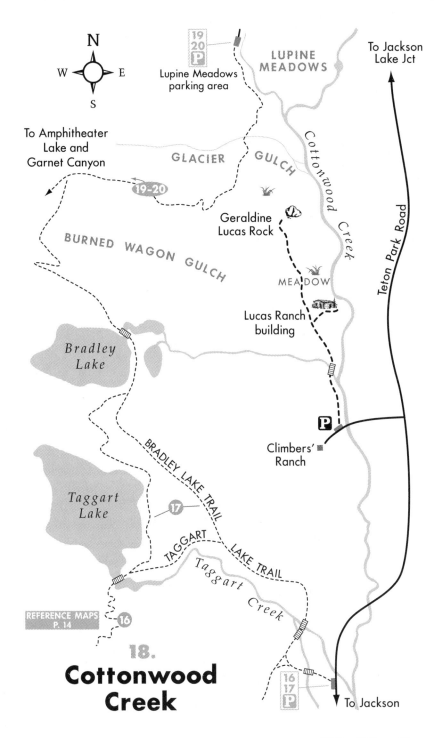

N
W   E
S

To Jackson
Lake Jct

19
20
P
Lupine Meadows
parking area

LUPINE
MEADOWS

Cottonwood Creek

To Amphitheater
Lake and
Garnet Canyon

GLACIER   GULCH

19-20

Geraldine
Lucas Rock

Teton Park Road

BURNED WAGON GULCH

MEADOW

Lucas Ranch
building

Bradley
Lake

P

Climbers'
Ranch

BRADLEY LAKE TRAIL

Taggart
Lake

17

TAGGART   LAKE TRAIL

Taggart Creek

REFERENCE MAPS
P. 14

16

18.
**Cottonwood
Creek**

16
17
P

To Jackson

19. Surprise and Amphitheater Lakes
LUPINE MEADOWS TRAILHEAD

Hiking distance: 9.6 miles round trip
Hiking time: 5 hours
Configuration: out-and-back
Elevation gain: 3,000 feet
Difficulty: strenuous
Exposure: exposed flats, forested slopes, and high alpine meadows
Dogs: not allowed
Maps: U.S.G.S. Moose and Grand Teton · Adventure Maps: Jackson Hole
      Beartooth Publishing: Grand Teton National Park map

The Lupine Meadows trailhead is the access point into Garnet Canyon, a steep, backcountry canyon that drains from the park's centerpiece Teton peaks. The trails from Lupine Meadows—Hikes 19 and 20—begin in the level Jackson Hole Valley, then strenuously climb for thousands of feet towards the peaks.

Surprise and Amphitheater Lakes sit on a high bench beneath the cliffs and snow-covered slopes of Disappointment Peak. Surprise Lake, at an elevation of 9,550 feet, is a circular tarn in a beautiful subalpine setting. Amphitheater Lake, at 9,700 feet, sits in a rugged, steep-walled cirque at the eastern base of the towering peak. The high mountain lakes are located only a quarter mile apart. The majestic peaks of the Teton Range, including Grand Teton, Mount Owen, and Tepee Pillar, surround the lakes. The hike begins on the valley floor in Lupine Meadows, just south of Jenny Lake, and climbs to the lakes through sage-covered meadows, forested moraines, flower-filled slopes, and alpine tundra. From the trail are beautiful views in every direction. The Teton peaks rise dramatically to the west. Blacktail Butte, Taggart Lake, Bradley Lake, and Jenny Lake lie below in the expansive Jackson Hole Valley.

To the trailhead

From the national park entrance at Moose, drive 6.2 miles to Lupine Meadows Road on the left (west). Turn left and continue 1.6 miles to the Lupine Meadows parking lot at the end of the road.

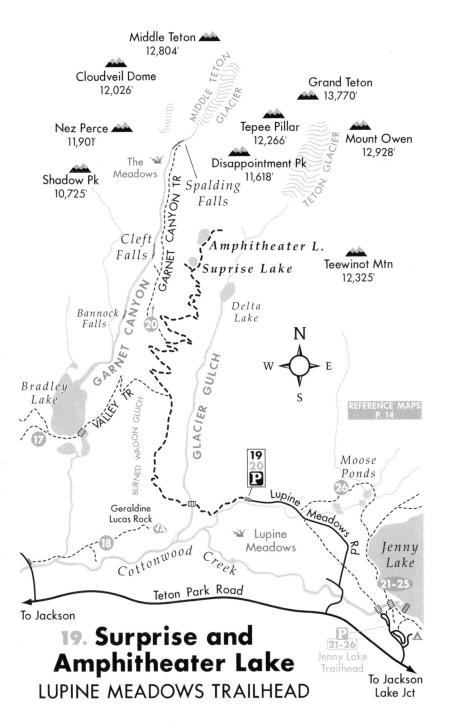

Middle Teton ▲▲
12,804'

Cloudveil Dome ▲▲
12,026'

Grand Teton
▲ 13,770'

Nez Perce ▲▲
11,901'

Tepee Pillar ▲▲
12,266'

Mount Owen ▲▲
12,928'

MIDDLE TETON GLACIER

The ☙
Meadows

Disappointment Pk ▲▲
11,618'

Shadow Pk ▲▲
10,725'

*Spalding
Falls*

GARNET CANYON TR

TETON GLACIER

*Cleft
Falls*

Amphitheater L.

Suprise Lake

Teewinot Mtn ▲▲
12,325'

GARNET CANYON

*Bannock
Falls*

20

*Delta
Lake*

N

W   E

S

*Bradley
Lake*

VALLEY TR

BURNED WAGON GLUCH

GLACIER GULCH

REFERENCE MAPS
P. 14

17

*Moose
Ponds*

26

19
20
P

Lupine Meadows Rd

Geraldine
Lucas Rock

*Jenny
Lake*

18

☙ Lupine
Meadows

21-25

Cottonwood Creek

Teton Park Road

To Jackson

P
21-26
Jenny Lake
Trailhead

△

To Jackson
Lake Jct

19. **Surprise and Amphitheater Lake**
LUPINE MEADOWS TRAILHEAD

From the South Jenny Lake turnoff, Lupine Meadows Road is 0.8 miles south on the right (west).

The hike

Cross the sage flats, heading south to the base of the lateral moraine. Cross a bridge over the Glacier Gulch drainage, meltwater from Teton Glacier 4,000 feet above. At one mile, curve west (right) and climb the forested ridge between Glacier Gulch and Burned Wagon Gulch. At 1.7 miles, pass a signed junction with the Valley Trail on the left, which heads south to Bradley Lake. The trail begins to steeply ascend the mountain on long, sweeping switchbacks between Glacier Gulch and Garnet Canyon. Bradley and Taggart Lakes can be seen to the south and Jenny Lake to the north. Continue climbing to a posted junction at 3 miles, located near a southern switchback at 8,400 feet.

The Garnet Canyon Trail branches left to Spalding Falls (Hike 20). Stay to the right, climbing more switchbacks through a forest of Douglas fir, subalpine fir, and Engelmann spruce. The trail finally levels out at 4.4 miles, where whitebark pine becomes dominant and views open up to the surrounding mountains. In less than a quarter mile, the trail reaches the east tip of Surprise Lake. For a great view of Surprise Lake and the surrounding peaks, leave the main trail, and follow the footpath south along the lake. Climb up the 200-foot pinnacle just southeast of the lake.

Return to the main trail, and continue across the north end of Surprise Lake for 0.2 miles to the east end of Amphitheater Lake. The lake is nestled beneath the craggy rock walls of Disappointment Peak, jutting up from the water's edge. The trail follows the eastern shoreline beyond the north tip of the lake to a saddle overlooking Glacier Gulch. After enjoying the wonderful views, return along the same trail. ▨

20. Garnet Canyon to Spalding Falls
LUPINE MEADOWS TRAILHEAD

Hiking distance: 10 miles round trip
Hiking time: 5 hours
Configuration: out-and-back
Elevation gain: 2,600 feet
Difficulty: strenuous
Exposure: exposed flats, forested slopes, and high alpine meadows
Dogs: not allowed
Maps: U.S.G.S. Moose and Grand Teton · Adventure Maps: Jackson Hole
Beartooth Publishing: Grand Teton National Park map

**map
page 75**

Garnet Canyon is a rugged, narrow, V-shaped canyon draining from the upper Teton peaks. The canyon is surrounded by Disappointment Peak, Tepee Pillar, Middle Teton, and Nez Perce. Garnet Creek, formed by runoff from Middle Teton Glacier, cascades through the canyon on its journey to Bradley Lake.

This hike follows the creek up to Spalding Falls at an elevation of 10,000 feet. It is the highest named waterfall in the Grand Tetons. The falls cascades 80 feet off the rocky cliffs into The Meadows, a boulder-strewn meadow framed by the jagged peaks. Below The Meadows, at the mouth of Garnet Canyon, the creek cascades another 50 feet over Cleft Falls. The hike begins in Lupine Meadows and follows the strenuous route to Surprise and Amphitheater Lakes before veering west into Garnet Canyon. The Garnet Canyon Trail is primarily used by rock climbers tackling Middle Teton, Tepee Pillar, or Grand Teton.

All off-trail hiking requires registration at the ranger station. To hike past Cleft Falls, register at the ranger station

To the trailhead

From the national park entrance at Moose, drive 6.2 miles to Lupine Meadows Road on the left (west). Turn left and continue 1.6 miles to the Lupine Meadows parking lot at the end of the road.

From the South Jenny Lake turnoff, Lupine Meadows Road is 0.8 miles south on the right (west).

The hike

Cross the sage flats, heading south to the base of the lateral moraine. Cross a bridge over the Glacier Gulch drainage, meltwater from Teton Glacier 4,000 feet above. At one mile, curve west (right) and climb the forested ridge between Glacier Gulch and Burned Wagon Gulch. At 1.7 miles, pass a signed junction with the Valley Trail on the left, which heads south to Bradley Lake. The trail begins to steeply ascend the mountain on long, sweeping switchbacks between Glacier Gulch and Garnet Canyon. Bradley and Taggart Lakes can be seen to the south and Jenny Lake to the north. Continue climbing to a posted junction at 3 miles, located near a southern switchback at 8,400 feet.

The trail to Surprise and Amphitheater Lakes heads to the right. Take the Garnet Canyon Trail to the left and traverse the mountain. Nez Perce sits straight ahead, while Bradley and Taggart Lakes can be seen far below. The trail soon curves right and heads into the mouth of the canyon, where views open to Middle Teton at the head of the canyon. An off-trail spur on the left drops down through a rock field to the creek below Cleft Falls. Switchbacks lead up a talus slope to the end of the designated Garnet Canyon Trail at 4.1 miles, located at a massive boulder field on the canyon floor near Cleft Falls.

If you registered at the ranger station, continue on the climbers' path, traversing the boulder field while staying close to Garnet Creek. At 0.6 miles, the path reaches The Meadows, a boulder-strewn alpine meadow surrounded by the magnificent Teton peaks. At the head of the meadow, backed by the 12,804-foot Middle Teton, Spalding Falls drops off the rocky cliff to the grassy basin floor. Return along the same trail. ▓

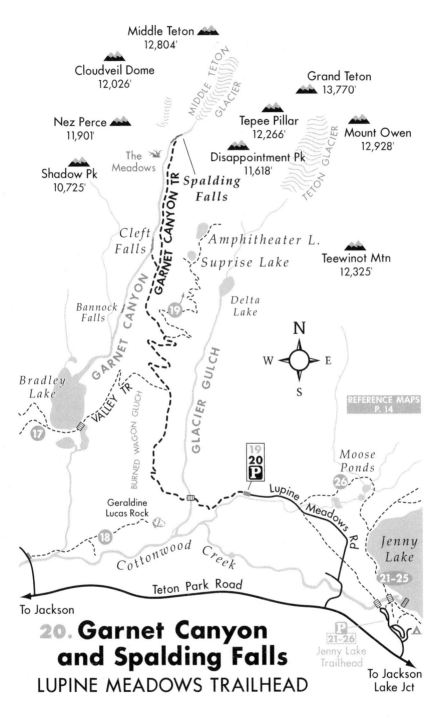

Middle Teton ▲ 12,804'

Cloudveil Dome 12,026'

Grand Teton ▲ 13,770'

Nez Perce ▲ 11,901'

Tepee Pillar 12,266'

Mount Owen 12,928'

MIDDLE TETON GLACIER

The Meadows

Shadow Pk 10,725'

Disappointment Pk 11,618'

Spalding Falls

GARNET CANYON TR

TETON GLACIER

Cleft Falls

Amphitheater L.

Suprise Lake

Teewinot Mtn 12,325'

GARNET CANYON

Bannock Falls

19

Delta Lake

N
W ✦ E
S

Bradley Lake

VALLEY TR

GLACIER GULCH

BURNED WAGON GLUCH

17

REFERENCE MAPS
P. 14

Moose Ponds

19
20
P

Lupine Meadows Rd

26

Geraldine Lucas Rock

18

Jenny Lake

21-25

Cottonwood Creek

Teton Park Road

To Jackson

P
21-26

Jenny Lake Trailhead

To Jackson Lake Jct

20. **Garnet Canyon and Spalding Falls**
LUPINE MEADOWS TRAILHEAD

Jenny Lake • Leigh Lake
CENTRAL GRAND TETON

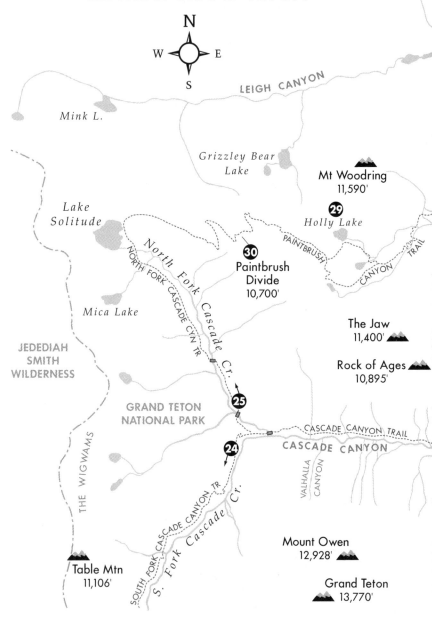

N
W ✦ E
S

LEIGH CANYON

Mink L.

Grizzley Bear
Lake

Mt Woodring
11,590'

Lake
Solitude

29

Holly Lake

PAINTBRUSH

North Fork Cascade Cr.

NORTH FORK CASCADE CYN TR

30
Paintbrush
Divide
10,700'

CANYON TRAIL

Mica Lake

The Jaw
11,400'

JEDEDIAH
SMITH
WILDERNESS

Rock of Ages
10,895'

GRAND TETON
NATIONAL PARK

25

CASCADE CANYON TRAIL

24

CASCADE CANYON

THE WIGWAMS

VALHALLA
CANYON

SOUTH FORK CASCADE CANYON TR

S. Fork Cascade Cr.

Mount Owen
12,928'

Table Mtn
11,106'

Grand Teton
13,770'

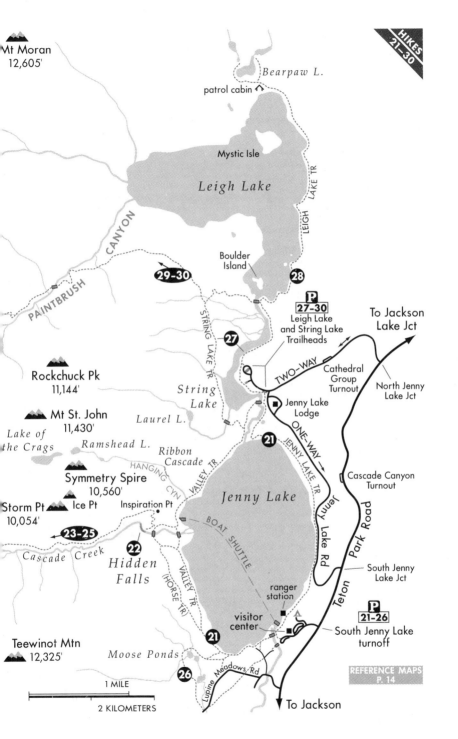

Mt Moran
12,605'

Bearpaw L.

patrol cabin

Mystic Isle

Leigh Lake

LEIGH LAKE TR

Boulder
Island

29-30

PAINTBRUSH CANYON

STRING LAKE TR

28

P
27-30
Leigh Lake
and String Lake
Trailheads

To Jackson
Lake Jct

27

TWO-WAY

Cathedral
Group
Turnout

North Jenny
Lake Jct

Rockchuck Pk
11,144'

*String
Lake*

Laurel L.

Jenny Lake
Lodge

Mt St. John
11,430'

*Lake of
the Crags*

Ramshead L.

*Ribbon
Cascade*

ONE-WAY

21

JENNY LAKE TR

Symmetry Spire
10,560'

HANGING CYN

VALLEY TR

Cascade Canyon
Turnout

Storm Pt   Ice Pt
10,054'

Inspiration Pt

Jenny Lake

BOAT SHUTTLE

23-25

Cascade Creek

22

*Hidden
Falls*

VALLEY TR
(HORSE TR)

ranger
station

South Jenny
Lake Jct

Teton Park Road

visitor
center

South Jenny Lake
turnoff

P
21-26

Teewinot Mtn
12,325'

21

Moose Ponds

26

Lupine Meadows Rd

REFERENCE MAPS
P. 14

1 MILE

2 KILOMETERS

To Jackson

21. Jenny Lake Loop
from SOUTH JENNY LAKE TRAILHEAD

Hiking distance: Via boat shuttle: 5-mile loop
(boat shuttle leaves every 20 minutes)
Walk perimeter: 7-mile loop
Hiking time: 2.5 hours—4 hours
Configuration: loop
Elevation gain: level
Difficulty: moderate
Exposure: mostly exposed with shaded areas
Dogs: not allowed
Maps: U.S.G.S. Jenny Lake · Adventure Maps: Jackson Hole
Beartooth Publishing: Grand Teton National Park map
National Geographic Trails Illustrated: Grand Teton Nat'l. Park

Jenny Lake sits in a glacial moraine at the mouth of Cascade Canyon beneath the spectacular Teton peaks. The lake is the second largest lake in Grand Teton National Park. (Jackson Lake is the largest.) It stretches 2.5 miles along the Teton Range with a width

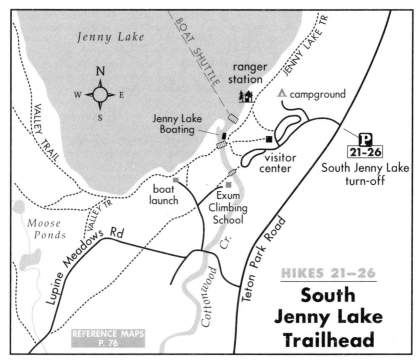

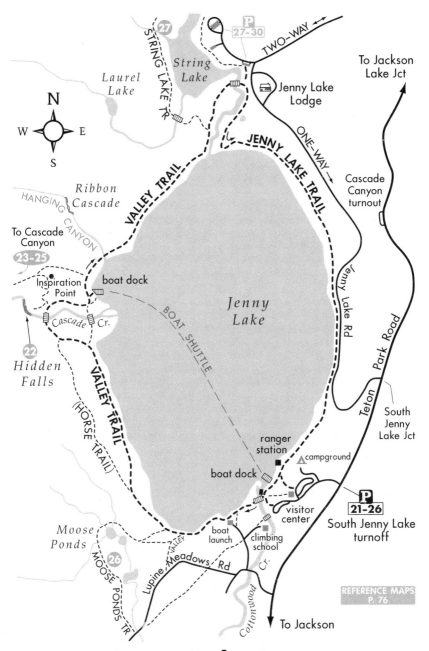

21. **Jenny Lake Loop**
SOUTH JENNY LAKE TRAILHEAD

of 1.5 miles. This popular hike circles the perimeter of gorgeous Jenny Lake on a level, well-trodden trail surrounded by magnificent scenery. On the west shore of the lake, an optional side trip leads to Hidden Falls, a waterfall that drops 200 feet along tumbling Cascade Creek. The hike may be shortened two miles by taking the boat shuttle across the lake from the Jenny Lake Ranger Station to the west shore.

To the trailhead

From the national park entrance at Moose, continue 7 miles on Teton Park Road to the South Jenny Lake turnoff and turn left (west). Park in the lot by the ranger station.

The South Jenny Lake turnoff is 13 miles south of Jackson Lake Junction and 3.2 miles south of North Jenny Lake Junction.

The hike

From the parking lot, take the paved path along Jenny Lake to the boat dock. The boat shuttle may be taken to the west shore of Jenny Lake. There is a fee for the boat ride.

If you prefer to hike, cross the long footbridge over Cottonwood Creek, and walk around the south shore of the lake. Pass the Valley Trail and Moose Ponds Trail on the left, staying near the lake. Head to the bridge crossing Cascade Creek near the west shore dock at 2 miles. For a side trip, take the left trail to Hidden Falls and Inspiration Point (Hike 22).

If you have taken the boat over to the west side of the lake, take the well-defined trail from the boat dock to the left toward Hidden Falls. In a short distance is a trail junction. For the side trip to Hidden Falls and Inspiration Point, take the trail to the left.

To continue hiking clockwise around the lake, take the trail to the north, parallel to the west shoreline of Jenny Lake. At the north end of the lake, the trail winds around the waterway that connects String Lake to Jenny Lake. Pass the String Lake Trail on the left, cross a bridge over the wide outlet stream, and loop south (right), back towards Jenny Lake. Follow the path along the more developed east side of Jenny Lake back to the ranger station and parking lot. ▦

22. Hidden Falls and Inspiration Point
SOUTH JENNY LAKE TRAILHEAD
to CASCADE CANYON

Hiking distance: Via boat shuttle: 1.8 miles round trip
(boat shuttle leaves every 20 minutes)
Walk south shore: 5.8 miles round trip

map page 83

Hiking time: 1.5—3 hours
Configuration: out-and-back (or loop with boat shuttle)
Elevation gain: 450 feet
Difficulty: easy to moderate
Exposure: mostly exposed with shaded areas
Dogs: not allowed
Maps: U.S.G.S. Jenny Lake · Adventure Maps: Jackson Hole
Beartooth Publishing: Grand Teton National Park map
National Geographic Trails Illustrated: Grand Teton Nat'l. Park

This hike is one of the most popular trails in the national park. Inspiration Point, on the west edge of Jenny Lake, sits atop an outcropping on a glacial bench more than 400 feet above the lake. The magnificent overlook rests near the mouth of Cascade

---

Jenny Lake Boat Shuttle

Operates May 15 — September 30

For current hours of operation,
call the marina at (307) 734-9227
jennylakeboating.com

Shuttle rates at the time of this printing:
(subject to change)

Adult round trip $10 · Adult one way $7

Child round trip $5 · Child one way $5

Shuttles run approximately every 20 minutes.

Boat dock is located at the South Jenny Lake area.

Reservations are not required. Handicapped-accessible.

Canyon beneath Ice Point, Storm Point, and Symmetry Spire on Mount St. John. The pinnacles of Teewinot Mountain tower across the canyon. The views stretch out across Jenny Lake and the Snake River Valley to the Gros Ventre Mountains east of Jackson Hole. Beautiful Hidden Falls, surrounded by spruce and fir, drops 200 feet along Cascade Creek before tumbling into Jenny Lake. This hike begins on the east shore of Jenny Lake and can be shortened two miles by taking the boat shuttle from the Jenny Lake Ranger Station to the west shore.

To the trailhead

From the national park entrance at Moose, continue 7 miles on Teton Park Road to the South Jenny Lake turnoff and turn left (west). Park in the lot by the ranger station.

The South Jenny Lake turnoff is 13 miles south of Jackson Lake Junction and 3.2 miles south of North Jenny Lake Junction.

The hike

From the parking lot, take the paved path along Jenny Lake to the boat dock. You may take the boat shuttle or hike to Hidden Falls and Inspiration Point. There is a fee for the boat shuttle, but the ride allows for great photo opportunities and shortens the hike by four miles (2 miles each way).

If you have taken the boat over to the west side of the lake, a well-defined trail to the left (south) follows Cascade Creek to a footbridge. The trail to the right (west) leads 0.2 miles towards Hidden Falls. Near two other footbridges over Cascade Creek is a side trail to the left for an excellent view of the falls. Continue another half mile up switchbacks to Inspiration Point.

If you prefer to hike from the south Jenny Lake trailhead, cross the long footbridge over Cottonwood Creek, and walk around the south shore of the lake. Pass the Valley Trail and Moose Ponds Trail on the left, staying near the lake. Head to the bridge crossing Cascade Creek near the west shore dock at 2 miles. Cross the bridge and take the trail to the left towards Hidden Falls. After savoring the views, return on the same path or enjoy the boat ride back to the trailhead. ▪

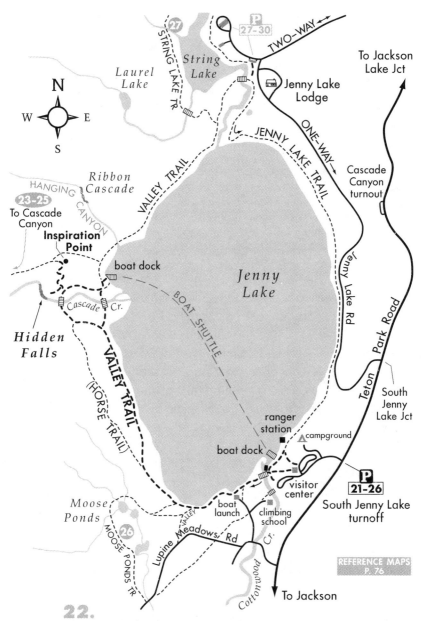

Hidden Falls–Inspiration Loop
SOUTH JENNY LAKE TRAILHEAD
to CASCADE CANYON

23. Cascade Canyon to the Canyon Fork

SOUTH JENNY LAKE TRAILHEAD

Hiking distance: 9.2 miles round trip (4 miles less with boat shuttle)
Hiking time: 5 hours
Configuration: out-and-back
Elevation gain: 1,100 feet
Difficulty: strenuous
Exposure: a mix of open meadow and forested canyon
Dogs: not allowed
Maps: U.S.G.S. Jenny Lake and Mount Moran
 Adventure Maps: Jackson Hole
 Beartooth Publishing: Grand Teton National Park map
 National Geographic Trails Illustrated: Grand Teton Nat'l. Park

map page 86

Cascade Canyon is a U-shaped, glacial-carved canyon with a wide, expansive floor and steep, mile-high walls. The hike up the canyon is one of the most popular and beautiful hikes in Grand Teton National Park. (The farther you hike, the less crowded the trail.) From the west end of Jenny Lake, the trail gently climbs up the magnificent canyon along Cascade Creek in the shadow of the Grand Teton. The towering peaks of the Teton Range loom above throughout the hike. The hike can be shortened by taking the boat shuttle from the Jenny Lake Ranger Station to the west shore.

To the trailhead

From the national park entrance at Moose, continue 7 miles on Teton Park Road to the South Jenny Lake turnoff and turn left (west). Park in the lot by the ranger station.

 The South Jenny Lake turnoff is 13 miles south of Jackson Lake Junction and 3.2 miles south of North Jenny Lake Junction.

The hike

From the parking lot, take the paved path along Jenny Lake to the boat dock. You may take the boat shuttle or hike to Hidden Falls and Inspiration Point. There is a fee for the boat shuttle, but the ride allows for great photo opportunities and shortens the hike by four miles (2 miles each way).

If you have taken the boat over to the west side of the lake, a well-defined trail to the left (south) follows Cascade Creek to a footbridge. The trail to the right (west) leads 0.2 miles towards Hidden Falls. Near two other footbridges over Cascade Creek is a side trail to the left for an excellent view of the falls. Continue on the main trail for another half mile up switchbacks to Inspiration Point.

If you prefer to hike from the south Jenny Lake trailhead, cross the long footbridge over Cottonwood Creek, and walk around the south shore of the lake. Pass the Valley Trail and Moose Ponds Trail on the left, staying near the lake. Head to the bridge crossing Cascade Creek near the west shore dock at 2 miles. Cross the bridge and take the trail to the left towards Hidden Falls. Continue another half mile up switchbacks to Inspiration Point.

After enjoying the views at Inspiration Point, take the main trail west through the forest and across talus slopes, climbing 0.6 miles to the mouth of Cascade Canyon. The trail—the Cascade Canyon Trail—levels out and gently heads up the wide canyon floor on the north side of Cascade Creek. Continue through open meadows, boulder fields, and forests of Engelmann spruce and Douglas fir. The steep-walled mountains tower a mile above the trail. Valhalla Canyon can be seen nestled between Mount Owen and Grand Teton, where a long, narrow cascade tumbles off the south canyon wall. At 3.6 miles from Inspiration Point, the canyon splits into a north and south drainage and Cascade Creek divides. Cross a footbridge over the North Fork to a trail split a quarter mile ahead. This is the turn-around spot.

To hike farther, trails continue up both the north and south canyons. Hike 24 heads south to Hurricane Pass. Hike 25 heads north to Lake Solitude, climbing 1,200 feet in 2.7 miles, and then another 2.4 miles up to Paintbrush Divide. Hike 25 can be combined with Hike 30 for a 19-mile loop through Paintbrush Canyon, the next canyon to the north. ▪

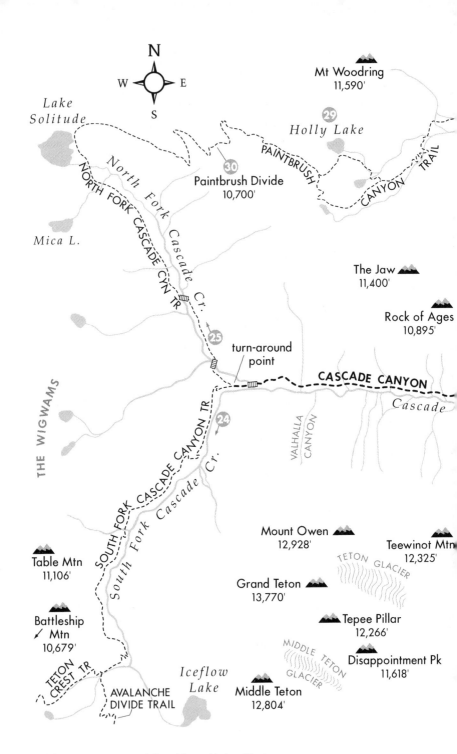

N
W E
S

Lake Solitude

Mt Woodring
11,590'

Holly Lake

29

30
Paintbrush Divide
10,700'

PAINTBRUSH

CANYON TRAIL

North Fork

NORTH FORK CASCADE CYN TR

Cascade Cr.

Mica L.

The Jaw
11,400'

Rock of Ages
10,895'

25

turn-around point

CASCADE CANYON

Cascade

THE WIGWAMS

SOUTH FORK CASCADE CANYON TR

South Fork Cascade Cr.

24

VALHALLA CANYON

Mount Owen
12,928'

Teewinot Mtn
12,325'

TETON GLACIER

Table Mtn
11,106'

Grand Teton
13,770'

Tepee Pillar
12,266'

Battleship Mtn
10,679'

MIDDLE TETON GLACIER

Disappointment Pk
11,618'

TETON CREST TR

Iceflow Lake

AVALANCHE DIVIDE TRAIL

Middle Teton
12,804'

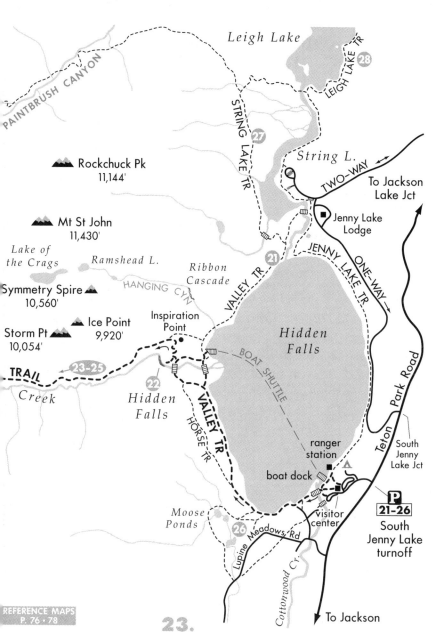

Leigh Lake

PAINTBRUSH CANYON

STRING LAKE TR

LEIGH LAKE TR

28

27

🔺 Rockchuck Pk
11,144'

String L.

TWO-WAY

To Jackson
Lake Jct

🔺 Mt St John
11,430'

■ Jenny Lake
Lodge

*Lake of
the Crags*

Ramshead L.

*Ribbon
Cascade*

HANGING CYN

JENNY LAKE TR

ONE-WAY

21

VALLEY TR

Symmetry Spire 🔺
10,560'

🔺 Ice Point
9,920'

Inspiration
Point

*Hidden
Falls*

Storm Pt 🔺
10,054'

23-25

TRAIL

Creek

22

*Hidden
Falls*

BOAT SHUTTLE

VALLEY TR

HORSE TR

Teton Park Road

ranger
station

South
Jenny
Lake Jct

boat dock

*Moose
Ponds*

26

Lupine Meadows Rd

visitor
center

P
21-26

South
Jenny Lake
turnoff

Cottonwood Cr.

To Jackson

23.

Cascade Canyon
to the Canyon Fork
SOUTH JENNY LAKE TRAILHEAD

24. South Fork Cascade Canyon to Hurricane Pass

SOUTH JENNY LAKE TRAILHEAD

Hiking distance: 19 miles round trip (4 miles less with boat shuttle)
Hiking time: 10 hours
Configuration: out-and-back
Elevation gain: 3,600 feet
Difficulty: very strenuous
Exposure: a mix of open meadow and forested canyon
Dogs: not allowed
Maps: U.S.G.S. Jenny Lake, Mount Moran, Grand Teton
　　　 Adventure Maps: Jackson Hole
　　　 Beartooth Publishing: Grand Teton National Park map
　　　 National Geographic Trails Illustrated: Grand Teton Nat'l. Park

**map
page 90**

Hurricane Pass sits at the head of the South Fork of Cascade Canyon at 10,372 feet. The pass is on the national park boundary on the west side of the park's centerpiece Teton peaks. From this magnificent perch are awesome 360-degree vistas, including a "back" view of the Grand, Middle, and South Tetons. Also in view are Table Mountain, Mount Moran, Battleship Mountain, Avalanche Divide, the limestone cliffs of The Wall, and the gradual slope of the west-facing Tetons. Below is a bird's-eye view of Schoolroom Glacier, a crescent-shaped glacier with a small lake.

To the trailhead

From the national park entrance at Moose, continue 7 miles on Teton Park Road to the South Jenny Lake turnoff and turn left (west). Park in the lot by the ranger station.

The South Jenny Lake turnoff is 13 miles south of Jackson Lake Junction and 3.2 miles south of North Jenny Lake Junction.

The hike

From the parking lot, take the paved path along Jenny Lake to the boat dock. You may take the boat shuttle or hike to Hidden Falls and Inspiration Point. There is a fee for the boat shuttle, but the ride allows for great photo opportunities and shortens the hike by four miles (2 miles each way).

If you have taken the boat over to the west side of the lake, a well-defined trail to the left (south) follows Cascade Creek to a footbridge. The trail to the right (west) leads 0.2 miles towards Hidden Falls. Near two other footbridges over Cascade Creek is a side trail to the left for an excellent view of the falls. Continue on the main trail for another half mile up switchbacks to Inspiration Point.

If you prefer to hike from the south Jenny Lake trailhead, cross the long footbridge over Cottonwood Creek, and walk around the south shore of the lake. Pass the Valley Trail and Moose Ponds Trail on the left, staying near the lake. Head to the bridge crossing Cascade Creek near the west shore dock at 2 miles. Cross the bridge and take the trail to the left towards Hidden Falls. Continue another half mile up switchbacks to Inspiration Point.

After enjoying the views at Inspiration Point, take the main trail west through the forest and across talus slopes, climbing 0.6 miles to the mouth of Cascade Canyon. The trail—the Cascade Canyon Trail—levels out and gently heads up the wide canyon floor on the north side of Cascade Creek. Continue through open meadows, boulder fields, and forests of Engelmann spruce and Douglas fir. The steep-walled mountains tower a mile above the trail. Valhalla Canyon can be seen nestled between Mount Owen and Grand Teton, where a long, narrow cascade tumbles off the south canyon wall. At 3.6 miles from Inspiration Point, the canyon splits into a north and south drainage and Cascade Creek divides. Cross a footbridge over the North Fork to a trail split a quarter mile ahead.

The right fork—North Fork Cascade Canyon Trail—climbs up the north fork to Lake Solitude (Hike 25). Take the left fork—South Fork Cascade Canyon Trail—into the south fork. Switchbacks lead up the canyon to views of the steep east ridge of Table Mountain. Follow the tumbling whitewater of the South Fork of Cascade Creek. Pass through a few flower-filled meadows, continually gaining elevation. Two miles up the canyon, enter a forest of whitebark pine, breaking out above the treeline at 3.5 miles. Climb a quarter mile up steep switchbacks to a junction in a meadow with the Avalanche Divide Trail on the left, which

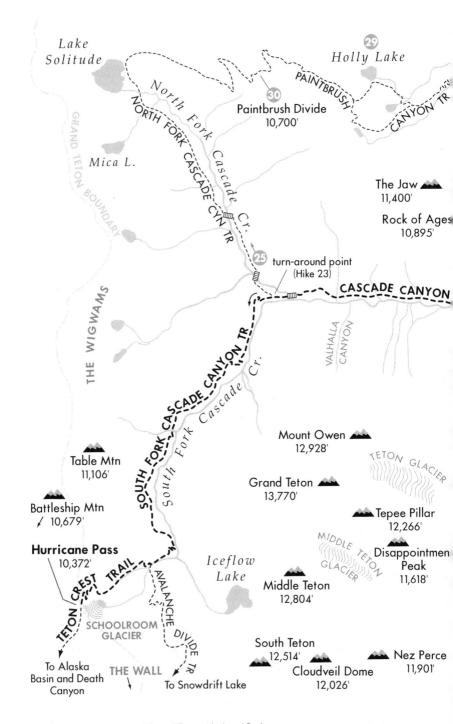

Lake Solitude

Holly Lake

29

Mica L.

North Fork Cascade Cr.

NORTH FORK CASCADE CYN TR

PAINTBRUSH

CANYON TR

30

Paintbrush Divide
10,700'

The Jaw ▲
11,400'

Rock of Ages
10,895'

25

turn-around point
(Hike 23)

CASCADE CANYON

GRAND TETON BOUNDARY

THE WIGWAMS

SOUTH FORK CASCADE CANYON TR

South Fork Cascade Cr.

VALHALLA CANYON

Mount Owen ▲
12,928'

TETON GLACIER

Table Mtn ▲
11,106'

Grand Teton ▲
13,770'

Battleship Mtn ▲
/ 10,679'

Tepee Pillar ▲
12,266'

Hurricane Pass
10,372'

Iceflow
Lake

MIDDLE TETON GLACIER

Disappointmen
Peak
11,618'

TETON CREST TRAIL

AVALANCHE DIVIDE TR

Middle Teton ▲
12,804'

SCHOOLROOM GLACIER

South Teton ▲
12,514'

Nez Perce ▲
11,901'

To Alaska
Basin and Death
Canyon

THE WALL

To Snowdrift Lake

Cloudveil Dome
12,026'

leads to Snowdrift Lake at the base of The Wall. Stay to the right, passing through talus slopes to the bottom (north) end of Schoolroom Glacier in a stark cirque. Zigzag up the headwall through limestone scree and possible snowfields. The trail tops out on Hurricane Pass at 9.5 miles, where there are sweeping views in every direction. This is the turn-around spot.

To hike farther, the trail descends into Alaska Basin on the Teton Crest Trail, leaving the national park. The trail connects with Death Canyon (Hike 8) for a multi-day loop hike. ■

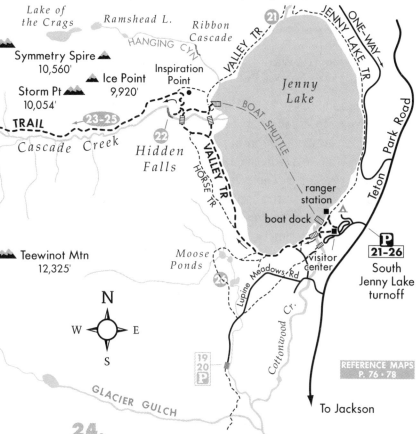

24.
South Fork Cascade Canyon to Hurricane Pass
SOUTH JENNY LAKE TRAILHEAD

25. North Fork Cascade Canyon to Lake Solitude

SOUTH JENNY LAKE TRAILHEAD

Hiking distance: 14.5 miles round trip (4 miles less with boat shuttle)
Hiking time: 7 hours
Configuration: out-and-back
Elevation gain: 2,300 feet
Difficulty: very strenuous
Exposure: a mix of open meadow and forested canyon
Dogs: not allowed
Maps: U.S.G.S. Jenny Lake and Mount Moran
Adventure Maps: Jackson Hole
Beartooth Publishing: Grand Teton National Park map
National Geographic Trails Illustrated: Grand Teton Nat'l. Park

**map
page 94**

Lake Solitude is a gorgeous high mountain lake at the head of the North Fork of Cascade Canyon. The 50-acre lake sits in a glacial depression at an elevation of 9,035 feet. It is ringed by scoured mountain walls in a stunning, backcountry cirque. The trail heads up the North Fork of Cascade Canyon in the heart of the Tetons, then climbs through sub-alpine forests, talus slopes, and meadows filled with wild flowers. Throughout the hike are magnificent views of the Cathedral Group: Teewinot Mountain, Mount Owen, and Grand Teton.

To the trailhead

From the national park entrance at Moose, continue 7 miles on Teton Park Road to the South Jenny Lake turnoff and turn left (west). Park in the lot by the ranger station.

The South Jenny Lake turnoff is 13 miles south of Jackson Lake Junction and 3.2 miles south of North Jenny Lake Junction.

The hike

From the parking lot, take the paved path along Jenny Lake to the boat dock. You may take the boat shuttle or hike to Hidden Falls and Inspiration Point. There is a fee for the boat shuttle, but the ride allows for great photo opportunities and shortens the hike by four miles (2 miles each way).

If you have taken the boat over to the west side of the lake, a well-defined trail to the left (south) follows Cascade Creek to a footbridge. The trail to the right (west) leads 0.2 miles towards Hidden Falls. Near two other footbridges over Cascade Creek is a side trail to the left for an excellent view of the falls. Continue on the main trail for another half mile up switchbacks to Inspiration Point.

If you prefer to hike from the south Jenny Lake trailhead, cross the long footbridge over Cottonwood Creek, and walk around the south shore of the lake. Pass the Valley Trail and Moose Ponds Trail on the left, staying near the lake. Head to the bridge crossing Cascade Creek near the west shore dock at 2 miles. Cross the bridge and take the trail to the left towards Hidden Falls. Continue another half mile up switchbacks to Inspiration Point.

After enjoying the views at Inspiration Point, take the main trail west through the forest and across talus slopes, climbing 0.6 miles to the mouth of Cascade Canyon. The trail—the Cascade Canyon Trail—levels out and gently heads up the wide canyon floor on the north side of Cascade Creek. Continue through open meadows, boulder fields, and forests of Engelmann spruce and Douglas fir. The steep-walled mountains tower a mile above the trail. Valhalla Canyon can be seen nestled between Mount Owen and Grand Teton, where a long, narrow cascade tumbles off the south canyon wall. At 3.6 miles from Inspiration Point, the canyon splits into a north and south drainage and Cascade Creek divides. Cross a footbridge over the North Fork to a trail split a quarter mile ahead.

From this posted trail junction, take the right trail—North Fork Cascade Canyon Trail—into the North Fork of Cascade Canyon, heading steadily uphill to the northwest. The first mile climbs through Engelmann spruce and Douglas fir, crossing two footbridges over the North Fork of Cascade Creek. Parallel the west side of the creek up the classic U-shaped, glaciated canyon, alternating between sub-alpine forest, talus slopes, and alpine meadows. The Wigwams rise high on the west wall of the canyon, and Paintbrush Divide can be seen to the right. The grade steepens as the trail zigzags up the moraine to Lake Solitude. The trail follows the east side of the beautiful lake, surrounded by the eroded, semicircular canyon walls that are sparsely dotted with random trees. At the north shore is a world-class view down canyon of Teewinot Mountain, Mount Owen, and the Grand Teton. This is our turn-around spot.

To turn the hike into a strenuous 19-mile loop, the trail continues up a series of steep switchbacks to Paintbrush Divide (Hike 30), gaining 1,700 feet in 2.4 miles. The trail returns to the valley through Paintbrush Canyon and back to Jenny Lake. ▣

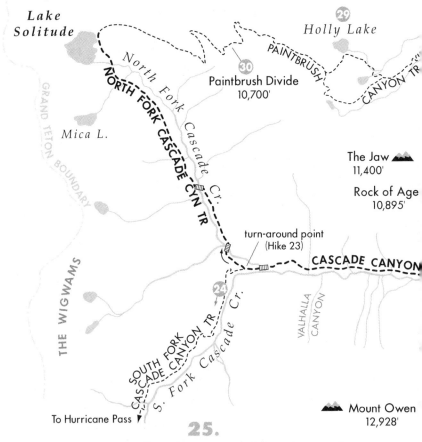

25.

North Fork Cascade Canyon to Lake Solitude

SOUTH JENNY LAKE TRAILHEAD

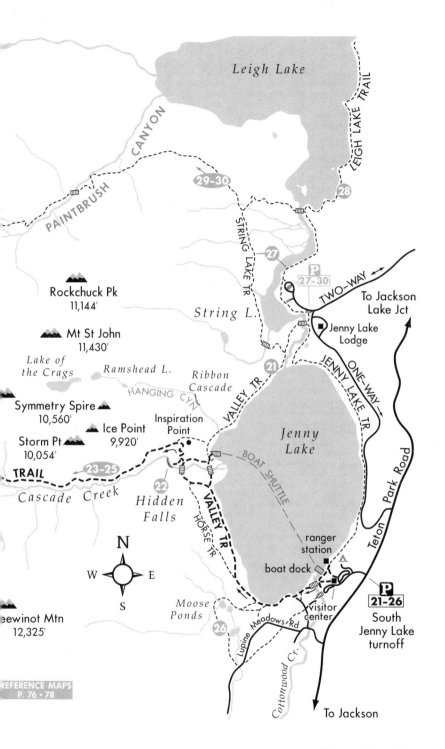

Leigh Lake

LEIGH LAKE TRAIL

29-30

28

STRING LAKE TR.

27

P
27-30

TWO-WAY

To Jackson
Lake Jct

Rockchuck Pk
11,144'

String L.

Jenny Lake
Lodge

Mt St John
11,430'

Lake of
the Crags

Ramshead L.

Ribbon
Cascade

21

VALLEY TR.

JENNY LAKE TR.

ONE-WAY

Symmetry Spire
10,560'

HANGING CYN

Inspiration
Point

Ice Point
9,920'

Storm Pt
10,054'

Jenny
Lake

TRAIL

23-25

BOAT SHUTTLE

Cascade Creek

22

Hidden
Falls

VALLEY TR.

HORSE TR.

ranger
station

boat dock

N

W   E

S

eewinot Mtn
12,325'

Moose
Ponds

26

Lupine Meadows Rd

visitor
center

P
21-26

South
Jenny Lake
turnoff

Teton Park Road

Cottonwood Cr.

To Jackson

26. Moose Ponds

SOUTH JENNY LAKE TRAILHEAD

Hiking distance: 3 miles round trip
Hiking time: 1.5 hours
Configuration: loop
Elevation gain: 150 feet
Difficulty: easy
Exposure: mostly exposed meadows
Dogs: not allowed
Maps: U.S.G.S. Jenny Lake and Moose · Adventure Maps: Jackson Hole
    Beartooth Publishing: Grand Teton National Park map
    National Geographic Trails Illustrated: Grand Teton Nat'l. Park

The Moose Ponds are a set of three ponds in a lush, stream-fed marshy bowl. The ponds sit near the south end of Jenny Lake beneath the jagged spires of Teewinot Mountain. The area provides an ideal habitat for moose, deer, and waterfowl, making it an excellent place to observe wildlife. This loop trail follows the south end of Jenny Lake, then circles the ponds and crosses Lupine Meadows.

To the trailhead

From the national park entrance at Moose, continue 7 miles on Teton Park Road to the South Jenny Lake turnoff and turn left (west). Park in the lot by the ranger station.

The South Jenny Lake turnoff is 13 miles south of Jackson Lake Junction and 3.2 miles south of North Jenny Lake Junction.

The hike

Take the paved path along Jenny Lake to the boat dock. Cross the long footbridge over Cottonwood Creek, and take the trail towards Cascade Canyon and Hidden Falls. Follow the south edge of Jenny Lake past the boat launch to a signed junction with the Valley Trail on the left at one mile. Continue straight ahead a short distance to another signed junction near the top of the moraine. Take the Moose Ponds Trail to the left to an overlook of the ponds. Descend to the willow flats and the three ponds. The path circles the ponds, crossing two footbridges and three streams. At the south end of the meadow, the trail enters a fir and spruce forest. At two miles the path breaks out of the forest into Lupine Meadows at the unpaved Lupine Meadows Road. Follow the road 30 yards to the left, and pick up the un-signed trail across the road on the right. Walk northeast through the sagebrush meadow and recross the road. The trail leads toward the Exum Climbing School. Curve left around the back of the building on a faint path. A short distance ahead is a horse bridge crossing Cottonwood Creek. Cross the creek to return to the parking lot. ▪

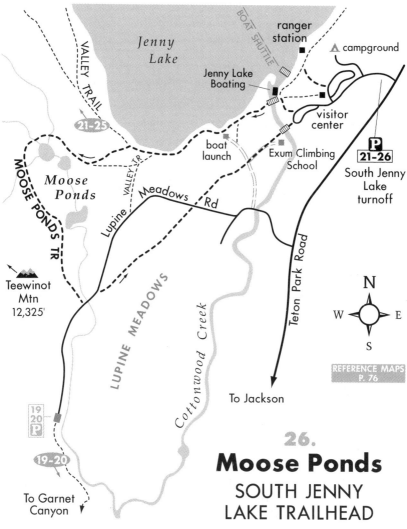

26.
Moose Ponds
SOUTH JENNY LAKE TRAILHEAD

27. String Lake Loop
STRING LAKE TRAILHEAD

Hiking distance: 3.6-mile loop
Hiking time: 2 hours
Configuration: loop
Elevation gain: 200 feet
Difficulty: easy
Exposure: a mix of open meadows and shaded forest
Dogs: not allowed
Maps: U.S.G.S. Jenny Lake · Adventure Maps: Jackson Hole
Beartooth Publishing: Grand Teton National Park map
National Geographic Trails Illustrated: Grand Teton Nat'l. Park

String Lake is a long and narrow lake connecting Jenny Lake to Leigh Lake along the base of the Teton peaks. String Lake is a shallow, sandy lake that warms up from the sun, making it popular for swimming. This easy hike circles String Lake, crossing bridges over streams and offering some of the best views of the Tetons.

To the trailhead

From the national park entrance at Moose, continue 10.2 miles on Teton Park Road to the North Jenny Lake Junction and turn left (west). Drive 0.9 miles to the String Lake Picnic Area and turn right. Drive 0.1 mile and turn left into the parking lot.

The hike

From the parking lot, take the trail west, crossing the wooden footbridge over the String Lake outlet stream. At 0.3 miles is a junction with the Valley Trail to Jenny Lake (Hike 21). Take the right fork on the String Lake Trail. At 0.5 miles, the trail crosses a bridge over an inlet stream from Laurel Lake, sitting 700 feet above the trail. After crossing, the trail heads north. Gradually gain 200 feet to another bridge over an inlet stream. At the crest of the hill is a junction with the Paintbrush Canyon Trail (Hikes 29 and 30). Take the right fork, heading downhill 0.8 miles to a bridge over the Leigh Lake outlet stream. Cross the bridge and take the right fork south along the shore of String Lake. Pass the picnic area and continue to the parking lot, completing the loop. ▧

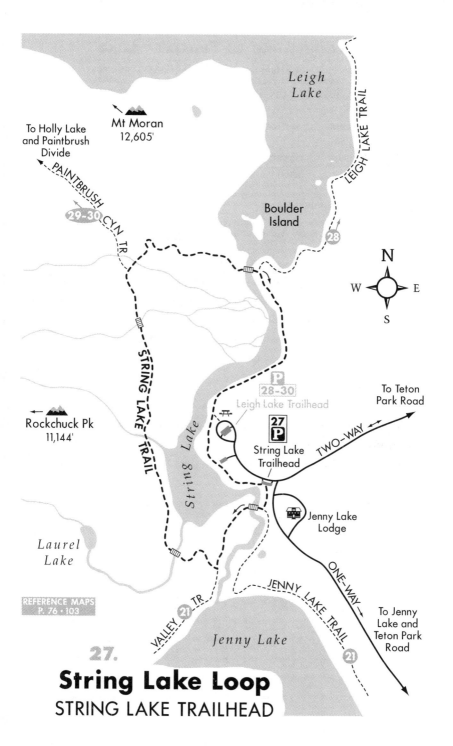

Leigh
Lake

LEIGH LAKE TRAIL

Mt Moran
12,605'

To Holly Lake
and Paintbrush
Divide

PAINTBRUSH CYN TR

29-30

Boulder
Island

28

N
W · E
S

STRING LAKE TRAIL

P
28-30
Leigh Lake Trailhead

To Teton
Park Road

Rockchuck Pk
11,144'

27
P
String Lake
Trailhead

TWO-WAY

Jenny Lake
Lodge

String Lake

ONE-WAY

Laurel
Lake

To Jenny
Lake and
Teton Park
Road

REFERENCE MAPS
P. 76 · 103

VALLEY 21 TR

JENNY LAKE TRAIL

21

Jenny Lake

27.
String Lake Loop
STRING LAKE TRAILHEAD

28. Leigh Lake to Bearpaw Lake
LEIGH LAKE TRAILHEAD

Hiking distance: 7.4 miles round trip
Hiking time: 3.5 hours
Configuration: out-and-back
Elevation gain: level
Difficulty: easy to moderate
Exposure: a mix of open meadows and shaded forest
Dogs: not allowed
Maps: U.S.G.S. Jenny Lake · Adventure Maps: Jackson Hole
　　　Beartooth Publishing: Grand Teton National Park map
　　　National Geographic Trails Illustrated: Grand Teton Nat'l. Park

This level hike meanders along the east shore of Leigh Lake to Bearpaw Lake, a tree-lined lake at the base of Mount Moran. The trail offers magnificent views of Mount Moran and the Cathedral Group—the three Teton peaks of Teewinot, Grand Teton, and Mount Owen. There are sandy beaches on the east side of Leigh Lake. This area is popular for canoeing, swimming, and hiking.

To the trailhead

From the national park entrance at Moose, continue 10.2 miles on Teton Park Road to the North Jenny Lake Junction and turn left (west). Drive 0.9 miles to the String Lake picnic area and turn right. Park a short distance ahead in the parking lot at the end of the loop.

The hike

From the parking lot, several asphalt walking paths lead to the trailhead at String Lake. This trail closely follows the shore of String Lake for 0.9 miles to the southern tip of Leigh Lake. There are two trail junctions within 100 yards of each other. Take the right fork both times, staying on the Leigh Lake Trail. The trail continues north along the east shore. At 2.2 miles is the sandy East Shore Beach. As you approach the north end of Leigh Lake, a patrol cabin is on the left, then the trail splits. The right fork leads to the east side of Bearpaw Lake. The left fork curves westward around the lake to Trapper Lake. Return along the same path. ■

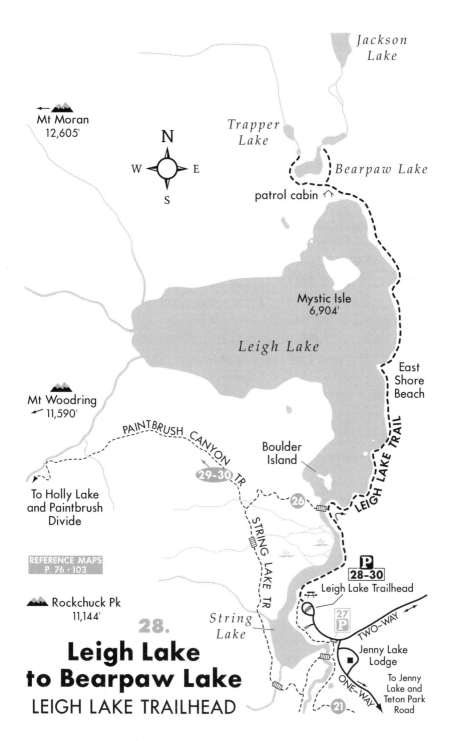

Jackson Lake

Mt Moran
12,605'

N
W · E
S

Trapper Lake

Bearpaw Lake

patrol cabin ⌂

Mystic Isle
6,904'

Leigh Lake

East Shore Beach

Mt Woodring
11,590'

PAINTBRUSH CANYON TR

29-30

Boulder Island

LEIGH LAKE TRAIL

To Holly Lake
and Paintbrush
Divide

26

STRING LAKE TR

REFERENCE MAPS
P. 76 · 103

Rockchuck Pk
11,144'

P
28-30
Leigh Lake Trailhead

28.

String Lake

27
P

TWO-WAY

Leigh Lake
to Bearpaw Lake
LEIGH LAKE TRAILHEAD

Jenny Lake Lodge

To Jenny
Lake and
Teton Park
Road

ONE-WAY

21

29. Paintbrush Canyon Trail to Holly Lake

LEIGH LAKE TRAILHEAD

Hiking distance: 12.6 miles round trip
Hiking time: 6 hours
Configuration: out-and-back
Elevation gain: 2,500 feet
Difficulty: strenuous
Exposure: mostly forested with some open meadows
Dogs: not allowed
Maps: U.S.G.S. Jenny Lake and Mount Moran
    Adventure Maps: Jackson Hole
    Beartooth Publishing: Grand Teton National Park map
    National Geographic Trails Illustrated: Grand Teton Nat'l. Park

**map
page 104**

Holly Lake is nestled in a gorgeous alpine setting within a glacial cirque at the base of Mount Woodring in Paintbrush Canyon.
The views from the glacial tarn include Rockchuck Peak, The Jaw,
Mount St. John, Leigh Lake, and Jackson Lake. Even though the
steep-walled Paintbrush Canyon is located in the central part of
the Teton Range, it is one of the quieter, less-traveled canyons.
The trail to Holly Lake begins between String and Leigh Lakes and
is a steady uphill climb through the canyon.

To the trailhead

From the national park entrance at Moose, continue 10.2 miles
on Teton Park Road to the North Jenny Lake Junction and turn
left (west). Drive 0.9 miles to the String Lake picnic area and turn
right. Park a short distance ahead in the parking lot at the end of
the loop.

The hike

Walk north along the east shore of String Lake. Continue 0.9 miles
to a bridge on the left, located just south of Leigh Lake. Cross
the wooden footbridge over the connector stream between the
two lakes. Head up the hillside through the woodland to a posted
junction on the lower slopes of Rockchuck Peak at 1.6 miles. The
left fork traverses the hillside overlooking String Lake and Jenny

Lake. Bear right and head west on the Paintbrush Canyon Trail through a dense forest of lodgepole pines, Engelmann spruce, Douglas fir, and subalpine fir. The trail reaches Paintbrush Canyon Creek near the mouth of the canyon at just over 3 miles. Views extend down canyon to Leigh Lake and Mystic Isle. Enter the high-walled, glacier-carved canyon, and cross a bridge to the north bank of the creek. Continue up canyon, crossing several tributary streams from Mount Woodring. Zigzag up a series of switchbacks to a trail junction at 5.8 miles. The left fork continues through the camping zone below the divide. Take the Holly Lake Trail to the right, and climb a few switchbacks. Cross an outlet stream on the east side of a small lake, reaching the south end of Holly Lake a half mile from the junction. After enjoying the high alpine lake, return along the same trail.

Paintbrush Divide—Hike 30—is 1.6 miles farther and 1,300 feet higher. ■

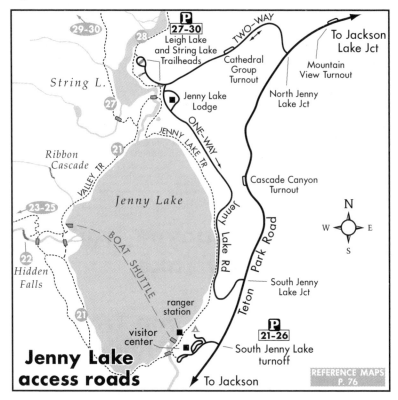

Jenny Lake access roads

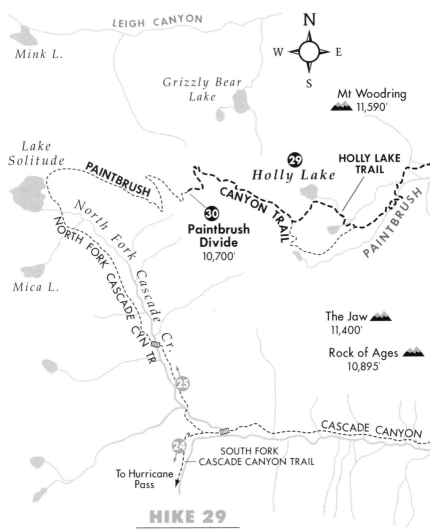

HIKE 29
Paintbrush Canyon Trail to Holly Lake

HIKE 30
Paintbrush Canyon Trail to Paintbrush Divide
LEIGH LAKE TRAILHEAD

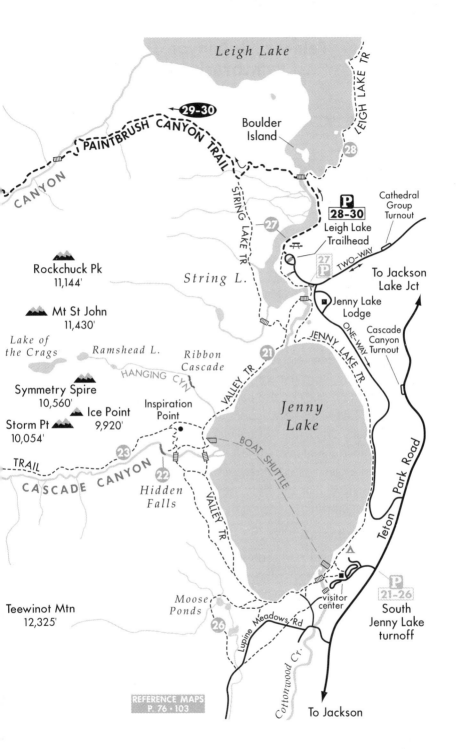

Leigh Lake

Boulder
Island

29-30

PAINTBRUSH CANYON TRAIL

LEIGH LAKE TR

CANYON

STRING LAKE TR

28

P
28-30
Leigh Lake
Trailhead

Cathedral
Group
Turnout

27

TWO-WAY

27
P

To Jackson
Lake Jct

▲▲ Rockchuck Pk
11,144'

String L.

Jenny Lake
Lodge

▲▲▲ Mt St John
11,430'

JENNY LAKE TR

ONE-WAY

Cascade
Canyon
Turnout

*Lake of
the Crags*

Ramshead L.

*Ribbon
Cascade*

HANGING CYN

VALLEY TR

21

▲ Symmetry Spire
10,560'

▲ Ice Point
9,920'

Inspiration
Point

*Jenny
Lake*

Storm Pt ▲▲
10,054'

23

BOAT SHUTTLE

TRAIL

CASCADE CANYON

22

*Hidden
Falls*

VALLEY TR

Teton Park Road

Teewinot Mtn
12,325'

*Moose
Ponds*

26

Lupine Meadows Rd

visitor
center

▲

P
21-26

South
Jenny Lake
turnoff

REFERENCE MAPS
P. 76 · 103

Cottonwood Cr.

To Jackson

30. Paintbrush Canyon Trail to Paintbrush Divide

LEIGH LAKE TRAILHEAD

Hiking distance: 15.8 miles round trip
Hiking time: 8 hours
Configuration: out-and-back
Elevation gain: 3,800 feet
Difficulty: very strenuous
Exposure: mostly forested canyon with exposed high meadows and rocky ridges
Dogs: not allowed
Maps: U.S.G.S. Jenny Lake and Mount Moran
Adventure Maps: Jackson Hole
Beartooth Publishing: Grand Teton National Park map
National Geographic Trails Illustrated: Grand Teton Nat'l. Park

map
page 104

Paintbrush Divide is in the rocky backcountry of the central Teton Range. The 10,700-foot divide lies at the upper end of Paintbrush Canyon between Leigh Canyon to the north and Cascade Canyon to the south. From the summit are sweeping vistas of the lakes beyond the mouth of the canyon, the winding Snake River, the Jackson Hole valley, and spectacular 360-degree views of the Teton peaks. Snowfields usually cover sections of the trail in the upper canyon until mid-August.

The hike can be combined with Cascade Canyon (Hike 25) as a 19-mile loop. For the best views of the Tetons, hike counter-clockwise, starting on the Paintbrush Canyon Trail.

To the trailhead

From the national park entrance at Moose, continue 10.2 miles on Teton Park Road to the North Jenny Lake Junction and turn left (west). Drive 0.9 miles to the String Lake picnic area and turn right. Park a short distance ahead in the parking lot at the end of the loop.

The hike

Walk north along the east shore of String Lake. Continue 0.9 miles to a bridge on the left, located just south of Leigh Lake. Cross the wooden footbridge over the connector stream between the two lakes. Head up the hillside through the woodland to a posted junction on the lower slopes of Rockchuck Peak at 1.6 miles. The left fork traverses the hillside overlooking String Lake and Jenny Lake. Bear right and head west on the Paintbrush Canyon Trail through a dense forest of lodgepole pines, Engelmann spruce, Douglas fir, and subalpine fir. The trail reaches Paintbrush Canyon Creek near the mouth of the canyon at just over 3 miles. Views extend down canyon to Leigh Lake and Mystic Isle. Enter the high-walled, glacier-carved canyon, and cross a bridge to the north bank of the creek. Continue up canyon, crossing several tributary streams from Mount Woodring. Zigzag up a series of switchbacks to a trail junction at 5.8 miles. The left fork continues through the camping zone below the divide. Take the Holly Lake Trail to the right, and climb a few switchbacks. Cross an outlet stream on the east side of a small lake, reaching the south end of Holly Lake a half mile from the junction.

After taking a rest at Holly Lake, continue hiking southwest above the lake, and rejoin the main Paintbrush Canyon Trail in a quarter mile. Veer to the right and head uphill to the west. Watch for Grizzly Bear Lake to the north, sitting in a cirque 1,000 feet above the floor of Leigh Canyon. Traverse a rocky meadow dotted with subalpine fir and whitebark pine. Climb above timberline through meadows surrounded by high, jagged peaks and barren, craggy cliffs. Switchbacks lead through scree and snow patches to the windswept 10,700-foot divide, where you are rewarded with spectacular views. This is the turn-around spot.

The trail continues 2.4 miles downhill to Lake Solitude, the headwaters for the North Fork of Cascade Canyon (Hike 25). The trail then descends through Cascade Canyon back to Jenny Lake on the valley floor. The Cascade Canyon and Paintbrush Canyon trails can be hiked together as a 19-mile loop. ■

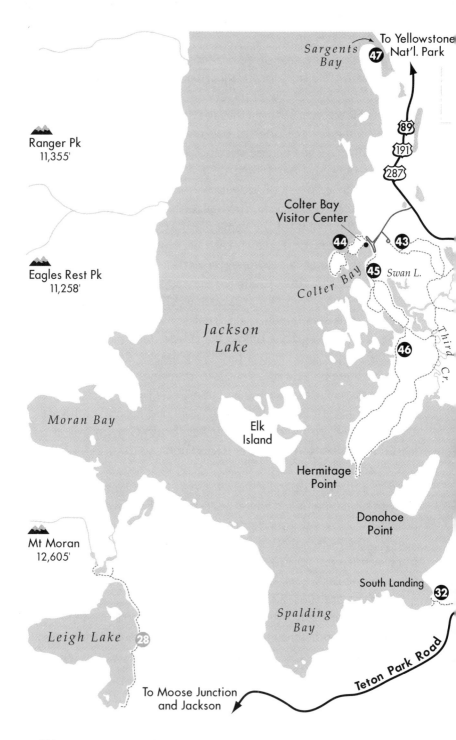

Lower Jackson Lake area

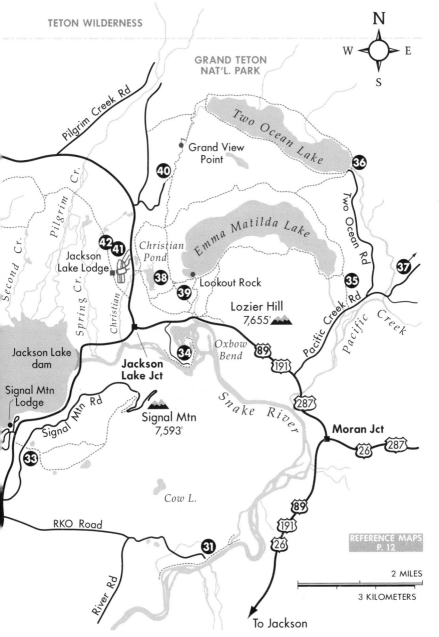

TETON WILDERNESS

N
W ◆ E
S

GRAND TETON
NAT'L. PARK

Two Ocean Lake

Grand View
Point

40

36

Two Ocean Rd

Emma Matilda Lake

42 **41**

*Christian
Pond*

Jackson
Lake Lodge

38

39

Lookout Rock

37

35

Pacific Creek Rd

Lozier Hill
7,655'

Pacific Creek

Pilgrim Creek Rd

Pilgrim Cr.

Second Cr.

Pilgrim Cr.

Spring Cr.

Christian

Jackson Lake
dam

Signal Mtn
Lodge

34

*Oxbow
Bend*

89

191

**Jackson
Lake Jct**

Signal Mtn Rd

Signal Mtn
7,593'

Snake River

287

Moran Jct

26 **287**

33

Cow L.

RKO Road

89

191

31

26

River Rd

To Jackson

REFERENCE MAPS
P. 12

2 MILES

3 KILOMETERS

31. Snake River Fisherman's Trail

Hiking distance: 1—2 miles round trip
Hiking time: 30 minutes—1 hour
Configuration: out-and-back
Elevation gain: level
Difficulty: easy
Exposure: a mix of forest and meadow
Dogs: not allowed
Maps: U.S.G.S. Moran

The Snake River Fisherman's Trail follows the serpentine Snake River along an unofficial angler and animal path. This hike is an opportunity to stroll along the banks of the river in the solitude of a quiet, private setting with dramatic views of the Tetons (and perhaps do a little fishing). The trail winds through stands of cottonwood, aspen, fir, pine, and spruce trees.

To the trailhead

From the national park entrance at Moose, continue 14.8 miles on Teton Park Road to the unsigned dirt road on the right, the RKO Road. Turn right (east) and drive 3.6 miles across the open meadow to a parking area at the end of the road by the Snake River.

RKO Road is 1.3 miles south of Signal Mountain Lodge.

The hike

Walk east through the tall evergreen forest on the clearly defined path to the banks of the Snake River. Unmaintained faint paths lead along the shoreline in both directions through forests and meadows. To the left (upstream), the trail heads across flat sagebrush benches. To the right (downstream), the path follows the river through a dense forest. (Notice the trees cut down by beavers.) At a quarter mile, the trail breaks out of the trees into an open meadow with fantastic views of the Tetons. In each direction are small islands, gravel bars, and side channels that make wading across the river easier. Choose your own route and turn-around spot. ▪

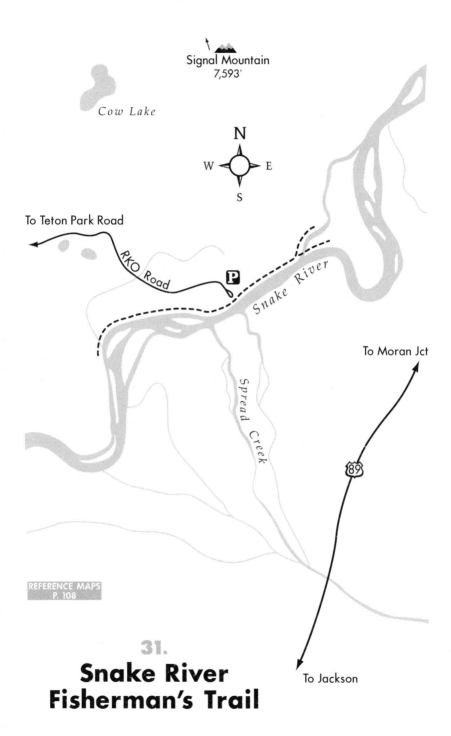

Signal Mountain
7,593'

Cow Lake

N
W E
S

To Teton Park Road

RKO Road

P

Snake River

To Moran Jct

Spread Creek

89

REFERENCE MAPS
P. 108

To Jackson

31.
Snake River
Fisherman's Trail

32. South Landing
JACKSON LAKE

Hiking distance: 1 mile round trip
Hiking time: 30 minutes
Configuration: out-and-back
Elevation gain: 100 feet
Difficulty: very easy
Exposure: a mix of forest and open shoreline
Dogs: not allowed
Maps: U.S.G.S. Moran and Jenny Lake

South Landing is a rounded cove near the south end of 25,000-acre Jackson Lake by Signal Mountain. The secluded bay has gorgeous views of the park's largest lake as well as Elk Island, Donoho Point (also an island), small Marie Island, Hermitage Point, and the stunning peaks of the Teton Range. The trail descends through a lodgepole pine forest to the shoreline, rimmed with rounded rocks.

To the trailhead

From the national park entrance at Moose, continue 14.8 miles on Teton Park Road to the unsigned dirt road on the right (RKO Road). The trailhead parking area is directly across from the dirt road on the west side of Teton Park Road.

RKO Road is 1.3 miles south of Signal Mountain Lodge.

The hike

Follow the posted trail south across the arid, sage-covered flat. Curve right on the old road, and drop into a shaded grove of evergreens, where the road becomes a footpath. Wind downhill through the dense forest to a picnic area at the far east end of the wide, rounded cove. A full frontal view of Mount Moran sits straight west. Rounded rocks line the beach surrounding the cove, backed by a ring of trees. Follow the shoreline north as views open up of Donoho Point and Hermitage Point. Return by retracing your steps. ■

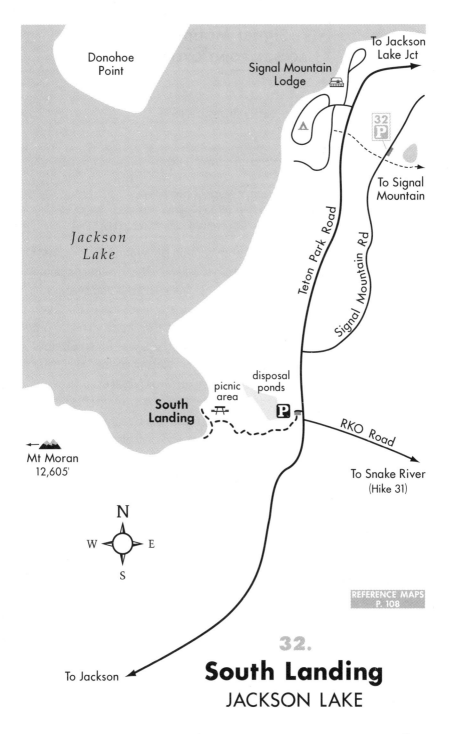

Donohoe
Point

Signal Mountain
Lodge

To Jackson
Lake Jct

32 P

To Signal
Mountain

*Jackson
Lake*

Teton Park Road

Signal Mountain Rd

disposal
ponds

picnic
area

**South
Landing**

P

RKO Road

To Snake River
(Hike 31)

Mt Moran
12,605'

N

W   E

S

REFERENCE MAPS
P. 108

To Jackson

32.

South Landing
JACKSON LAKE

33. Signal Mountain
JACKSON POINT OVERLOOK

Hiking distance: 5.4 miles round trip
Hiking time: 2.5 hours
Configuration: out-and-back with central loop
Elevation gain: 700 feet
Difficulty: moderate
Exposure: a mix of forest and meadows
Dogs: not allowed
Maps: U.S.G.S. Moran · Adventure Maps: Jackson Hole
　　　　Beartooth Publishing: Grand Teton National Park map
　　　　National Geographic Trails Illustrated: Grand Teton Nat'l. Park

Signal Mountain is a 7,593-foot mountain between the southeast side of Jackson Lake and the Snake River. The isolated summit towers 800 feet above Jackson Hole Valley, providing sweeping views. The hike up Signal Mountain leads to Jackson Point Overlook, a scenic viewing area that takes in the great vistas. From the overlook are views of Jackson Lake, the Snake River, Oxbow Bend, the Teton Wilderness, the flat glacial plains, and four mountain ranges—the Teton, Absaroka, Gros Ventres, and Wind River Ranges. This hike begins near the Signal Mountain Lodge and Jackson Lake, then continues up the mountain through a forest to the overlook. The paved Signal Mountain Road also winds up to the overlook, so don't be surprised to discover people at the summit after hiking through the quiet solitude of the forest.

To the trailhead

From the national park entrance at Moose, drive 15 miles on Teton Park Road to the signed Signal Mountain Summit turnoff on the right (east). Continue 1.1 mile on Signal Mountain Road to the signed trailhead on the right. Park in the parking area on the right 30 yards ahead by the pond.

　　Signal Mountain Road is 1.1 mile south of Signal Mountain Lodge.

The hike

Head east past the trail sign along the south side of the pond that is covered with lily pads. Ascend a small rise through the

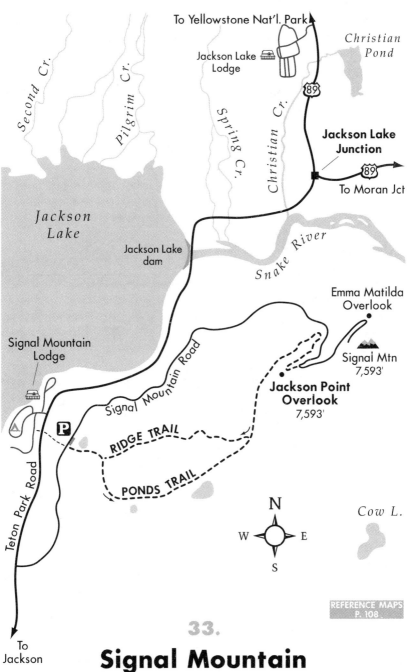

To Yellowstone Nat'l. Park

Christian Pond

Jackson Lake Lodge

89

Jackson Lake Junction

To Moran Jct

Second Cr.

Pilgrim Cr.

Spring Cr.

Christian Cr.

89

Jackson Lake

Jackson Lake dam

Snake River

Emma Matilda Overlook

Signal Mountain Lodge

Signal Mtn 7,593'

Signal Mountain Road

Jackson Point Overlook 7,593'

P

RIDGE TRAIL

PONDS TRAIL

Cow L.

Teton Park Road

N
W · E
S

To Jackson

33.

Signal Mountain
JACKSON POINT OVERLOOK

forest to a signed junction, beginning the loop. The left fork, the Ridge Trail, will be the return route. Take the right fork along the Ponds Trail through the open forest of aspen and conifer. The trail weaves through the forest past two ponds on the right. At 1.7 miles, the two routes merge. Bear to the right for a one-mile ascent. Head uphill through large stands of Douglas fir. Near the top, the trail breaks out of the forest to stunning views at Jackson Point Overlook. From the overlook, a paved path leads 70 yards to a parking area.

After enjoying the vast views of the landscape, return one mile downhill to the signed junction with the Ridge Trail. The trail rises and drops over several ridges through the forest and meadows while offering excellent views of the Teton Range. At the junction with the Ponds Trail, bear right, back to the trailhead. ▪

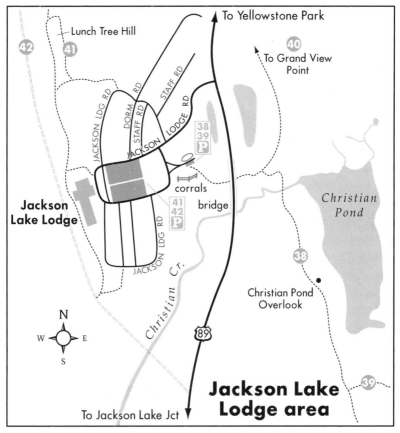

34. Oxbow Bend
SNAKE RIVER

Hiking distance: 1 mile round trip
Hiking time: 40 minutes
Configuration: out-and-back
Elevation gain: level
Difficulty: very easy
Exposure: mostly exposed
Dogs: not allowed
Maps: U.S.G.S. Moran · Adventure Maps: Jackson Hole
      Beartooth Publishing: Grand Teton National Park

map
page 118

Oxbow Bend is a scenic section of the Snake River that is named after the U-shaped collar of an ox. The slow-moving, crescent-shaped bend, located near Jackson Lake Junction, is a superb habitat for moose, elk, beaver, muskrat, and a wide variety of waterfowl. The river curves around the northern flank of Signal Mountain near its outlet from Jackson Lake. Mount Moran, a pinnacle peak of the Teton Range, dominates the landscape.

This hike begins at the former location of Cattlemans Bridge, a popular boat-launching site. The bridge, constructed in the mid-1950s, was used by ranchers for herding cattle across the Snake River from the Potholes area, south of Signal Mountain. When grazing ceased, the bridge remained and became a popular hiking and fishing access route. The bridge has since deteriorated and was removed in 2001.

To the trailhead

The turnoff to Oxbow Bend is located between Jackson Lake Junction and Moran Junction. From Jackson Lake Junction, drive 0.5 miles east on Highway 89 to the unsigned road and turn right (south). From Moran Junction, drive 3.4 miles west on Highway 89 to the unsigned road and turn left (south). Drive one mile south to the end of the unpaved road. The parking area is near the river.

The hike

From the Cattlemans Bridge site at the base of Signal Mountain, footpaths lead downstream to the north and upstream to the west. The north route follows an open forest along the banks of a side channel of the Snake River. The path ends on a peninsula at Oxbow Bend. The west route follows the river along the base of Signal Mountain. ■

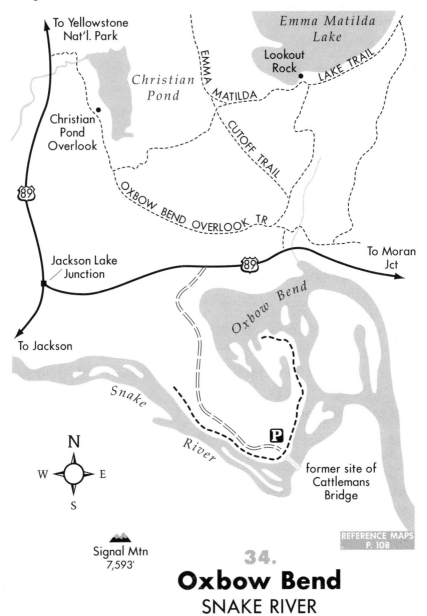

34.
Oxbow Bend
SNAKE RIVER

35. Emma Matilda Lake

Hiking distance: 10.3-mile loop
Hiking time: 5-6 hours
Configuration: loop
Elevation gain: 600 feet
Difficulty: moderate to somewhat strenuous
Exposure: a mix of exposed meadows and shaded forest
Dogs: not allowed
Maps: U.S.G.S. Moran and Two Ocean Lake
   Beartooth Publishing: Grand Teton National Park map

**map
page 120**

Emma Matilda Lake is a large, natural lake that lies straight east of Jackson Lake. The crescent-shaped lake, and Two Ocean Lake just to the north, were formed when receding glaciers gouged out the land. Melting glacial water gradually filled up the depressions. A trail circles the scenic lake, which stretches three miles long and a half mile wide.

The trail along the north side of Emma Matilda Lake follows an open ridge dotted with Douglas fir and stands of aspen. The ridge, 400 feet above the lake, separates Emma Matilda Lake from Two Ocean Lake. This area offers great vistas of the Teton Range, Jackson Lake, and Emma Matilda Lake. The south trail winds along the shore in a dense forest with towering Douglas fir, subalpine fir, and Engelmann spruce.

The lake can be accessed via a number of routes on the west end around Jackson Lake Lodge and from Two Ocean Lake on the northeast. This hike leads to the lake from a connector path off of Pacific Creek Road on the remote southeast corner of the lake. The trail is generally quiet and secluded except on the west end. Bears frequent the area, so use caution.

To the trailhead

The trailhead is along Pacific Creek Road between Jackson Lake Junction and Moran Junction. From Jackson Lake Junction, drive 2.7 miles east on Highway 89 to the signed Pacific Creek Road and turn left (north). From Moran Junction, drive 1.3 miles west on Highway 89 to Pacific Creek Road and turn right (north). Drive 1.4 miles on the dirt road to the trailhead parking area on the left.

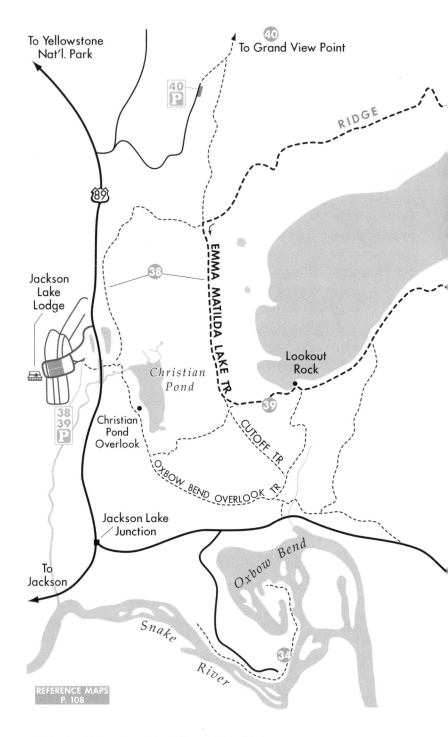

To Yellowstone Nat'l. Park

To Grand View Point

40

40 P

89

RIDGE

Jackson Lake Lodge

38

EMMA MATILDA LAKE TR.

Christian Pond

Lookout Rock

38 39 P

Christian Pond Overlook

39

CUTOFF TR.

OXBOW BEND OVERLOOK TR.

Jackson Lake Junction

To Jackson

Oxbow Bend

34

Snake River

REFERENCE MAPS P. 108

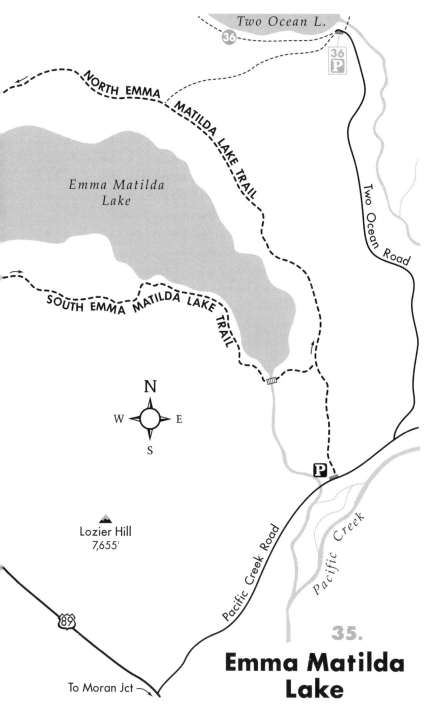

Two Ocean L.

36

36
P

NORTH EMMA MATILDA LAKE TRAIL

Emma Matilda
Lake

Two Ocean Road

SOUTH EMMA MATILDA LAKE TRAIL

N
W   E
S

P

Lozier Hill
7,655'

Pacific Creek Road

Pacific Creek

89

To Moran Jct

35.

Emma Matilda
Lake

The hike

Take the gravel road north, which quickly narrows to a footpath. Head up the forested slope, and climb through a flower-filled meadow to a posted junction at 0.6 miles. The South Emma Matilda Lake Trail—our return route—goes to the left. Begin the loop straight ahead on the North Emma Matilda Lake Trail. Gently climb through a mix of trees and meadows with obscured westward views of Emma Matilda Lake. Gradually curve left, crossing a small wetland, parallel to the out-of-view lake. The Teton Mountains move in and out of view. Top a slope to a great vista of Emma Matilda Lake backed by the majestic Teton Peaks. At 2.4 miles is a posted junction on the right that leads one mile to Two Ocean Lake.

Continue straight, staying on the North Emma Matilda Lake Trail. Head west above the north side of the lake. Pass through a grassland, then climb 300 feet through the fir forest to a 7,300-foot ridge. Follow the length of the ridge west while overlooking the scenic lake and Mount Leidy to the southeast. At the west end of the ridge, descend to the base of the mountain to a posted 4-way junction at 5.2 miles. The right fork leads 1.7 miles to Grand View Point and continues to Two Ocean Lake. Straight ahead leads 1.3 miles to Jackson Lake Lodge.

For this hike, bear left on the Emma Matilda Lake Trail. Walk south up the hill through open, rolling terrain, veering left at a distinct Y-fork. One hundred yards ahead is a posted junction. The right fork leads 0.7 miles to Christian Pond and continues to Jackson Lake Lodge. Stay to the left, passing another junction to Jackson Lake Lodge just after crossing a small bridge. Again stay to the left for 0.1 mile to Lookout Rock, a 6,887-foot knoll on the edge of the lake. After savoring the overlook views, curve right from the summit and continue east. Gently climb the forested hillside above the lake and continue east through the forest. Return lakeside through towering Douglas fir and Engelmann spruce. At the southeast end of Emma Matilda Lake, cross the lake's outlet stream on a wood bridge. Complete the loop in a grassy meadow at 9.7 miles. Bear right and retrace your steps to the trailhead. ■

36. Two Ocean Lake

Hiking distance: 6.4-mile loop
Hiking time: 3 hours
Configuration: loop
Elevation gain: 100 feet
Difficulty: easy to moderate
Exposure: rolling, open meadows and shaded forest
Dogs: not allowed
Maps: U.S.G.S. Two Ocean Lake · Adventure Maps: Jackson Hole
Beartooth Publishing: Grand Teton National Park map
National Geographic Trails Illustrated: Grand Teton Nat'l. Park

map
page 125

Two Ocean Lake and Emma Matilda Lake are two long, narrow lakes to the east of Jackson Lake. The forest-lined lakes sit in glacier-carved depressions. Snow melt filled the depressions, forming the lakes as the glacier retreated. This quiet, secluded hike around Two Ocean Lake traverses the rolling terrain through meadows lined with aspen groves and old-growth spruce, fir, and pines. Along the north shore are views of Jackson Lake and the Teton Range. At the west end of the lake is an alternative route to Grand View Point, which includes magnificent views of Two Ocean Lake, Jackson Lake, and the Grand Tetons. (Grand View Point may also be accessed via Hike 40.) Bears frequent the area, so use caution.

To the trailhead

The trailhead is along Pacific Creek Road between Jackson Lake Junction and Moran Junction. From Jackson Lake Junction, drive 2.7 miles east on Highway 89 to the signed Pacific Creek Road and turn left (north). From Moran Junction, drive 1.3 miles west on Highway 89 to Pacific Creek Road and turn right (north).

Drive 2.1 miles northeast on Pacific Creek Road to Two Ocean Road and turn left. Continue 2.4 miles on the unpaved road to the picnic grounds and parking area that overlook the lake at the end of the road.

The hike

Take the signed Two Ocean Lake Trail to the east, where the road enters the parking area. Cross a footbridge over the lake's outlet stream, and head through the forest. Cross a meadow lined with aspens. Curve left along the northern shore of Two Ocean Lake. At several unsigned trail forks, stay to the right to avoid the lower wetlands. Follow the well-defined path west through sage-covered meadows. The trail leaves the shoreline and crosses a creek. Traverse the meadows, crossing a second creek. At the west end of the lake is a signed junction with the Grand View Point Trail. The detour to Grand View Point will add two miles to the trip and is a wonderful side trip (see Hike 40). Continue around the south side of the lake. The path leads through the shade of a dense conifer forest, crossing two small meadows and bridges over inlet streams. The trail emerges from the forest at the parking area. ■

37. Pacific Creek Trail

Hiking distance: 6 miles (or more) round trip
Hiking time: 3 hours
Configuration: out-and-back
Elevation gain: 300 feet
Difficulty: easy to moderate
Exposure: mostly exposed with shady pockets
Dogs: allowed
Maps: U.S.G.S. Whetstone Mountain and Gravel Mountain
Adventure Maps: Jackson Hole
Beartooth Publishing: Grand Teton National Park map

map
page 127

Pacific Creek is a 30-mile-long waterway that drains from Two Ocean Plateau atop the Continental Divide. The creek flows into the Snake River at Moran Junction. This remote trail parallels Pacific Creek through designated wilderness that is rich with wildlife, including elk, grizzly bears, and wolves. The trail sees few hikers, except during hunting season. Access is from the northeast corner of Grand Teton National Park, but the trail is located in the

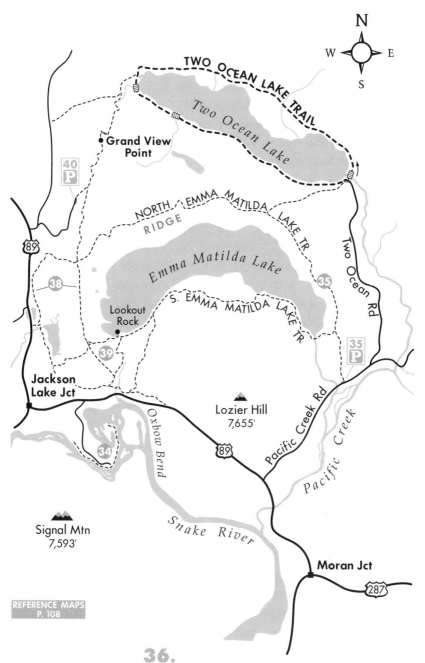

N
W   E
S

TWO OCEAN LAKE TRAIL

Two Ocean Lake

40 P

● **Grand View Point**

89

NORTH EMMA MATILDA LAKE TR

RIDGE

Emma Matilda Lake

38

35

Two Ocean Rd

Lookout Rock ●

S. EMMA MATILDA LAKE TR

39

35 P

Jackson Lake Jct

Oxbow Bend

▲ **Lozier Hill** 7,655'

Pacific Creek Rd

Pacific Creek

34

89

▲▲ **Signal Mtn** 7,593'

Snake River

■ **Moran Jct**

287

REFERENCE MAPS P. 108

36.
Two Ocean Lake

Teton Wilderness, part of the Bridger–Teton National Forest. The mostly level creekside trail travels through the wilderness to a broad valley with forests and large meadows. The area is only accessible via foot or horseback.

The hike included here follows the first 3 miles, from the wilderness boundary into the vast valley. En route, the trail crosses a couple tributary streams and crosses Whetstone Creek to the valley floor. The hike, which follows Pacific Creek for miles, may be lengthened or shorted at any point along the trail.

To the trailhead

The trailhead is at the end of Pacific Creek Road, located between Jackson Lake Junction and Moran Junction. From Jackson Lake Junction, drive 2.7 miles east on Highway 89 to the signed Pacific Creek Road and turn left (north). From Moran Junction, drive 1.3 miles west on Highway 89 to Pacific Creek Road and turn right (north). Drive 8.2 miles on the dirt road to the trailhead at the end of the road.

The hike

From the end of Pacific Creek Road, walk past the trailhead kiosk. Enter the Teton Wilderness within the Bridger–Teton National Forest. Pass through tree-rimmed meadows, and traverse the hillside above Pacific Creek. Follow the rolling landscape along numerous small dips and rises. Cross a tributary stream to a posted junction with the Whetstone Creek Trail on the left at 1.8 miles. The Whetstone Creek Trail heads north, parallel to the creek along the eastern base of Whetstone Mountain.

For this hike, stay on the Pacific Creek Trail straight ahead. Cross a second stream by a grotto to the left. Continue to an open expanse on a bench overlooking the rock-strewn creek. Pass through the meadow and hop over another stream. A couple of minutes ahead, cross Whetstone Creek, where expansive views open into the valley. Descend to the valley floor within the vast expanse. The trail (which becomes the Atlantic Pacific Creek Trail) parallels Pacific Creek and Enos Creek for 11 miles to Enos Lake and for 15 miles to Two Ocean Pass. Choose your own turn-around spot. ▦

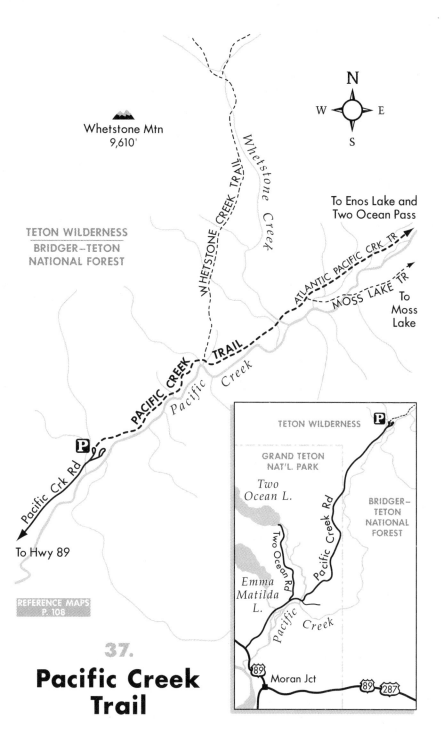

Whetstone Mtn
9,610'

TETON WILDERNESS
BRIDGER–TETON
NATIONAL FOREST

Whetstone Creek

WHETSTONE CREEK TRAIL

To Enos Lake and
Two Ocean Pass

ATLANTIC PACIFIC CRK TR

MOSS LAKE TR

To
Moss
Lake

PACIFIC CREEK TRAIL

Pacific Creek

Pacific Crk Rd

To Hwy 89

REFERENCE MAPS
P. 108

TETON WILDERNESS

GRAND TETON
NAT'L. PARK

*Two
Ocean L.*

Two Ocean Rd

*Emma
Matilda
L.*

BRIDGER–
TETON
NATIONAL
FOREST

Pacific Creek Rd

Pacific Creek

89

Moran Jct

89 287

37.
Pacific Creek Trail

38. Christian Pond Trail
JACKSON LAKE LODGE AREA

Hiking distance: 3.2 miles round trip
Hiking time: 1.5 hours
Configuration: loop
Elevation gain: 250 feet
Difficulty: easy
Exposure: a mix of open meadows and shaded forest
Dogs: not allowed
Maps: U.S.G.S. Moran and Two Ocean Lake
Beartooth Publishing: Grand Teton National Park map

Christian Pond is a waterfowl habitat and nesting area for trumpeter swan. It is located across the park road from Jackson Lake Lodge. The gentle Christian Pond Trail circles the pond through rolling hills covered in sage and stands of lodgepole pines. Open meadows offer commanding views of the Teton Range. Bring binoculars for bird watching and wildlife observation.

To the trailhead

From the national park entrance at Moose, continue 20 miles on Teton Park Road to Jackson Lake Junction and turn left (north). Drive one mile on Highway 89 to Jackson Lodge Road and turn left. Drive 0.2 miles and turn left towards the corrals. Park in the first parking area on the right.

The hike

From the parking lot follow the trail east, passing the horse corrals towards the highway bridge. The trail dips and crosses under the bridge to a signed trail junction in a willow-filled basin. Take the trail to the right 0.2 miles, crossing Christian Creek, to the Christian Pond Overlook. After enjoying the views, continue 0.3 miles to another signed trail junction. Take the trail to the left, which reads "via Emma Matilda Lake." Along this section of the trail are several unmarked Y-junctions. Stay left at each one. By staying left, you will loop around Christian Pond, returning to the highway bridge. Cross back under the bridge to the corrals and parking lot.

For a longer hike, include the loop to Lookout Rock—Hike 39. Connecting trails also lead to Emma Matilda Lake and Two Ocean Lake. ▦

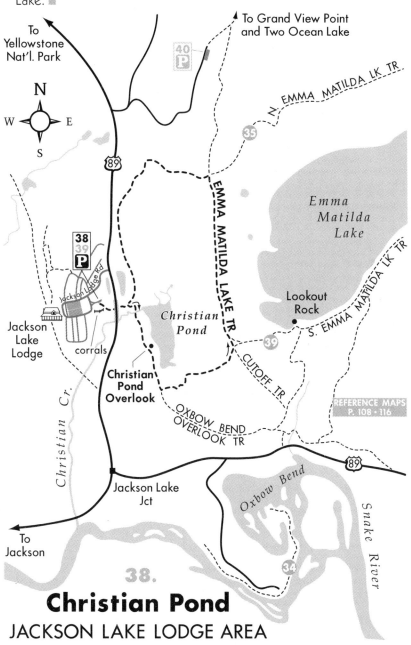

38.
Christian Pond
JACKSON LAKE LODGE AREA

39. Lookout Rock
JACKSON LAKE LODGE AREA

Hiking distance: 3.8 miles round trip
Hiking time: 2 hours
Configuration: out-and-back with loop
Elevation gain: 300 feet
Difficulty: easy
Exposure: a mix of open meadows and shaded forest
Dogs: not allowed
Maps: U.S.G.S. Moran and Two Ocean Lake
   Adventure Maps: Jackson Hole
   Beartooth Publishing: Grand Teton National Park map

Lookout Rock is a gorgeous overlook on the southwest corner of Emma Matilda Lake. The hike to Lookout Rock begins at Jackson Lake Lodge. En route to the lookout, the trail passes Christian Pond, a waterfowl habitat and nesting area for trumpeter swan. From the trail are great views of Jackson Lake and the dam, the island of Donoho Point, the Teton Range, the Oxbow Bend of the Snake River, and Emma Matilda Lake.

To the trailhead

From the national park entrance at Moose, continue 20 miles on Teton Park Road to Jackson Lake Junction and turn left (north). Drive one mile on Highway 89 to Jackson Lodge Road and turn left. Drive 0.2 miles and turn left towards the corrals. Park in the first parking area on the right.

The hike

Head east past the horse corrals and under the park road to a signed junction. Bear right toward Christian Pond, weaving through the meadow marbled with waterways. Climb the knoll to the Christian Pond Overlook, and continue south to a signed junction, beginning the loop. Bear right on the Oxbow Bend Overlook Trail, following the hillside ridge. As you top the hill, views open to Oxbow Bend, a slow-moving, crescent-shaped bend in the Snake River. Continue east to a junction with the Lookout Rock Cutoff Trail on the left. Stay to the right, traversing the hillside above Oxbow Bend. At the top of the hill, the trail levels out, curves north, and enters a fir and spruce forest. Walk through meadows with stands of conifers to a signed junction at 2.3 miles on the south shore of Emma Matilda Lake. Take the left fork 0.1 mile to Lookout Rock. Climb to the overlook of the lake. After enjoying the views, descend to the west along the lakeshore to a trail split. The right fork leads 2.7 miles to Grand View Point (Hike 40). Go left, completing the loop at the next junction. Return to the right past Christian Pond and back to the trailhead. ■

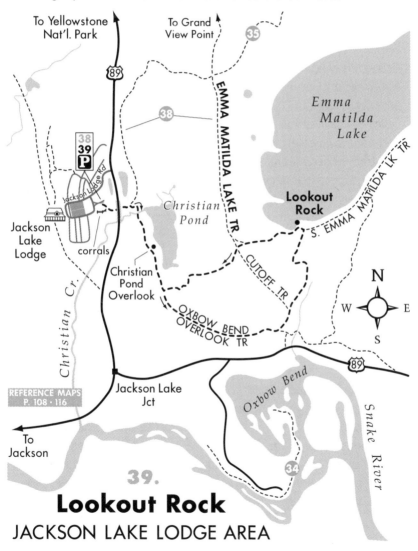

39.
Lookout Rock
JACKSON LAKE LODGE AREA

40. Grand View Point
JACKSON LAKE LODGE AREA

Hiking distance: 2.2 miles round trip
Hiking time: 1 hour
Configuration: out-and-back
Elevation gain: 600 feet
Difficulty: easy to moderate
Exposure: a mix of open meadows and shaded forest
Dogs: not allowed
Maps: U.S.G.S. Two Ocean Lake · Adventure Maps: Jackson Hole
Beartooth Publishing: Grand Teton National Park map

Grand View Point sits atop a reddish-colored volcanic rock near the west end of Two Ocean Lake. From the 7,586-foot summit are magnificent 360-degree panoramas that include Two Ocean Lake, Emma Matilda Lake, Jackson Lake, the Teton Wilderness, and an unsurpassed view of Mount Moran and the Teton Range. The trail crosses morainal ridges and passes through a wooded terrain of lodgepole pine, Douglas fir, and subalpine fir. The forested trail is short but strenuous, gaining 600 feet in 1.1 mile. The magnificent views at the top are well worth the effort.

To the trailhead

From the national park entrance at Moose, continue 20 miles on Teton Park Road to Jackson Lake Junction and turn left (north). Drive 1.9 miles on Highway 89 to an unmarked gravel road on the right (east). Turn right and continue 0.9 miles on the bumpy road to the trailhead parking area on the right.

The hike

From the parking area, head northeast past the trailhead sign into the forest. Make a short, steep ascent for less than a quarter mile to a junction. The right fork heads south to Emma Matilda Lake and Christian Pond. For this hike, take the left fork towards Grand View Point. Steadily climb through the evergreen forest. Pass a rocky knoll overlooking Emma Matilda Lake and Two Ocean Lake. Climb a short distance farther to Grand View Point, an exposed promontory with stunning views from 700 feet above Two Ocean Lake. After enjoying the scenery, return by retracing your steps.

The trail continues north for 1.3 miles (downhill) to Two Ocean Lake. To hike around Two Ocean Lake, reference Hike 36. ▨

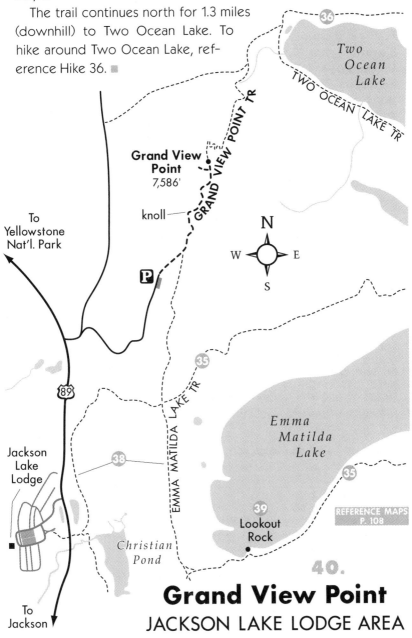

40.
Grand View Point
JACKSON LAKE LODGE AREA

41. Lunch Tree Hill Loop
JACKSON LAKE LODGE AREA

Hiking distance: 0.5-mile loop—2 miles round trip
Hiking time: 30 minutes—1 hour
Configuration: out-and-back with loop
Elevation gain: 80 feet
Difficulty: very easy
Exposure: mostly exposed
Dogs: not allowed
Maps: U.S.G.S. Two Ocean Lake
      National Geographic Trails Illustrated: Grand Teton Nat'l. Park

The Lunch Tree Hill Loop is an interpretive trail that begins at Jackson Lake Lodge. The trail climbs the hill to the north and circles the sagebrush-covered blufftop. Atop the small hill is a magnificent overlook and picnic area with panoramic vistas of the Willow Flats wetlands, Jackson Lake, and the entire Teton Range forming the backdrop. The overlook is the historic site where, in 1926, John D. Rockefeller Jr. and his family had lunch with Horace Albright, then superintendent of Yellowstone Park. (Rockefeller was instrumental in creating Grant Teton National Park.) En route to Lunch Tree Hill are interpretive panels about the area's history, geology, wildlife, and plant life.

To the trailhead

From the national park entrance at Moose, continue 20 miles on Teton Park Road to Jackson Lake Junction and turn left (north). Drive one mile on Highway 89 to Jackson Lodge Road and turn left (west). Park in the parking area near Jackson Lake Lodge.

The hike

Begin by walking through Jackson Lake Lodge and marveling at the close-up views of the entire Teton Range through the huge picture window. Head out to the walkway in front of the lodge. Follow the pathway to the right along the rail fence to the posted trailhead. Ascend the hill on the old paved path to a flat knoll at the summit. Along the path and at the summit are spectacular views of Willow Flats, Jackson Lake, the island of Donoho Point,

Hermitage Point, and the spectacular backdrop of the Teton Range. The trail loops around the summit. At the far end of the loop, an informal trail continues north, following the ridge along the top of the bluffs. The trail continues through sagebrush and pines to a north view of the wetland valley.

Back at the self-guided loop, pass a 1953 rock memorial to John D. Rockefeller Junior. Slowly descend, with views of prominent Signal Mountain straight ahead to the south. Stroll through an aspen grove, and return to the north side of Jackson Lake Lodge. ▪

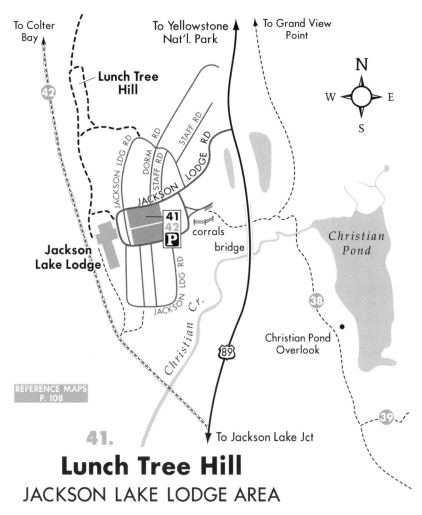

Lunch Tree Hill
JACKSON LAKE LODGE AREA

42. Willow Flats to Second Creek
JACKSON LAKE LODGE AREA

Hiking distance: 4.8 miles round trip
Hiking time: 2.5 hours
Configuration: out-and-back
Elevation gain: level
Difficulty: easy to slightly moderate
Exposure: a mix of open meadows and shaded forest
Dogs: not allowed
Maps: U.S.G.S. Two Ocean Lake · Adventure Maps: Jackson Hole
  Beartooth Publishing: Grand Teton National Park map
  National Geographic Trails Illustrated: Grand Teton Nat'l. Park

The hike to Second Creek starts at Jackson Lake Lodge and leads through the wildlife habitat of Willow Flats, a large marshy area with ponds and meadows. The area is frequented by moose, deer, elk, beaver, and coyotes. The trail follows a service road through stands of aspen, ponderosa pine, Douglas fir, spruce, and cottonwood trees. There are two stream crossings and spectacular views of the Teton Range.

To the trailhead

From the national park entrance at Moose, continue 20 miles on Teton Park Road to Jackson Lake Junction and turn left (north). Drive one mile on Highway 89 to Jackson Lodge Road and turn left (west). Park in the parking area near Jackson Lake Lodge.

The hike

Facing towards Jackson Lake Lodge, take the service road heading to the left (south) of the lodge. A posted trail sign leads to an asphalt walking path. Take this path downhill to the service road, and head to the right (north) along the road. At 0.5 miles there is a log crossing over a stream. Continue 1.8 miles to a bridge that crosses the wide, rocky creek bed of Pilgrim Creek. Within minutes of crossing Pilgrim Creek, the view opens to Mount Moran. At 2.4 miles is a posted junction. Take the left fork towards Second Creek Spring. The right fork leads to Colter Bay, as does another junction 0.3 miles ahead (Hike 43). At 2.9

miles, just beyond the picnic tables, is Second Creek Spring. This is the turn-around spot. Return along the same trail. ■

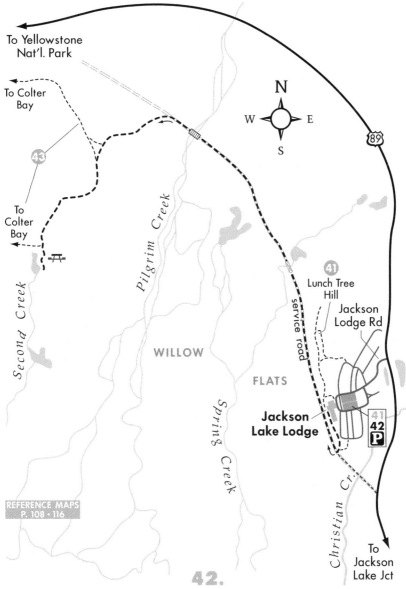

To Yellowstone Nat'l. Park

To Colter Bay

N
W ◆ E
S

89

43

To Colter Bay

Pilgrim Creek

Second Creek

WILLOW

FLATS

Spring Creek

service road

41
Lunch Tree Hill

Jackson Lodge Rd

Jackson Lake Lodge

41
42
P

Christian Cr.

To Jackson Lake Jct

REFERENCE MAPS
P. 108 • 116

42.

Willow Flats to Second Creek
JACKSON LAKE LODGE AREA

43. Willow Flats Loop
COLTER BAY • JACKSON LAKE

Hiking distance: 6.5-mile loop
Hiking time: 3 hours
Configuration: double loop
Elevation gain: level
Difficulty: easy to slightly moderate
Exposure: a mix of open meadows and shaded forest
Dogs: not allowed
Maps: U.S.G.S. Colter Bay and Two Ocean Lake
　　　Adventure Maps: Jackson Hole
　　　Beartooth Publishing: Grand Teton National Park map
　　　National Geographic Trails Illustrated: Grand Teton Nat'l. Park

Willow Flats is a large freshwater marsh interspersed with cotton-wood, spruce, and fir forests. The extensive grassy wetlands and ponds provide a habitat for moose, elk, beaver, and waterfowl. A network of trails crosses Willow Flats, connecting Colter Bay with Jackson Lake Lodge. This hike begins and ends at the Colter Bay corrals, forming a double loop through Willow Flats. From the trail, the Tetons can be seen across Jackson Lake.

To the trailhead

From the national park entrance at Moose, continue 20 miles on Teton Park Road to Jackson Lake Junction and turn left (north). Drive 5.4 miles to Colter Bay Road and turn left (west). Continue 0.6 miles to a stop sign. Turn left and head 0.5 miles to the horse corrals and parking area.

The hike

Follow the unpaved service road past the corrals to the signed trail for Jackson Lake Lodge. Leave the road and take the foot-path to the left, beginning the first loop. Wind through the for-est, and cross the wide meadow in full view of the Teton Range. Traverse the side of the hill along the east edge of the meadow. Reenter the forest to a signed four-way junction at 1.2 miles, the beginning of the second loop.

　　Bear left on the service road towards Jackson Lake Lodge. Follow the old road east through open forests, crossing Third

Creek. At 2.5 miles is a signed junction. Take the right fork a short distance towards Second Creek Spring to another signed junction. Again head to the right. Cross the large grassy meadows of Willow Flats to a three-way junction. The sharp left fork leads to Swan Lake and Heron Pond. Curve to the right, crossing a long wooden bridge over Third Creek, and return to the four-way junction at the service road. Take the left fork along the old road, passing the disposal ponds, and return to the Colter Bay corrals. ▨

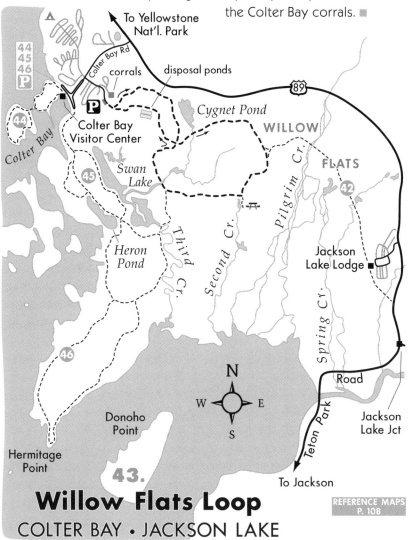

43.

Willow Flats Loop
COLTER BAY · JACKSON LAKE

REFERENCE MAPS
P. 108

44. Lakeshore Trail at Colter Bay
COLTER BAY • JACKSON LAKE

Hiking distance: 2-mile loop
Hiking time: 1 hour
Configuration: double loop
Elevation gain: level
Difficulty: easy
Exposure: a mix of open meadows and shaded forest
Dogs: not allowed
Maps: U.S.G.S. Colter Bay • Adventure Maps: Jackson Hole
        Beartooth Publishing: Grand Teton National Park map
        National Geographic Trails Illustrated: Grand Teton Nat'l. Park

The Lakeshore Trail follows a section of shoreline along Colter Bay and 25,000-acre Jackson Lake, the second largest lake in the Greater Yellowstone region. The trail crosses an isthmus and circles a forested peninsula protruding into Jackson Lake. The entire hike stays close to the shoreline. Throughout the double-loop trail are views of islands, other bays, and close-up vistas of the northern Teton Mountain Range, highlighted by massive Mount Moran and its distinctive Skillet Glacier.

To the trailhead

From the national park entrance at Moose, continue 20 miles on Teton Park Road to Jackson Lake Junction and turn left (north). Drive 5.4 miles to Colter Bay Road and turn left (west). At the end of the road, one mile ahead, park by the Colter Bay Visitor Center.

The hike

From the parking lot, walk behind the visitor center to the shoreline. Follow the paved trail to the right along the north shore of the marina through the lodgepole pine trees. At 0.5 miles is a sign marking the Lakeshore Foot Trail junction—go right. A short distance ahead, cross an isthmus that separates Jackson Lake and Colter Bay. Follow the trail to the left, which circles the perimeter of the peninsula in a clockwise direction. The beach at the far end of the peninsula is a wonderful area for a picnic. The trail continues along the shoreline back to the isthmus. After crossing, take the trail to the left, following the shoreline of Jackson Lake back to the Colter Bay Visitor Center. ■

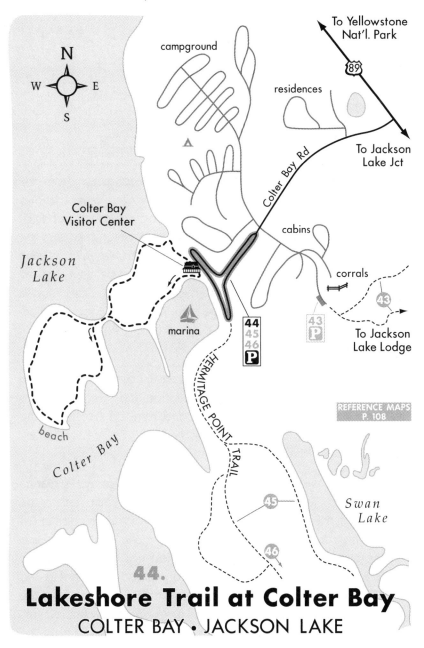

44.
Lakeshore Trail at Colter Bay
COLTER BAY • JACKSON LAKE

45. Swan Lake and Heron Pond
COLTER BAY · JACKSON LAKE

Hiking distance: 3 miles round trip
Hiking time: 1.5 hours
Configuration: out-and-back with large loop
Elevation gain: level
Difficulty: easy
Exposure: a mix of open meadows and shaded forest
Dogs: not allowed
Maps: U.S.G.S. Colter Bay · Adventure Maps: Jackson Hole
Beartooth Publishing: Grand Teton National Park map
National Geographic Trails Illustrated: Grand Teton Nat'l. Park

The trail to Swan Lake and Heron Pond heads south from the Colter Bay Visitor Center towards Hermitage Point, a peninsula on Jackson Lake. The pristine path strolls through stands of lodgepole pines with views of Colter Bay, Jackson Lake, and the ever-present Teton peaks. Both Swan Lake and Heron Pond have abundant water lilies and water fowl, including pelicans, osprey, trumpeter swan, cranes, heron, Canada geese, and ducks. Moose and elk are frequently seen in the area. This 3-mile loop is the beginning of the longer 9-mile loop to Hermitage Point (Hike 46).

To the trailhead

From the national park entrance at Moose, continue 20 miles on Teton Park Road to Jackson Lake Junction and turn left (north). Drive 5.4 miles to Colter Bay Road and turn left (west). At the road's end, one mile ahead, park by the Colter Bay Visitor Center.

The hike

The trailhead is on the south end of the parking lot by the marina boat launch. Take the signed Hermitage Point Foot Trail to the right along the Colter Bay shoreline. There is a trail junction at 0.4 miles. Take the trail to the right, staying close to the shoreline. A short distance ahead is an optional loop to the Jackson Lake Overlook on the right. Both trails merge ahead at the north end of Heron Pond, one mile from the trailhead. Continue along the shore of Heron Pond to another trail junction. Follow the left trail for this hike, which loops back towards Swan Lake. (The trail to the right leads south to Hermitage Point, Hike 46.) The trail heads north, then continues along the west shore of Swan Lake. A short distance ahead, complete the loop and return to the Colter Bay parking lot. ■

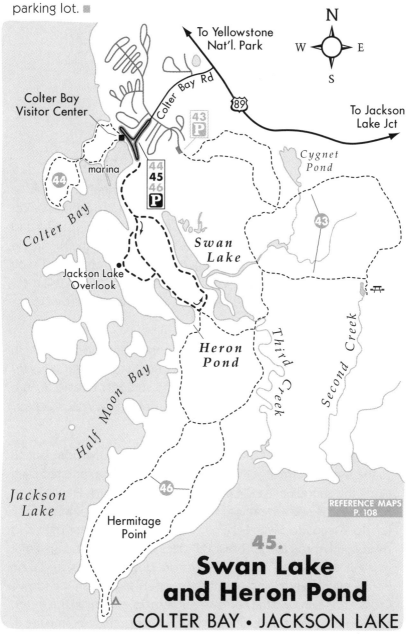

To Yellowstone Nat'l. Park

N
W · E
S

Colter Bay Rd
89

To Jackson Lake Jct

Colter Bay Visitor Center

43
P

Cygnet Pond

marina

44

44
45
46
P

Colter Bay

Swan Lake

43

Jackson Lake Overlook

Half Moon Bay

Heron Pond

Third Creek

Second Creek

Jackson Lake

46

REFERENCE MAPS
P. 108

Hermitage Point

45.
Swan Lake
and Heron Pond
COLTER BAY · JACKSON LAKE

46. Hermitage Point
COLTER BAY · JACKSON LAKE

Hiking distance: 8.8-mile loop
Hiking time: 4 hours
Configuration: double or triple loop
Elevation gain: 150 feet
Difficulty: moderate
Exposure: a mix of open meadows and shaded forest
Dogs: not allowed
Maps: U.S.G.S. Colter Bay, Two Ocean Lake, Jenny Lake
   Adventure Maps: Jackson Hole
   Beartooth Publishing: Grand Teton National Park map
   National Geographic Trails Illustrated: Grand Teton Nat'l. Park

The Hermitage Point Trail loops around the perimeter of a large peninsula that extends into Jackson Lake. The trail begins at Colter Bay and meanders across the rolling terrain through forests and meadows, passing ponds and creeks to the tip of the peninsula. Throughout the hike are stunning views of the Tetons and their majestic peaks. Most people return after the first loop (Hike 45), leaving the peninsula to be explored away from the crowds.

To the trailhead

From the national park entrance at Moose, continue 20 miles on Teton Park Road to Jackson Lake Junction and turn left (north). Drive 5.4 miles to Colter Bay Road and turn left (west). At the road's end, one mile ahead, park by the Colter Bay Visitor Center.

The hike

From the south end of the parking lot, head past the boat launch to the signed Hermitage Point Foot Trail. Follow the forested path along the shoreline. At 0.4 miles, bear right towards Heron Pond. Follow the eastern shore of Heron Pond to a signed junction. The left fork leads to Swan Lake for the return route. Bear right and head south through the forest 0.8 miles towards Hermitage Point to a cut-across trail. Take the right fork down the forested peninsula, eventually giving way to the open sagebrush meadows. Cross a ridge around the narrow southern tip, and begin the return to the north past stands of Douglas fir and a primitive campsite at

4.7 miles. Follow the shoreline, then curve inland into the forest to the cut-across trail. Bear right and follow the west edge of the meadow adjacent to Third Creek. At the next junction, bear left over a small hill to the Heron Pond/Swan Lake junction. Take the right fork along the western shore of Swan Lake, returning to the first trail junction. Head right, back to the trailhead. ■

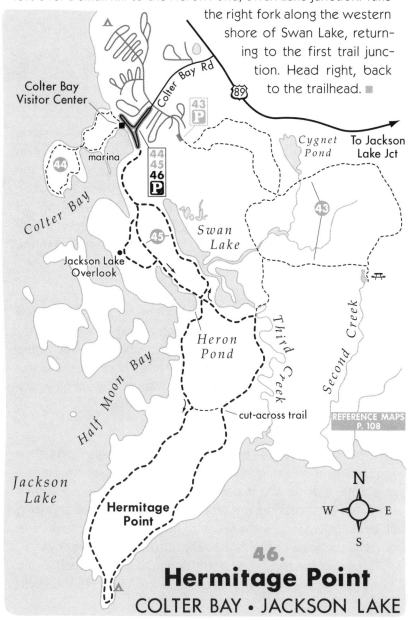

Colter Bay Visitor Center

Colter Bay Rd

89

43 P

Cygnet Pond

To Jackson Lake Jct

marina

44

44
45
46 P

Colter Bay

45

Swan Lake

43

Jackson Lake Overlook

Heron Pond

Third Creek

Second Creek

Half Moon Bay

cut-across trail

REFERENCE MAPS
P. 108

Jackson Lake

Hermitage Point

N
W · E
S

46.
Hermitage Point
COLTER BAY · JACKSON LAKE

47. Sargents Bay
JACKSON LAKE

Hiking distance: 1—2 miles round trip
Hiking time: 1 hour
Configuration: out-and-back
Elevation gain: 50 feet
Difficulty: easy
Exposure: some shaded forest and open shoreline
Dogs: not allowed
Maps: U.S.G.S. Colter Bay

Jackson Lake is the second largest lake in the greater Yellowstone area. Sargents Bay, north of Colter Bay, is a lightly visited bay on the east shore of the lake that offers impressive views of the Teton Range. The bay was formed between 1910 and 1916 when the Jackson Lake Dam raised the water level. The trail is an old wagon road that is used primarily by fishermen. It follows a gully for a quarter mile to the enclosed bay. Pebble beaches rim the shoreline, backed by the forested sloping hills.

To the trailhead

From the national park entrance at Moose, continue 20 miles on Teton Park Road to Jackson Lake Junction and turn left (north). Drive 8.3 miles to a parking pullout on the west (left) side of the road. The unmarked trail is located 2.9 miles north of the Colter Bay turnoff and 12.7 miles south of Flagg Ranch. It is the only turnout for a long distance in either direction.

The hike

Take the unsigned but distinct path down the gently sloping draw. The path meanders through an open pine forest with small meadows. Enter a dense forest along the east ridge of the ravine, then drop into and cross the ravine. Two routes lead to the shoreline at Sargents Bay. Follow the ravine to the mouth of the small cove, or climb the knoll on the path to the north edge of the cove.

To extend the hike, head north along the sandy beach to the mouth of the bay, with views across Jackson Lake. To the south,

the beach leads to the southernmost end of the bay. Choose
your own route and distance. ■

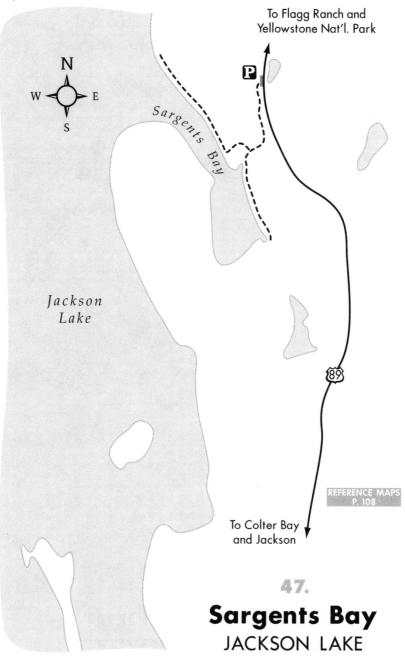

To Flagg Ranch and
Yellowstone Nat'l. Park

N
W   E
S

Sargents Bay

Jackson
Lake

REFERENCE MAPS
P. 108

To Colter Bay
and Jackson

47.

Sargents Bay
JACKSON LAKE

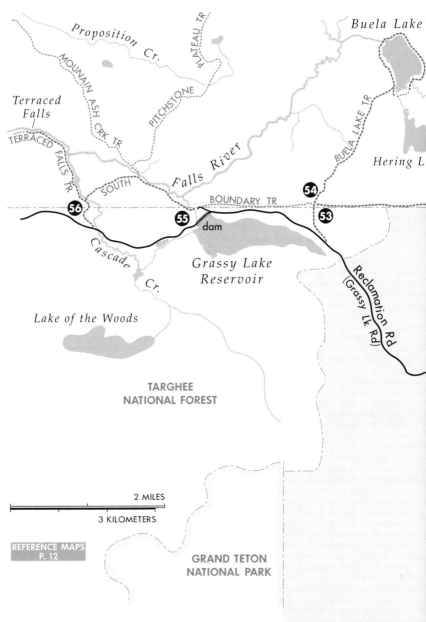

Proposition Cr.

Buela Lake

PLATEAU TR.

Terraced Falls

MOUNAIN ASH CRK. TR.

PITCHSTONE

TERRACED FALLS TR.

Falls River

Buela Lake Tr.

Hering L

SOUTH

BOUNDARY TR

54

56

55

dam

53

Cascade Cr.

Grassy Lake Reservoir

Reclamation Rd (Grassy Lk Rd)

Lake of the Woods

TARGHEE
NATIONAL FOREST

2 MILES

3 KILOMETERS

REFERENCE MAPS
P. 12

GRAND TETON
NATIONAL PARK

HIKES 48–56

John D. Rockefeller Jr. Memorial Parkway

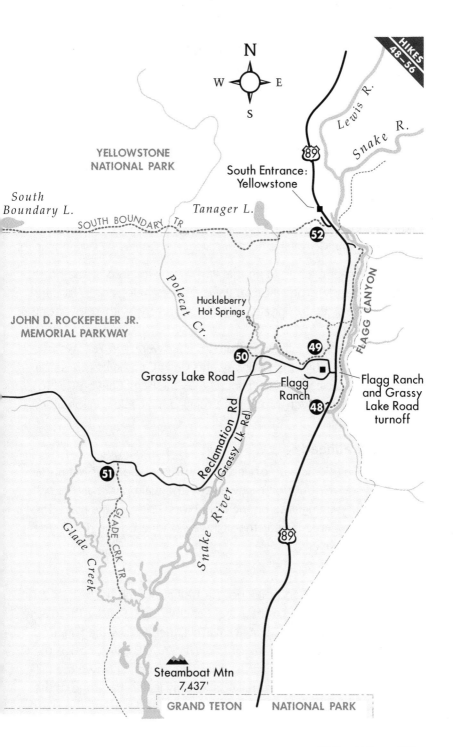

N

W   E

S

HIKES 48-56

YELLOWSTONE NATIONAL PARK

South Entrance: Yellowstone

South Boundary L.

Tanager L.

SOUTH BOUNDARY TR

52

JOHN D. ROCKEFELLER JR. MEMORIAL PARKWAY

Polecat Cr.

Huckleberry Hot Springs

Lewis R.

Snake R.

89

FLAGG CANYON

50

49

Grassy Lake Road

Flagg Ranch

Flagg Ranch and Grassy Lake Road turnoff

48

Reclamation Rd (Grassy Lk Rd)

51

Snake River

GLADE CRK TR

Glade Creek

89

Steamboat Mtn 7,437'

GRAND TETON   **NATIONAL PARK**

48. Flagg Canyon Trail along the Snake River

JOHN D. ROCKEFELLER JR. MEMORIAL PARKWAY

Hiking distance: 5 miles round trip
Hiking time: 2.5 hours
Configuration: out-and-back
Elevation gain: 100 feet
Difficulty: easy to slightly moderate
Exposure: a mix of shaded forest and open meadows
Dogs: not allowed
Maps: U.S.G.S. Flagg Ranch and Lewis Canyon
　　　　National Geographic Trails Illustrated: Old Faithful/SW Yellowstone

John D. Rockefeller Jr. Memorial Parkway is located at the north end of Grand Teton National Park, an undeveloped, 37-square-mile corridor that connects the Grand Tetons with Yelowstone National Park.

The Snake River emerges from its headwaters in Yellowstone, then flows through the parkway and Flagg Canyon before entering Jackson Lake. This riverfront hike on the Flagg Canyon Trail follows the Snake River through the rugged, volcanic canyon along the cliff's edge.

To the trailhead

From the Flagg Ranch turnoff in the John D. Rockefeller Jr. Memorial Parkway, drive south on Highway 89 (the main park road) a half mile to the parking area on the right (west) side of the road. The large parking area is near the highway bridge on the north side of the Snake River.

The hike

Cross the highway and pick up the trail along the north bank of the Snake River next to the Flagg Ranch Bridge. Follow the river upstream to the north. Climb a small hill, then follow the forested bluffs above the west bank of the river. At 0.8 miles, notice the cascades and waterfalls across the river, tumbling down the hillside tributary stream. The trail temporarily leaves the edge of the cliffs and winds through a conifer forest. At 1.2 miles, the path returns to the edge of the cliffs at a signed junction with the Polecat Creek Loop connector trail (Hike 49). Stay to the right, following the river past another beautiful cascade on the opposite river bank at 1.5 miles. At this point, the river narrows and swiftly flows through the steep-walled gorge of rhyolite and volcanic rock. At 2.5 miles, the trail ends at a boat launch and picnic area just south of the Yellowstone National Park boundary. Return by retracing your steps. ■

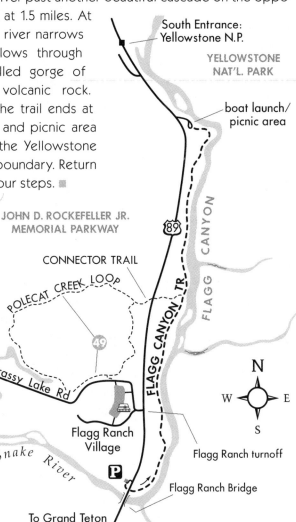

South Entrance: Yellowstone N.P.

YELLOWSTONE NAT'L. PARK

boat launch/ picnic area

JOHN D. ROCKEFELLER JR. MEMORIAL PARKWAY

CONNECTOR TRAIL

FLAGG CANYON

89

POLECAT CREEK LOOP

FLAGG

50

Huckleberry Hot Springs

49

FLAGG CANYON TR.

Grassy Lake Rd

N

W · E

S

Flagg Ranch Village

Flagg Ranch turnoff

Snake River

P

Flagg Ranch Bridge

To Grand Teton Nat'l. Park

48.

Flagg Canyon Trail along the Snake River
JOHN D. ROCKEFELLER JR. MEM. PARKWAY

49. Polecat Creek Loop
from Flagg Ranch

JOHN D. ROCKEFELLER JR. MEMORIAL PARKWAY

Hiking distance: 2.3-mile loop
Hiking time: 1 hour
Configuration: loop
Elevation gain: 100 feet
Difficulty: easy
Exposure: a mix of shaded forest and open meadows
Dogs: not allowed
Maps: U.S.G.S. Flagg Ranch
 National Geographic Trails Illustrated: Old Faithful/SW Yellowstone

Flagg Ranch is located in the John D. Rockefeller Jr. Memorial Parkway, two miles south of Yellowstone National Park and five miles north of Grand Teton. The small village lies between the Snake River and Polecat Creek, offering lodging, camping, horseback riding, float trips, fly-fishing, and hiking. The site was originally used as a military outpost for management of Yellowstone Park and was named after the flags that flew on the premises.

The headwaters of Polecat Creek begin in Yellowstone and flow south, joining the Snake River a mile west of Flagg Ranch. The Polecat Creek Loop is a leisurely walk that follows a ridge overlooking the lush marshy meadows along the creek. The wetlands are rich with waterfowl and songbirds. The trail traverses a lodgepole pine, subalpine fir, and Engelmann spruce forest with little gain in elevation.

To the trailhead

At the north end of Grand Teton National Park, in the John D. Rockefeller Jr. Memorial Parkway, turn west at the Flagg Ranch/ Grassy Lake Road turnoff at Flagg Ranch Village. Make a quick right onto Grassy Lake Road. Park at the northeast end of the visitor center parking lot, across from the horse stables on the south side of Grassy Lake Road.

The hike

Walk 40 yards to the left (west) along Grassy Lake Road to the unsigned footpath on the right. The footpath connects with the signed Polecat Creek Loop 20 yards ahead. Bear left, parallel to Grassy Lake Road, hiking the loop clockwise through a lodge-pole pine forest. Cross an unpaved service road and continue to the west. A short distance ahead, curve right and follow Polecat Creek above the wet, green meadow. At 1.3 miles, the path recrosses the service road to a signed junction with the Flagg Canyon Connector Trail on the left. Stay on the main trail to the right, completing the loop at Grassy Lake Road 0.5 miles ahead. ■

Polecat Creek Loop
from Flagg Ranch
JOHN D. ROCKEFELLER JR. MEM. PARKWAY

50. Huckleberry Hot Springs
JOHN D. ROCKEFELLER JR. MEMORIAL PARKWAY

Hiking distance: 1 mile round trip
Hiking time: 30 minutes
Configuration: out-and-back
Elevation gain: level
Difficulty: easy, with exception of river crossing
Exposure: mostly open meadows
Dogs: not allowed
Maps: U.S.G.S. Flagg Ranch
National Geographic Trails Illustrated: Old Faithful/SW Yellowstone

Huckleberry Hot Springs, one mile west of Flagg Ranch, is a natural hot springs in a beautiful mountain meadow between Yellowstone and Grand Teton National Parks. The springs, in excess of 100 degrees Fahrenheit, has a series of pools, a waterfall, a grotto, and a natural bridge. The hot springs are located along a small tributary stream of Polecat Creek, which empties into the Snake River a couple of miles downstream. This short, easy hike is a popular cross-country ski route in the winter.

To the trailhead

At the north end of Grand Teton National Park, in the John D. Rockefeller Jr. Memorial Parkway, turn west at the Flagg Ranch/Grassy Lake Road turnoff at Flagg Ranch Village. Make a quick right onto Grassy Lake Road. Continue 1.1 mile to the unmarked trailhead parking pullout on the right, located immediately after crossing the bridge over Polecat Creek.

The hike

From the parking pullout, hike north on the abandoned road past the "no bikes and no dogs" undesignated trail sign. After 100 yards the trail splits. Bear to the right and wade through the 20-foot wide Polecat Creek. Careful footing is advised, as the current is stronger than it looks. After crossing, the trail leads into a meadow. Near the middle of the meadow is a stream. This is the beginning of the hot springs. Follow the stream to the left, heading upstream to a series of warm water pools. Return by retracing your steps. ▪

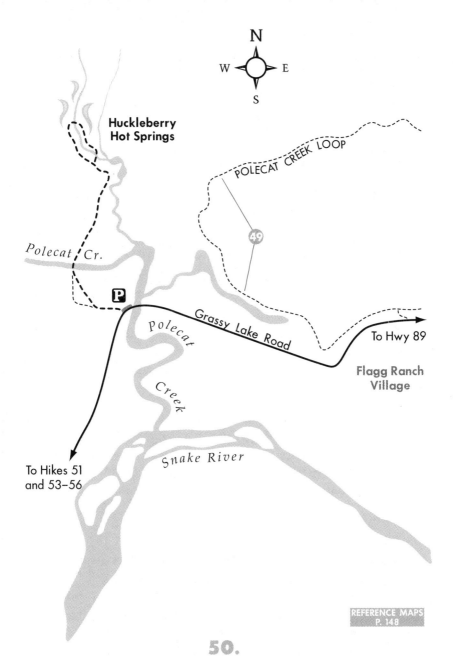

50.
Huckleberry Hot Springs
JOHN D. ROCKEFELLER JR. MEM. PARKWAY

51. Glade Creek Trail
JOHN D. ROCKEFELLER JR. MEMORIAL PARKWAY

Hiking distance: 3 miles round trip
Hiking time: 1.5 hours
Configuration: out-and-back
Elevation gain: 200 feet
Difficulty: easy
Exposure: mostly exposed with forested pockets
Dogs: not allowed
Maps: U.S.G.S. Flagg Ranch
National Geographic Trails Illustrated: Old Faithful/SW Yellowstone

Glade Creek begins just east of Grassy Lake in the John D. Rockefeller Jr. Memorial Parkway. The creek flows south, joining the Snake River above Jackson Lake. The Glade Creek Trail heads into Grand Teton National Park along the west side of Jackson Lake en route to Jenny Lake. This hike follows the first 1.5 miles to Glade Creek on an easy, well-defined path. The trail heads due south through a dense conifer forest en route to a wide valley overlooking the Snake River.

To the trailhead

At the north end of Grand Teton National Park, turn west at the Flagg Ranch/Grassy Lake Road turnoff at Flagg Ranch Village. Make a quick right onto Grassy Lake Road (which becomes Reclamation Road en route to the trailhead). Continue 4.4 miles to the trailhead parking area on the left.

The hike

Head south through the flat, open lodgepole pine forest. Cross a wooden footbridge over a small tributary stream of Glade Creek. The path heads down a long gradual descent. At 1.2 miles, views open up of the Snake River in a wide valley. Descend to the valley floor to a log footbridge over Glade Creek. This is the turnaround spot. To return, retrace your steps.

To hike farther, cross the bridge and traverse the meadow along the west edge of the marshes lining the Snake River. The trail reaches the Grand Teton National Park boundary at 3.5 miles and continues along Jackson Lake. The Glade Creek Trail connects with a series of trails leading west to Jackass Pass, Owl Creek, Berry Creek, and Webb Canyon. ■

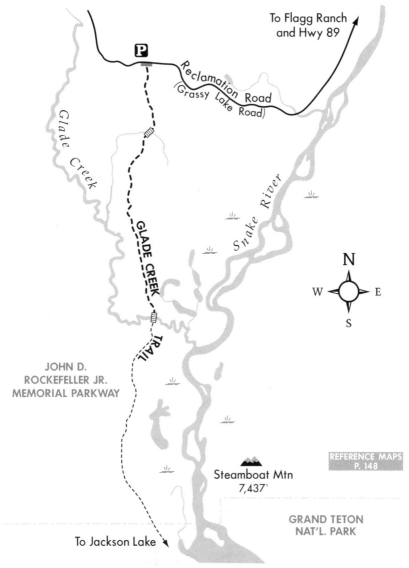

51. **Glade Creek Trail**
JOHN D. ROCKEFELLER JR. MEM. PARKWAY

52. South Boundary Lake
from the east

SOUTH BOUNDARY TRAIL from Y.N.P. SOUTH ENTRANCE

Hiking distance: Tanager Lake: 2 miles round trip
                             South Boundary Lake: 10 miles round trip
Hiking time: 1–5 hours
Configuration: out-and-back
Elevation gain: 150 feet to 500 feet
Difficulty: easy to moderate
Exposure: open meadows with forested pockets
Dogs: not allowed
Maps: U.S.G.S. Lewis Canyon and Grassy Lake Reservoir
               National Geographic Trails Illustrated: Old Faithful/SW Yellowstone

The South Boundary Trail crosses the entire south end of Yellowstone National Park. This hike begins outside the south entrance gate of Yellowstone near the John D. Rockefeller Jr.

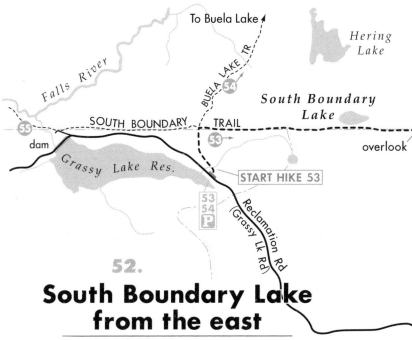

52.
South Boundary Lake
from the east
South Boundary Trail
from Yellowstone's South Entrance

Memorial Parkway and parallels the south boundary of the national park. En route to South Boundary Lake, the trail passes Tanager Lake, a 32-acre lake in a boggy, wetland meadow. The bucolic meadow is an excellent place for spotting moose and observing birds. Three miles farther west is South Boundary Lake, a forested 10-acre lake lined with pond lilies. The South Boundary Trail continues west, connecting with trails to the Pitchstone Plateau, Union Falls, and the Bechler Ranger Station. Hikes 52 and 53 can be combined for a one-way, 7-mile shuttle hike.

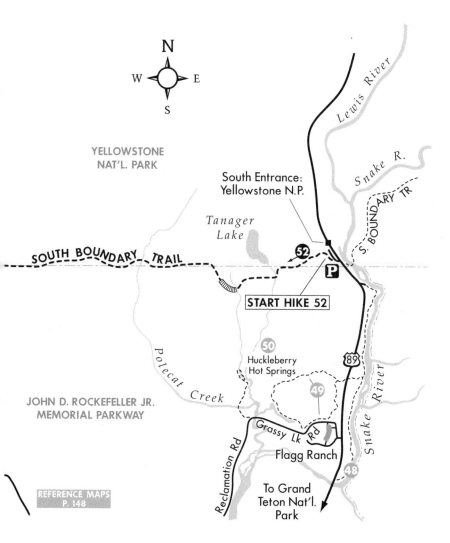

To the trailhead

At the north end of Grand Teton National Park, in the John D. Rockefeller Jr. Memorial Parkway, drive 2 miles north of Flagg Ranch towards Yellowstone National Park. Turn left across the road from the large Yellowstone National Park sign, and immediately pull into the parking spaces on the right. (The turnoff is 0.2 miles south of the Yellowstone entrance gate.)

The hike

Walk up the paved service road, past the Snake River Ranger Station, to the corrals on the left. Curve around the far (north) end of the corrals to the posted trailhead. Cross the tree-dotted meadow on the faint path. Within 30 yards, the trail becomes distinct and climbs 120 feet up the hillside to the Yellowstone boundary. Follow the level, tree-lined corridor west along the park boundary. At a half mile, make an easy, gradual descent through an open forest of young lodgepole pines. Curve south into John D. Rockefeller Jr. Memorial Parkway, and cross an old log footbridge over the Tanager Lake outlet stream. Stroll through the quiet backcountry, and cross the wetland on a long wooden footbridge. Skirt the south end of the meadow, and head back into the forest. Climb an 80-foot rise, returning to the park boundary at 1.8 miles. Continue west on the level path. At 2.5 miles, the trail steadily climbs through the forest to an over-look of the Snake River valley and Huckleberry Mountain in the east. At 5 miles, continuing straight west, the trail parallels the south edge of South Boundary Lake. Short side paths drop down to the shoreline. This is the turn-around spot.

The trail continues another 1.5 miles to the junction with the Buela Lake Trail for a one-way, 7-mile shuttle with Hike 53. ∎

53. South Boundary Lake from the west

SOUTH BOUNDARY TRAIL from GRASSY LAKE

Hiking distance: 4.4 miles round trip
Hiking time: 2.5 hours
Configuration: out-and-back
Elevation gain: 500 feet
Difficulty: easy
Exposure: a mix of open meadows and shaded forest
Dogs: not allowed
Maps: U.S.G.S. Grassy Lake Reservoir and Lewis Canyon
National Geographic Trails Illustrated: Old Faithful/SW Yellowstone

map
page 162

South Boundary Lake is an oval-shaped, 10-acre lake on the south boundary of Yellowstone National Park. The forested lake is lined with pond lilies and rimmed with lodgepole pines. Utilizing the South Boundary Trail, South Boundary Lake can be accessed from the west—near Grassy Lake—or from the east, at the south entrance to Yellowstone (Hike 52). This hike begins from Grassy Lake and climbs over a small, forested ridge to the park boundary. The trail parallels the boundary to the south edge of the lake, following along the shoreline. Hikes 52 and 53 can be combined for a one-way, 7-mile shuttle hike.

To the trailhead

At the north end of Grand Teton National Park, in the John D. Rockefeller Jr. Memorial Parkway, turn west at the Flagg Ranch/ Grassy Lake Road turnoff at Flagg Ranch Village. Make a quick right onto Grassy Lake Road. Continue 9.3 miles to the unsigned Buela Lake turnout on the right side of the road. (Grassy Lake Road becomes Reclamation Road en route to the trailhead.) The turnout is a quarter mile past the Targhee National Forest sign.

The hike

Walk past the Buela Lake Trail sign, and ascend the forested ridge to an overlook of the entire 1.8-mile-long Grassy Lake. At a half mile, atop a plateau, is a posted 4-way junction with the South Boundary Trail. The route straight ahead leads to Buela Lake (Hike 54). To the left, the South Boundary Trail leads to the Mountain Ash Creek Trail (Hike 55).

Take the right fork and head east on the old access road, slowly being reclaimed by vegetation. The nearly straight path follows the south boundary of Yellowstone National Park through lodgepole pines, Engelmann spruce, and subalpine fir. At 1.5 miles, the old road becomes a single track and descends into the deep

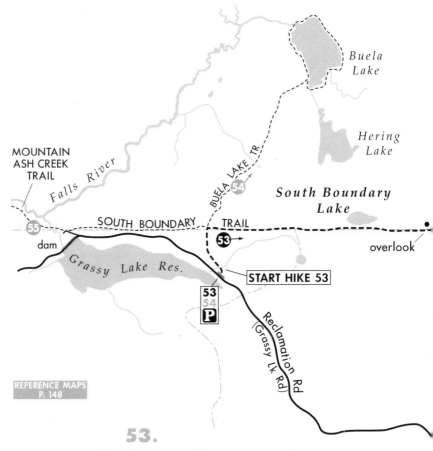

53.

South Boundary Lake from the west

South Boundary Trail from Grassy Lake

forest, reaching the southwest end of South Boundary Lake at 2 miles. The trail parallels the south side of the lake, with a few short side paths dropping down to the shoreline. This is the turn-around spot.

The trail continues another 5 miles to the Snake River Ranger Station at the south entrance to Yellowstone for a one-way, 7-mile shuttle with Hike 52. ■

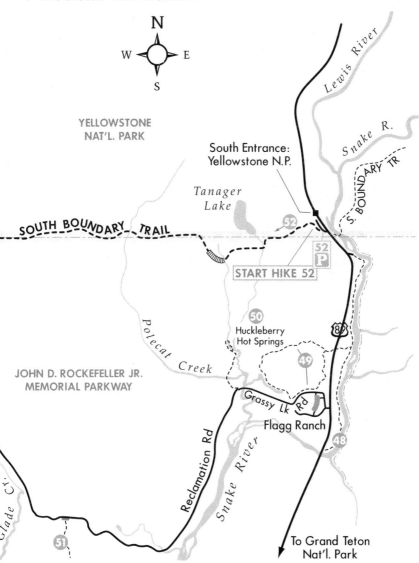

54. Buela Lake

Hiking distance: 5 miles round trip
Hiking time: 2.5 hours
Configuration: out-and-back
Elevation gain: 400 feet
Difficulty: easy to slightly moderate
Exposure: a mix of open meadows and shaded forest
Dogs: not allowed
Maps: U.S.G.S. Grassy Lake Reservoir
      National Geographic Trails Illustrated: Old Faithful/SW Yellowstone

Buela Lake is a beautiful 107-acre backcountry lake that sits at an elevation of 7,400 feet near the south end of Yellowstone National Park. The lake is surrounded by forested hills. Yellow pond lilies grow along its marshy south end, where a stream from Hering Lake feeds the lake. The outlet stream at the northwest end of Buela Lake forms the headwaters of Falls River. Access to the trailhead is through the John D. Rockefeller Jr. Memorial Parkway and Targhee National Forest. The well-defined trail gently winds through lodgepole pines and parallels the western shoreline past two designated campsites.

To the trailhead

At the north end of Grand Teton National Park, in the John D. Rockefeller Jr. Memorial Parkway, turn west at the Flagg Ranch/ Grassy Lake Road turnoff at Flagg Ranch Village. Make a quick right onto Grassy Lake Road. Continue 9.3 miles to the unsigned Buela Lake turnout on the right side of the road. (Grassy Lake Road becomes Reclamation Road en route to the trailhead.) The turnout is a quarter mile past the Targhee National Forest sign.

The hike

Walk past the trailhead sign, and ascend the hill to an overlook of the entire 1.8-mile-long Grassy Lake. At a half mile, atop a plateau, is a posted 4-way junction with the South Boundary Trail, which parallels the Yellowstone National Park boundary. Continue straight ahead through a young forest of lodgepole pines and aspens. Cross the gently rolling terrain, heading north

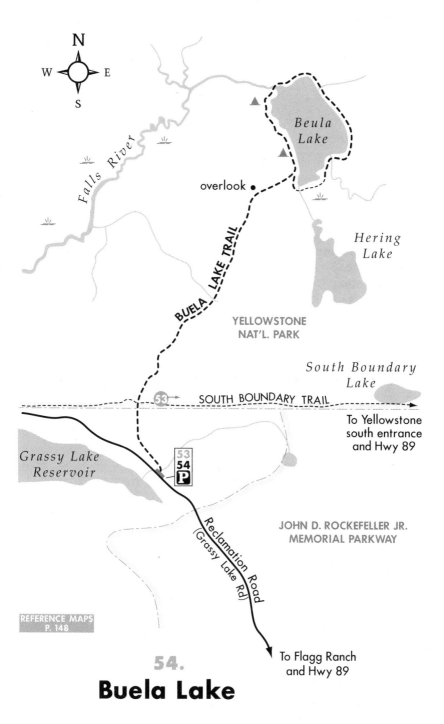

N
W ● E
S

Falls River

▲

Beula Lake

▲

overlook ●

Hering Lake

BUELA LAKE TRAIL

YELLOWSTONE
NAT'L. PARK

South Boundary Lake

53 SOUTH BOUNDARY TRAIL

To Yellowstone
south entrance
and Hwy 89

53
54
P

Grassy Lake Reservoir

JOHN D. ROCKEFELLER JR.
MEMORIAL PARKWAY

Reclamation Road
(Grassy Lake Rd)

REFERENCE MAPS
P. 148

To Flagg Ranch
and Hwy 89

54.
Buela Lake

inside the national park. At 2.2 miles, curve east to an overlook of Buela Lake. Descend 150 feet to the forested shoreline and a view across the lake. To the right is a swampy wetland and inlet stream from Hering Lake, a ten-minute walk to the south. The main trail curves north and follows the western shoreline past two campsites. Wild blueberries line the lakeside path, which circles the lake. ■

55. Mountain Ash Creek—Cascade Creek Loop

Hiking distance: 4.3-mile loop
Hiking time: 2 hours
Configuration: loop
Elevation gain: 200 feet
Difficulty: easy to slightly moderate
Exposure: shaded forest and open slopes
Dogs: not allowed
Maps: U.S.G.S. Grassy Lake Reservoir
       National Geographic Trails Illustrated: Old Faithful/SW Yellowstone

The Mountain Ash Creek Trail begins near the south boundary of Yellowstone National Park below the Grassy Lake Dam spillway. The trail leads deep into the backcountry to Mountain Ash Creek, Union Falls, Bechler Meadows, and the Falls River Basin. This hike follows the first portion of the trail to Falls River and makes a loop back along Cascade Creek and Reclamation Road.

To the trailhead

At the north end of Grand Teton National Park, in the John D. Rockefeller Jr. Memorial Parkway, turn west at the Flagg Ranch/Grassy Lake Road turnoff at Flagg Ranch Village. Make a quick right onto Grassy Lake Road (which becomes Reclamation Road en route to the trailhead). Continue 10.9 miles to the Grassy Lake Dam at the west end of Grassy Lake. Before crossing the dam, turn right. Drive 0.2 miles downhill and park at the posted Mountain Ash Creek Trail.

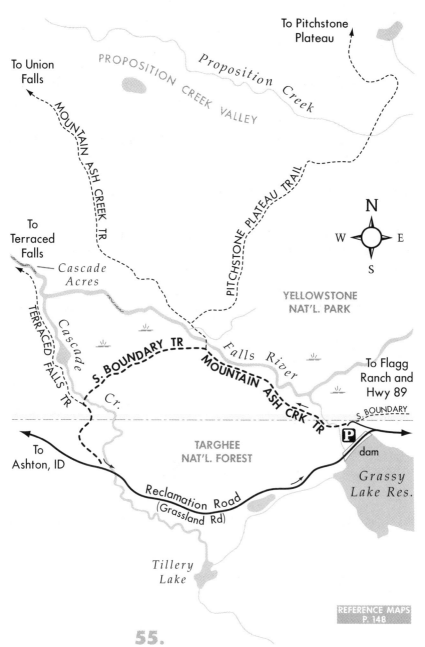

To Pitchstone Plateau

To Union Falls

PROPOSITION CREEK VALLEY

Proposition Creek

MOUNTAIN ASH CREEK TR

To Terraced Falls

Cascade Acres

PITCHSTONE PLATEAU TRAIL

N
W E
S

YELLOWSTONE NAT'L. PARK

TERRACED FALLS TR

Cascade

S. BOUNDARY TR

Falls River

MOUNTAIN ASH CRK TR

To Flagg Ranch and Hwy 89

S. BOUNDARY

Cr.

P

dam

To Ashton, ID

TARGHEE NAT'L. FOREST

Grassy Lake Res.

Reclamation Road (Grassland Rd)

Tillery Lake

REFERENCE MAPS
P. 148

55.
Mountain Ash Creek–Cascade Creek Loop

The hike

Cross over the spillway to the Mountain Ash Creek Trail sign. Go to the right, heading through the open forest 0.1 mile to the Yellowstone National Park boundary. Continue into the park, reaching Falls River at a half mile. Curve left and follow the river downstream to a posted junction at 1.1 mile. The Mountain Ash Creek Trail fords Falls River and continues 6.5 miles to Union Falls. Take the South Boundary Trail to the left, skirting the southwest edge of a wetland meadow. Wind through the forest and drop down to tumbling Cascade Creek at a rock wall. Cross the creek to a junction at 2 miles. The right fork parallels Cascade Creek and Falls River to Terraced Falls (Hike 56). This hike stays to the left and ascends the hill. Steadily gain elevation, leaving Yellowstone National Park, to Grassy Lake Road in the Targhee National Forest. Bear left on the unpaved road and cross over Cascade Creek. Follow the road 1.6 miles back to the Grassy Lake dam. Cross the dam and bear left on the road, descending back to the trailhead. ▓

56. Cascade Creek Trail to Terraced Falls

Hiking distance: 3.8 miles round trip
Hiking time: 2 hours
Configuration: out-and-back
Elevation gain: 300 feet
Difficulty: easy to slightly moderate
Exposure: open slopes with forested pockets
Dogs: not allowed
Maps: U.S.G.S. Grassy Lake Reservoir
      National Geographic Trails Illustrated: Old Faithful/SW Yellowstone

map
page 170

Cascade Creek is a short but stunning creek that connects Tillery Lake to Falls River. The trail begins in the Targhee National Forest, adjacent to Grand Teton, and heads into the remote, south end of Yellowstone National Park. The trail parallels the creek past a steady series of whitewater cascades and waterfalls en route to Terraced Falls. The falls is a six-tiered cataract on the Falls River which plunges 140 feet between steep volcanic columns of rock. The trail to Terraced Falls also passes a series of magnificent waterfalls and powerful whitewater cascades along both Cascade Creek and Falls River. Below the confluence of the two creeks is Cascade Acres, a segmented set of rapids dropping 30 feet over a 200-yard stretch of the creek.

To the trailhead

At the north end of Grand Teton National Park, turn west at the Flagg Ranch/Grassy Lake Road turnoff at Flagg Ranch Village. Make a quick right onto Grassy Lake Road (which becomes Reclamation Road en route to the trailhead). Continue 10.9 miles to the Grassy Lake Dam at the west end of Grassy Lake. Cross the dam and drive another 1.7 miles to the trailhead on the right, just after crossing the bridge over Cascade Creek.

The hike

Head downhill on the Cascade Creek Trail, a narrow, rocky road overlooking the Proposition Creek valley. Stay on the west side of Cascade Creek, entering Yellowstone National Park at 0.35 miles.

Drop down to a posted junction at Cascade Creek. The right fork (South Boundary Trail) crosses the creek to Falls River (Hike 55). Bear left on the Terraced Falls Trail, and parallel Cascade Creek through an open lodgepole pine forest. Pass cascades over long slabs of rock, a rock grotto, and a series of waterfalls. At 1.2 miles,

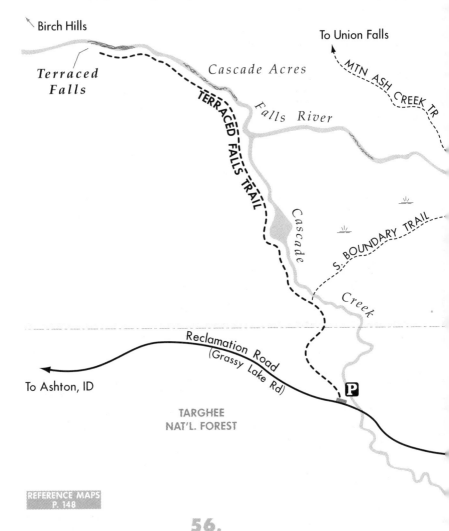

REFERENCE MAPS
P. 148

56.

Cascade Creek Trail to Terraced Falls

the trail reaches the confluence of Cascade Creek and Falls River at a wide, sweeping S-bend in the river. Follow the 80-foot wide river downstream past Cascade Acres, a 200-yard cascade by large rock formations and caves. Traverse the hillside high above the river, and slowly descend to the riverbank. The trail ends on the edge of the steep cliffs at an overlook of Terraced Falls, the river, and Birch Hills. ▪

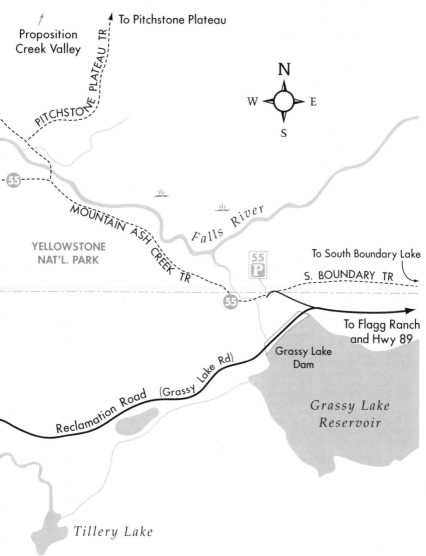

57. Cunningham Cabin

Hiking distance: 0.5-mile loop
Hiking time: 20 minutes
Configuration: loop
Elevation gain: level
Difficulty: very easy
Exposure: open flatlands
Dogs: not allowed
Maps: U.S.G.S. Moran
        Cunningham Cabin Guide

Cunningham Cabin was the 160-acre homestead ranch of J. Pierce and Margaret Cunningham from the 1880s. The homestead is located just south of Spread Creek in the flatlands overlooking the Snake River between Moose Junction and Moran Junction. The ranch was primarily used for grazing cattle and cultivating hay. All that remains of the historic homesite are buck-and-rail fences, foundation stones, broken posts, and depressions. The existing cabin, built in the 1950s, is a replica of the original 1880s cabin. The half-mile, self-guiding trail circles the cabin, foundation, and surrounding grounds.

To the trailhead

From the intersection of Highway 89 and Teton Park Road at Moose Junction (located 12 miles north of Jackson), drive 12.4 miles north on Highway 89 to the posted Cunningham Cabin on the left. The turnoff is between mile markers 178 and 179. Turn left and continue 0.4 miles to the parking lot at the end of the road.

From Moran Junction, the turnoff to the cabin is 5.3 miles south on Highway 89.

The hike

Walk through the buck-and-rail fence, overlooking the expansive flatlands of Jackson Hole and the entire Teton Range. Head northwest through the open grasslands. Curve right and cross a bridge over the creek to the low, three-room cabin with a sod roof. Continue past the cabin, passing depressions and remnants of foundations while sensing the history associated with the area. The trail returns along the back side of the cabin and completes the loop. ▪

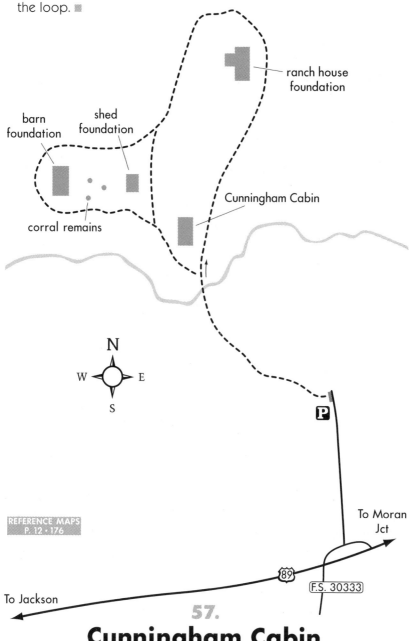

ranch house foundation

barn foundation

shed foundation

corral remains

Cunningham Cabin

N
W ⬥ E
S

P

To Moran Jct

REFERENCE MAPS
P. 12 • 176

89

F.S. 30333

To Jackson

57.
Cunningham Cabin

58. Toppings Lakes Trail

Hiking distance: 3.6 miles round trip
(plus optional 1.2 miles for spur trail)
Hiking time: 2 hours
Configuration: out-and-back
Elevation gain: 1,100 feet
Difficulty: moderate
Exposure: mix of shaded forest and exposed meadows
Dogs: allowed
Maps: U.S.G.S. Davis Hill and Mount Leidy
Beartooth Publishing: Grand Teton National Park map

Toppings Lakes are two lakes on the west side of Mount Leidy in the Bridger-Teton National Forest, located just outside of the east Grand Teton boundary. The high mountain lakes sit in a depression surrounded by forests and meadows at an elevation of 8,500 feet. The two lakes are connected by a stream and drain to the east down through Coal Creek, a tributary of Spread Creek. The Toppings Lakes Trail follows a ridge through lodgepole pines and parallels a stream to a large meadow and the lakes. A side path leads a half mile to a ridge and an overlook of Mount Leidy and the lakes below.

To the trailhead

From the intersection of Highway 89 and Teton Park Road at Moose Junction (located 12 miles north of Jackson), drive 12.4 miles north on Highway 89 to Forest Service Road 30333. The road is located directly across the road from Cunningham Cabin, between mile markers 178 and 179. Turn right on Forest Service Road 30333, and drive 0.8 miles to a Y-fork. Forest Service Road 30333 goes to the right. Veer left on Forest Service Road 30310 and go 2.4 miles to another Y-fork. Stay to the right and continue 1.5 miles uphill to the trailhead parking area (a wide pullout) on the right. The road is gated to vehicles just beyond the parking area.

From Moran Junction, the turnoff to the road is 5.3 miles south on Highway 89.

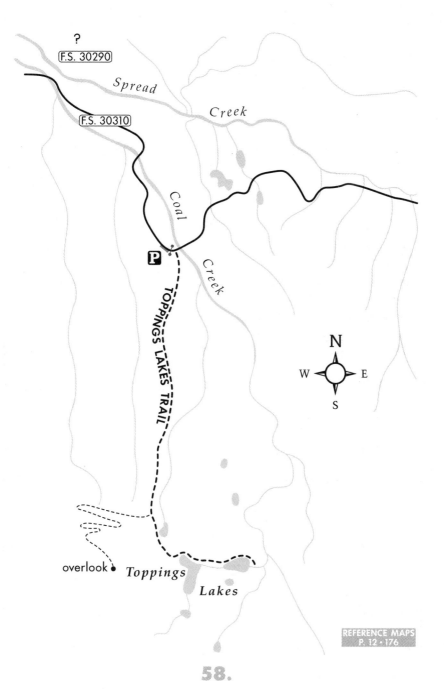

?

F.S. 30290

Spread

Creek

F.S. 30310

Coal

P

Creek

TOPPINGS LAKES TRAIL

N

W · E

S

overlook · *Toppings*

Lakes

REFERENCE MAPS
P. 12 · 176

58.

Toppings Lakes Trail

The hike

Head up the dirt road, passing the vehicle gate. Walk 200 yards to an unsigned footpath on the right. Take the trail and enter the dense lodgepole pine forest. Climb the narrow ridge through the dense forest between two steep embankments. The stream on the left is the outlet stream from a pond below the lakes. At 1.1 mile is a trail split. The right fork climbs 0.6 miles to the 9,100-foot ridge and an overlook of Toppings Lakes.

For this hike, stay to the left on the posted Toppings Lakes Trail. Descend past the pond on the left, dropping into an open meadow. Walk through the meadow above the pond to the first Toppings Lake. Skirt around the north side, traversing the hillside past the first lake. Follow the outlet stream to the lower lake, a large oblong lake surrounded by forest. The footpath follows the north side of the lake to its outlet on the east end. Return by retracing your steps. ▬

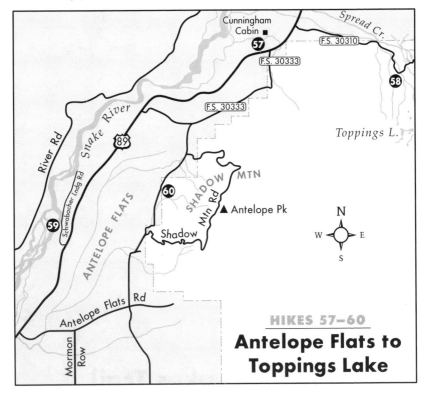

59. Schwabacher's Landing

Hiking distance: 1 to 4 miles round trip
Hiking time: 30 minutes to 2 hours
Configuration: out-and-back
Elevation gain: level
Difficulty: easy
Exposure: open forest and riparian vegetation
Dogs: not allowed
Maps: U.S.G.S. Moose

map
page 178

Schwabacher's Landing is a launch site on the Snake River between Moose Junction and Moran Junction, popular with anglers and river rafters. This flat river area is home to moose, elk, deer, antelope, coyote, beaver, otter, eagles, and abundant waterfowl. The trail meanders along the banks of the Snake River past beaver dams and partially chewed trees. Throughout the hike are picturesque views of the Tetons and their reflection in the water (cover photo).

To the trailhead

From the intersection of Highway 89 and Teton Park Road at Moose Junction (located 12 miles north of Jackson), drive 4 miles north to Schwabacher Landing Road on the left. Turn left onto the gravel road, and continue 0.6 miles to a road split. The left fork leads 0.1 mile to a parking area. The right fork leads 0.4 miles farther to another parking area.

The hike

From either parking area, the unmaintained network of trails is well defined. Used by animals and people, the trails follow along the riverbank and side channels of the Snake River through a forest of cottonwood and willow trees. With the river to the west and the highway and sagebrush flats to the east, you may easily wander upstream or downstream without getting lost. ■

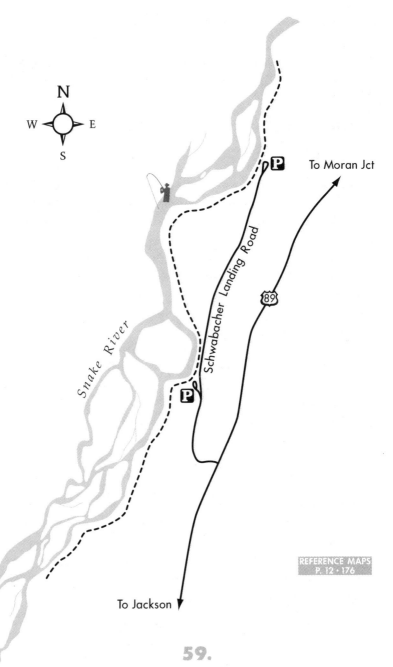

N
W · E
S

P

To Moran Jct

Schwabacher Landing Road

89

Snake River

P

To Jackson

REFERENCE MAPS
P. 12 · 176

59.

Schwabacher's Landing

60. Shadow Mountain Trail to Antelope Peak

Hiking distance: 5 miles round trip
Hiking time: 2.5 hours
Configuration: out-and-back
Elevation gain: 1,400 feet
Difficulty: moderate
Exposure: mix of open meadows and shaded forest
Dogs: allowed
Maps: U.S.G.S. Shadow Mountain · Adventure Maps: Jackson Hole
    Beartooth Publishing: Grand Teton, Jackson Hole, Teton Valley

map
page 181

Shadow Mountain rises up from Antelope Flats along the eastern boundary of Grand Teton National Park in the Teton National Forest. The Shadow Mountain Trail begins at the base of the mountain at the park boundary. The trail winds up a small canyon in the center of the mountain through a mixed forest of evergreens and aspen. The hike ends at Shadow Mountain Road by Antelope Peak, the mountain's 8,252-foot summit. From a large meadow near the summit are far-reaching views across Antelope Flats and the cottonwood-lined Snake River to Jackson Lake. These are some of the finest vistas of the Teton Range.

Antelope Peak can also be accessed from Shadow Mountain Road (where this trail ends). The road is a memorable automobile side trip that is also a popular biking route and cross-country skiing area.

To the trailhead

From the intersection of Highway 89 and Teton Park Road at Moose Junction (located 12 miles north of Jackson), drive 1.2 miles north on Highway 89 to Antelope Flats Road. Turn right on Antelope Flats Road, and drive 3.3 miles to a 4-way intersection. Turn left and continue 1.6 miles to a signed road split. Veer left, following the "National Forest Access" sign, and go 1.9 miles on the dirt road to the trailhead parking area on the right.

As a side note, at 0.7 miles is a junction with Shadow Mountain Road (Forest Service Road 30340) by an information kiosk and

Shadow Mountain Campground. This road winds up the mountain to the unsigned trailhead on the left of the upper end of the Shadow Mountain Trail. It is located near the mountain summit at 3.6 miles, directly across from Forest Service Road 30340F on the right. The drive is an exceptional experience surrounded by flower-filled meadows and some of the best vistas of the jagged Teton Range and Jackson Hole.

The hike

Two trails depart from the trailhead. One path steeply climbs the ridge to the east. For this hike, take the lower and more attractive trail to the south. Cross the sage-covered meadow to the mouth of the canyon. Follow the two-track trail through aspen groves, slowly gaining elevation. Continue up the draw as a mix of evergreens, including Douglas fir, subalpine fir, limber pine, lodgepole pine, and spruce, dot the landscape. Steadily climb on the gentle grade, weaving through the forest. At 2 miles, the trail breaks out of the forest to flower-filled meadows on a bench, with sweeping panoramas of the Teton Range, the Snake River, and Jackson Hole. Weave through the meadow to the end of the trail atop Shadow Mountain Road at Antelope Peak, the mountain's summit. ▪

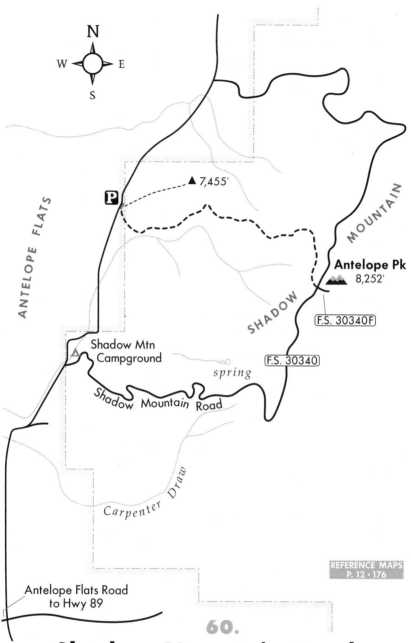

N
W E
S

ANTELOPE FLATS

P

▲ 7,455'

MOUNTAIN

Antelope Pk
8,252'

SHADOW

F.S. 30340F

F.S. 30340

Shadow Mtn
Campground

spring

Shadow Mountain Road

Carpenter Draw

Antelope Flats Road
to Hwy 89

REFERENCE MAPS
P. 12 · 176

60.
Shadow Mountain Road
to Antelope Peak summit

61. Lower Slide Lake

GROS VENTRE SLIDE INTERPRETIVE TRAIL

GROS VENTRE WILDERNESS

Hiking distance: 1.2 miles round trip
Hiking time: 1 hour
Configuration: small loop with inter-connecting paths
Elevation gain: 200 feet
Difficulty: easy
Exposure: mostly exposed
Dogs: allowed
Maps: U.S.G.S. Shadow Mountain
  Earthwalk Press: Grand Teton National Park, Wyoming

The Gros Ventre River, a tributary of the Snake River, winds into Jackson Hole through Antelope Flats, forming a portion of the southern boundary of Grand Teton National Park. On June 23, 1925, a 2,000-foot avalanche from Sheep Mountain, on the south side of the river valley, blocked the canyon and formed a natural dam 225-feet high and a mile wide. The dam blocked the Gros Ventre River, creating Lower Slide Lake. The three-mile-long lake covers over 1,100 acres and is now a popular recreation site. The Gros Ventre Slide Interpretive Trail is a 0.8-mile hike along a self-guided nature trail. The trail overlooks the largest natural landslide of historical record in North America. Informative signs along the trail discuss the geology and flora of the area.

To the trailhead

From the town square in downtown Jackson, drive 7 miles north on Highway 89 to the posted Gros Ventre Junction. Turn right on Gros Ventre Road and drive 8 miles, passing through the small town of Kelly, to the T-intersection where the signed Gros Ventre Road heads to the right. Turn right and continue 4.7 miles to the trailhead. The parking turnout is on the right.

From Moose Junction, the Gros Ventre Junction is 5.5 miles south on Highway 89.

The hike

Follow the trail southeast from the parking area. As you hike down the hill, other trail options appear. They all weave around and re-connect with the main loop. Benches are provided throughout the hike. The fisherman trails that lead beyond the interpretive trail to Lower Slide Lake are worth exploring. Return along the same route back to the parking area. ■

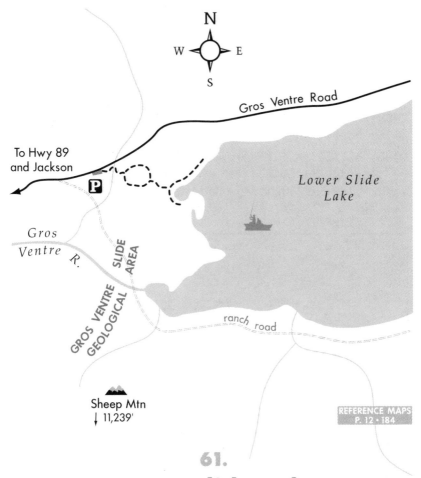

61.

Lower Slide Lake
Gros Ventre Slide Interpretive Trail
GROS VENTRE WILDERNESS

62. Horsetail Creek Trail
GROS VENTRE WILDERNESS

Hiking distance: 3.4 miles round trip
Hiking time: 1.5 hours
Configuration: out-and-back
Elevation gain: 600 feet
Difficulty: easy to slightly moderate
Exposure: exposed
Dogs: allowed
Maps: U.S.G.S. Mount Leidy · Adventure Maps: Jackson Hole
　　　　Beartooth Publishing: Grand Teton, Jackson Hole, Teton Valley

Horsetail Creek, a tributary of the Gros Ventre River, drains through the Lavender Hills in the Gros Ventre Mountains before emptying into Lower Slide Lake. The Horsetail Creek Trail begins at the mouth of the canyon directly across from Lower Slide Lake. The lightly used trail winds through the quiet of a beautiful forest. The trail parallels and crosses Horsetail Creek through gently rolling hills with flower-filled meadows, streams, and small canyons.

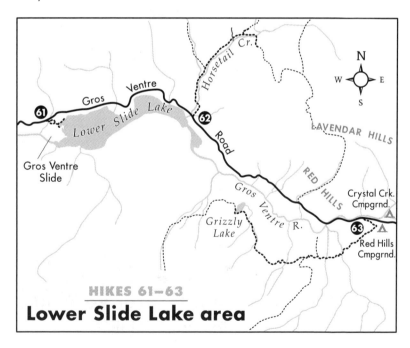

HIKES 61–63
Lower Slide Lake area

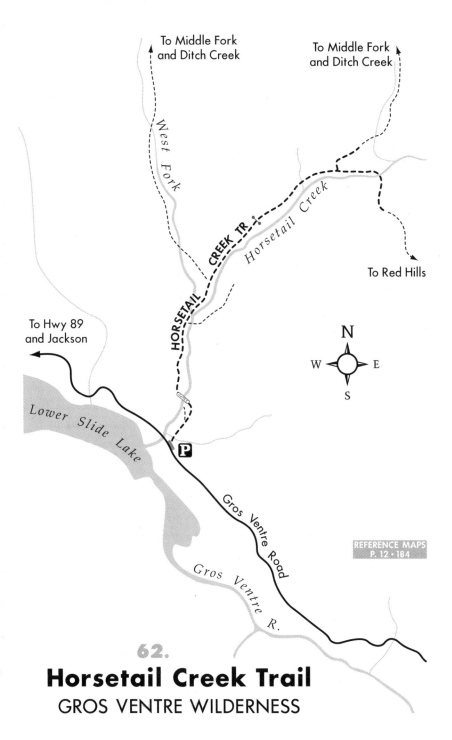

To Middle Fork
and Ditch Creek

To Middle Fork
and Ditch Creek

West Fork

Horsetail Creek

HORSETAIL CREEK TR.

To Red Hills

To Hwy 89
and Jackson

N
W · E
S

Lower Slide Lake

P

Gros Ventre Road

Gros Ventre R.

REFERENCE MAPS
P. 12 · 184

62.
Horsetail Creek Trail
GROS VENTRE WILDERNESS

To the trailhead

From the town square in downtown Jackson, drive 7 miles north on Highway 89 to the posted Gros Ventre Junction. Turn right on Gros Ventre Road and drive 8 miles, passing through the small town of Kelly, to the T-intersection where the signed Gros Ventre Road heads to the right. Turn right and continue 7.6 miles to the Horsetail Creek trailhead parking area on the left. The trailhead is located immediately after the road crosses Horsetail Creek.

From Moose Junction, the Gros Ventre Junction is 5.5 miles south on Highway 89.

The hike

From the parking area, hike north past the trailhead sign and into the draw. Rock hop across the stream. At 0.3 miles, the trail crosses Horsetail Creek. Just before reaching the creek, a footpath to the right leads to a log crossing. After crossing, return to the main trail. Continue up the canyon to a trail split at 0.8 miles. The right fork crosses Horsetail Creek and leads a short distance into a lush, narrow canyon. Return to the junction and continue on the left fork up a ridge to a fence and gate. Once past the gate, the gradient steepens, gaining 400 feet in the next 0.6 miles. As the trail levels off, it nears the creek and crosses a tributary stream to another trail split. This is our turn-around spot. Return by retracing your steps.

To hike farther, the left fork crosses a divide, then continues along the Middle Fork of Ditch Creek to a junction with the North Fork and Main Fork of Ditch Creek. The trail along the Middle Fork makes connections to the Mount Leidy Headlands to the east and Teton Science School to the west. The right fork leads to Slate Creek and the Red Hills. ▪

63. Grizzly Lake
GROS VENTRE WILDERNESS

Hiking distance: 9 miles round trip
Hiking time: 5 hours
Configuration: out-and-back
Elevation gain: 600 feet *
Difficulty: strenuous
Exposure: mostly exposed with forested pockets
Dogs: allowed
Maps: U.S.G.S. Grizzly Lake
         Adventure Maps: Jackson Hole
         Beartooth Publishing: Grand Teton, Jackson Hole, Teton Valley

**map
page 189**

Grizzly Lake sits in the northern foothills of the Gros Ventre Range. The oval-shaped lake is located just south of the Gros Ventre River and north of the Gros Ventre Mountains. The scenic lake, formed by an ancient landslide on the northern slope of the Gros Ventres, is tucked in a broad depression at 7,184 feet in elevation. The lake is surrounded by rolling, tree-dotted hills and grassy meadows. The hike crosses the glacial moraines through a mix of open sagebrush, grassy meadows, conifer forests, and aspen groves. Throughout most of the hike are vistas of the colorful Red Hills and Lavender Hills that lie across the river valley. En route to Grizzly Lake, the trail crosses several tributary streams of the Gros Ventre River and a water ditch.

*The actual elevation gain in this hike is about 600 feet, but the undulating path climbs and descends seven times, creating an elevation gain of over 1,400 feet each way.

To the trailhead

From the town square in downtown Jackson, drive 7 miles north on Highway 89 to the posted Gros Ventre Junction. Turn right on Gros Ventre Road and drive 8 miles, passing through the small town of Kelly, to the T-intersection where the signed Gros Ventre Road heads to the right. Turn right and continue 11.5 miles to the posted entrance to the Red Hills Campground. Park in the wide pullout on the right, in front of the sign and by the trailhead kiosk on the right.

From Moose Junction, the Gros Ventre Junction is 5.5 miles south on Highway 89.

The hike

Pass the trailhead map and head up the footpath. Join an old jeep road, and walk through a meadow with spectacular views of the Red Hills. A short distance ahead, veer right on the signed trail, leaving the old road. Climb through a lodgepole pine forest to an open rolling meadow with 360-degree vistas that include the Teton Peaks. Cross the open expanse and descend to a water ditch. Cross the ditch on a wood bridge, then wade across East Miner Creek. Follow the creek upstream, then zigzag up the slope, utilizing three switchbacks, to a minor ridge with more vistas. Follow the west rim of the East Miner Creek drainage. Curve left and drop down to West Miner Creek. Cross the creek on a one-log bridge and cross a small stream. Ascend the west canyon slope, then drop down to an unsigned fork. The trail straight ahead leads to a private ranch. Take the left fork and follow the waterway up canyon. Climb the slope again to a signed trail junction at 2.5 miles. The left fork leads 5 miles to Blue Miner Lakes.

Continue straight on the right fork. Skirt the south edge of a grassy wetland, and climb to a 7,600-foot saddle in a flower-filled meadow. Gently descend and contour to the right. Head down a minor drainage among open groves of aspens, limber pines, and lodgepole pines. At 4.4 miles is a Y-fork posted for Grizzly Lake, where the lake can be spotted below. The left branch leads to the lake's south and west shore, then continues to Redmond Creek and into the Gros Ventre Wilderness. The right branch drops directly down to Grizzly Lake's east shore. Return by retracing your steps. ▪

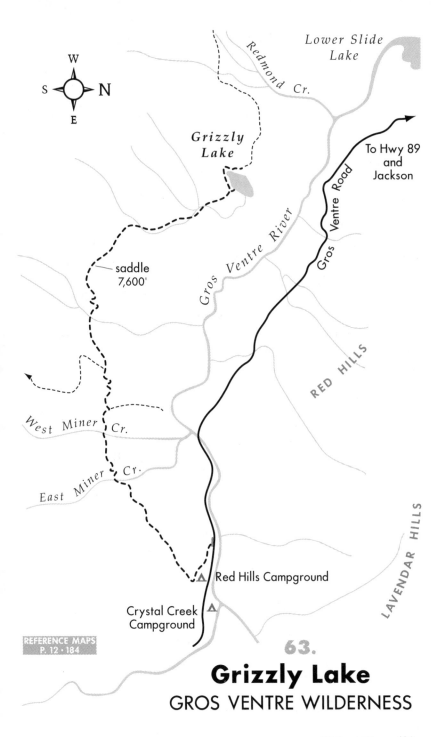

Lower Slide
Lake

Redmond Cr.

W
N
S ⊕ N
E

Grizzly
Lake

To Hwy 89
and
Jackson

Gros Ventre Road

Gros Ventre River

saddle
7,600'

RED HILLS

West Miner Cr.

East Miner Cr.

LAVENDAR HILLS

△ Red Hills Campground

Crystal Creek
Campground △

REFERENCE MAPS
P. 12 • 184

63.

Grizzly Lake
GROS VENTRE WILDERNESS

64. Lower Sheep Creek Canyon to Curtis Canyon Viewpoint

Hiking distance: 3 miles round trip
Hiking time: 1.5 hours
Configuration: two out-and-back trails
(or return along the road for a loop)
Elevation gain: 1,000 feet
Difficulty: easy to moderate
Exposure: a mix of open meadows and forested canyons
Dogs: allowed
Maps: U.S.G.S. Gros Ventre Junction

**map
page 192**

Lower Sheep Creek Canyon lies near the east end of the National Elk Refuge in the Teton National Forest. The access trail begins in the refuge and quickly enters the mouth of the canyon. The hike leads to two overlooks located on the west slope of the Gros Ventre Range. From the overlooks, perched 600 feet above the valley floor, are expansive views across the elk refuge, the Teton Range, the Snake River Range, Jackson Peak, Curtis Canyon, and into Sheep Creek Canyon.

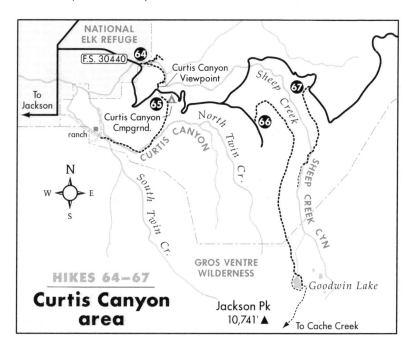

To the trailhead

From the town square in downtown Jackson, drive east on Broadway (the main street through Jackson) 0.9 miles to the end of Broadway. Turn left onto the gravel road into the National Elk Refuge. Drive 4.7 miles to an intersection and sign for Curtis Canyon Campground. Turn right and go 1.6 miles towards the campground. The trailhead is on the left by the Teton National Forest boundary sign, just before winding up the mountain to the campground.

The hike

Take the wide path across the open sage flats on the east end of the National Elk Refuge. Follow the west edge of the hillside 100 yards to the mouth of the canyon and a trail split. The left fork crosses the aspen-lined creek and zigzags up the north canyon wall to a 6,960-foot overlook of the elk preserve, the town of Jackson, and the Teton Range. Return to the trail split, and take the right fork (now on your left), staying in the canyon under the shade of pines and fir. The trail parallels the south side of Sheep Creek through the narrow canyon, steadily gaining elevation. The undulating path climbs the canyon wall to open meadows and returns to the creek in the shaded woodland. Pass a stream-fed side canyon across the creek on the vertical north canyon wall. A short distance ahead, the trail ends at the creek. A faint path heads up the canyon wall to the right. The steep climb ends at the Curtis Canyon Viewpoint by Curtis Campground. While climbing the hillside, the trail fades in and out, so when in doubt, curve to the right.

To turn the hike into a loop, descend on the unpaved road and enjoy the sweeping vistas to the west. The trailhead is at the base of the hill. ▧

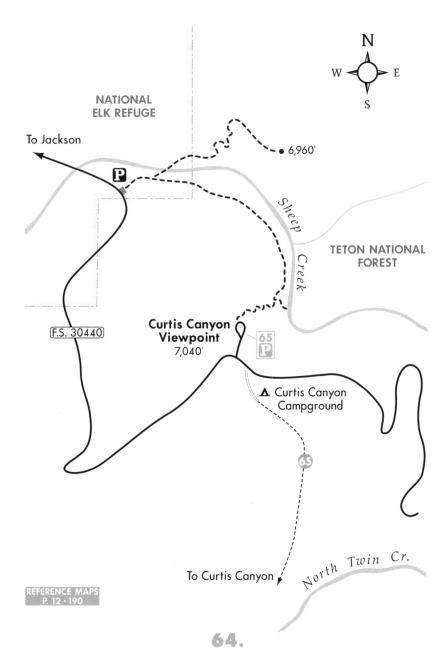

N
W   E
S

NATIONAL
ELK REFUGE

To Jackson

• 6,960'

P

Sheep Creek

TETON NATIONAL
FOREST

F.S. 30440

**Curtis Canyon
Viewpoint**
7,040'

65
P

▲ Curtis Canyon
Campground

65

To Curtis Canyon

North Twin Cr.

REFERENCE MAPS
P. 12 • 190

64.

Lower Sheep Creek Canyon
to Curtis Canyon Viewpoint

65. Curtis Canyon Trail from Curtis Canyon Viewpoint

Hiking distance: 3 miles round trip
Hiking time: 1.5 hours
Configuration: out-and-back
Elevation gain: 700 feet
Difficulty: easy to slightly moderate
Exposure: a mix of open meadows and forested canyons
Dogs: allowed
Maps: U.S.G.S. Gros Ventre Junction
Earthwalk Press: Grand Teton National Park, Wyoming

map
page 194

Curtis Canyon is a stream-fed canyon tucked into the Gros Ventre Mountains just outside the town of Jackson and adjacent to the National Elk Refuge. Access to Curtis Canyon is through the 25,000-acre elk refuge. The Curtis Canyon Trail is an old ranch road reclaimed by the grassy meadow. The two-track trail begins at the Curtis Canyon Campground and heads downhill through a narrow canyon parallel to North Twin Creek. There are four creek crossings and magnificent rock formations.

To the trailhead

From the town square in downtown Jackson, drive east on Broadway (the main street through Jackson) 0.9 miles to the end of Broadway. Turn left onto the gravel road into the National Elk Refuge. Drive 4.7 miles to an intersection and sign for Curtis Canyon Campground Turn right and go 2.7 miles to the signed Curtis Canyon Viewpoint. Park on the left in the overlook viewing area.

The hike

Head 30 yards up the road to the Curtis Canyon Campground on the right. Follow the road through the campground 0.2 miles to the far south end of the loop by campsite 10. Several unsigned paths leave the campground and join the easily visible main trail in the meadow. The two-track trail heads south down the draw fringed with conifers. Descend into the canyon along North Twin Creek. To the right are steep cliffs with sculpted rock formations.

At 0.7 miles, cross the creek and continue down the narrow canyon in the shade of the forest. Follow the watercourse through the forest, recrossing the creek at one mile. At the mouth of the canyon, cross the creek again, then emerge to wonderful views of the Tetons. At 1.6 miles the trail crosses South Twin Creek at an unpaved private road at the Twin Creek Ranch boundary. To return, hike back up the canyon along the same trail. ▨

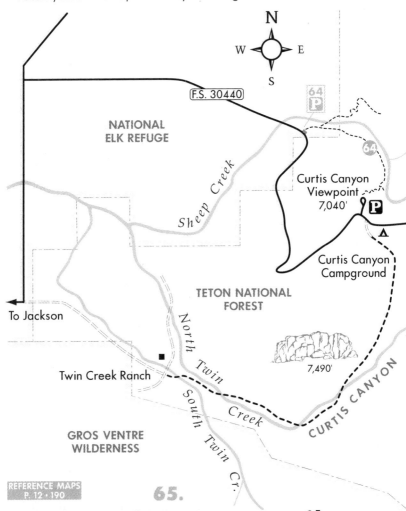

66. Goodwin Lake
GROS VENTRE WILDERNESS

Hiking distance: 6 miles round trip
Hiking time: 3 hours
Configuration: out-and-back
Elevation gain: 1,500 feet
Difficulty: moderate
Exposure: a mix of open meadows and forested canyons
Dogs: allowed
Maps: U.S.G.S. Gros Ventre Junction, Blue Miner Lake, Turquoise Lake
   Adventure Maps: Jackson Hole
   Beartooth Publishing: Grand Teton, Jackson Hole, Teton Valley

map
page 196

Goodwin Lake sits in a glacial cirque on the east flank of the prominent, cone-shaped Jackson Peak, directly east of the town of Jackson. The small timberline lake in the Gros Ventre Wilderness is rimmed with whitebark pine and Engelmann spruce on the north, east, and south shores. The steep talus slopes of Jackson Peak rise from the western shoreline. The trail to Goodwin Lake follows a narrow, 9,000-foot ridge through open forests—high above Sheep Creek Canyon—to the north end of the lake at the base of Jackson Peak.

To the trailhead

From the town square in downtown Jackson, drive east on Broadway (the main street through Jackson) 0.9 miles to the end of Broadway. Turn left on the gravel road into the National Elk Refuge. Drive 4.7 miles to an intersection and sign for Curtis Canyon Campground and turn right. At 6 miles, the road leaves the flatlands and enters the Teton National Forest. Wind 3 miles up the mountain—passing the campground—to a road split. Sheep Creek Road bears left (Hike 67). Take the right fork one mile towards Goodwin Lake to the trailhead on the left at the end of the road.

The hike

Pass the trailhead sign and climb through grassy meadows and open pine forest. Views of the elk preserve, the Teton peaks, and barren Jackson Peak tower above the forest. Near the top of the slope, curve to the right and head south. Follow the narrow, forested ridge above Sheep Creek Canyon on the left and the Twin Creek drainage on the right. At 2.2 miles, the trail enters the Gros Ventre Wilderness. Leave the narrow ridge 30 yards ahead, and traverse the east-facing cliffs perched high above Sheep Creek Canyon. Climb through the forest on the root- and rock-strewn path to the outlet stream of Goodwin Lake by a trail sign. Cross the creek to the left, and parallel the creek's east bank to the north end of the lake. The trail continues along the east side of the lake, passes Jackson Peak, and connects with the Cache Creek Trail (Hike 68). A path circles Goodwin Lake, but a portion of the trail on the west side crosses a steep talus slope along the base of Jackson Peak. Return along the same trail. ▪

N
W ◆ E
S

66.

Goodwin Lake
GROS VENTRE WILDERNESS

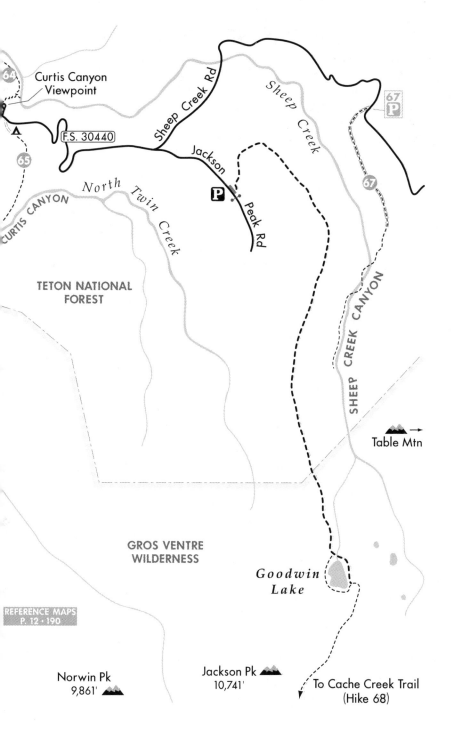

Curtis Canyon
Viewpoint

64

F.S. 30440

65

Sheep Creek Rd

Sheep Creek

67 P

67

Jackson

P

Peak Rd

CURTIS CANYON

North Twin Creek

TETON NATIONAL
FOREST

SHEEP CREEK CANYON

Table Mtn

GROS VENTRE
WILDERNESS

Goodwin
Lake

REFERENCE MAPS
P. 12 • 190

Norwin Pk
9,861'

Jackson Pk
10,741'

To Cache Creek Trail
(Hike 68)

67. Upper Sheep Creek Canyon

Hiking distance: 2.5 miles round trip
Hiking time: 1.5 hours
Configuration: out-and-back
Elevation gain: 200 feet
Difficulty: easy
Exposure: open meadow and forested slopes
Dogs: allowed
Maps: U.S.G.S. Blue Miner Lake and Turquoise Lake
   Adventure Maps: Jackson Hole
   Beartooth Publishing: Grand Teton, Jackson Hole, Teton Valley

Sheep Creek Canyon is located in the Gros Ventre Range nestled between a 400-foot-high ridge and Table Mountain. The stream-fed canyon flows through a beautifully forested grassland meadow with pine groves and wildflowers. The isolated trail follows the east side of the canyon down to the creek. The trail to Goodwin Lake (Hike 66) follows along the 400-foot ridge to the west of the trail.

To the trailhead

From the town square in downtown Jackson, drive east on Broadway (the main street through Jackson) 0.9 miles to the end of Broadway. Turn left on the gravel road into the National Elk Refuge. Drive 4.7 miles to an intersection and sign for Curtis Canyon Campground and turn right. At 6 miles, the road leaves the flatlands and enters the Teton National Forest. Wind 3 miles up the mountain—passing the campground—to a road split. The road to Goodwin Lake curves to the right (Hike 66). Take the Sheep Creek Road to the left, and drive 2.4 miles to an old jeep road veering off to the right. This is the trailhead. Park off the road.

The hike

Walk up the old jeep road through open brush and a mixed conifer forest. Gently climb to a ridge overlooking Sheep Creek Canyon, Jackson Peak (which looms over the canyon), and the Teton peaks in the distance. The ridge across the valley is the route to Goodwin Lake (Hike 66). Traverse the east edge of the canyon, gradually descending into the forest. The old jeep road ends at one mile in a meadow at the valley floor. Cross over a log barrier to a footpath leading to Sheep Creek. At the creek are open grasslands teeming with wildflowers and rimmed with pines. Meander through the riparian vegetation and pastoral surroundings. An old trail continues up the canyon, but it is not maintained and has become overgrown and difficult to follow. Return along the same trail. ▦

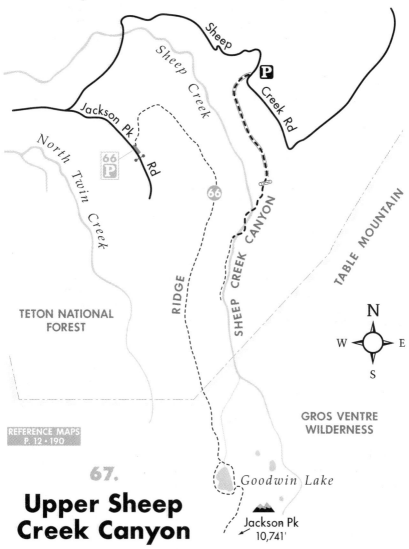

67.

Upper Sheep Creek Canyon

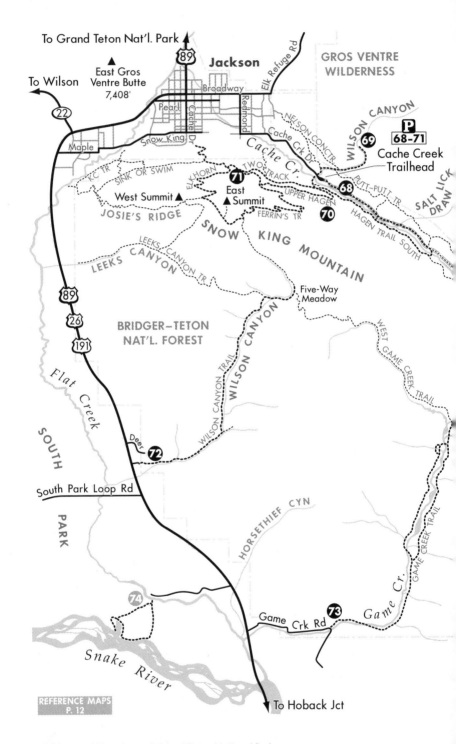

To Grand Teton Nat'l. Park

89

Jackson

▲ East Gros
Ventre Butte
7,408'

GROS VENTRE
WILDERNESS

To Wilson

22

Broadway

Elk Refuge Rd

WILSON CANYON

Pearl

Cache Dr

Redmond

NELSON CONCTR.

P
68-71
69
Cache Creek
Trailhead

Maple

Snow King Dr

Cache Cr.

Cache Ck Dr.

SALT LICK DRAW

KC TR

SINK OR SWIM

ELKHORN

71

TWO-TRACK

UPPER HAGEN

68

PUTT-PUTT TR

West Summit ▲

East
▲ Summit

FERRIN'S TR

70

HAGEN TRAIL SOUTH

JOSIE'S RIDGE

SNOW   KING   MOUNTAIN

LEEKS CANYON TR

LEEKS CANYON

WEST GAME CREEK TRAIL

Five-Way
Meadow

89

26

191

BRIDGER–TETON
NAT'L. FOREST

WILSON CANYON TRAIL

WILSON CANYON

Flat Creek

SOUTH

Deer

72

South Park Loop Rd

PARK

HORSETHIEF CYN

GAME CREEK TRAIL

Game Cr.

74

73

Game Crk Rd

Snake River

To Hoback Jct

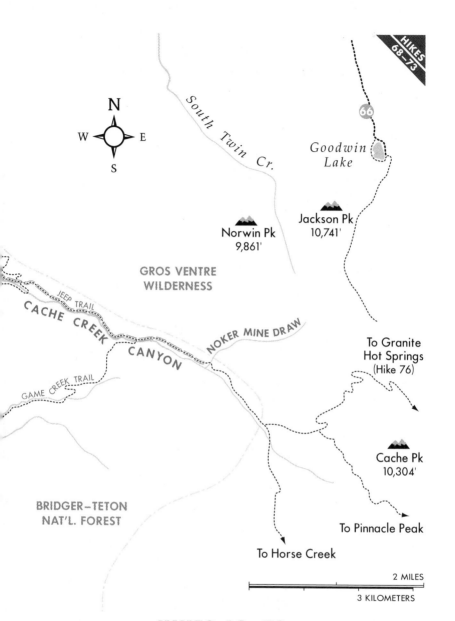

N
W   E
S

South Twin Cr.

66

Goodwin Lake

Jackson Pk
10,741'

Norwin Pk
9,861'

GROS VENTRE
WILDERNESS

JEEP TRAIL

CACHE CREEK CANYON

NOKER MINE DRAW

To Granite
Hot Springs
(Hike 76)

GAME CREEK TRAIL

Cache Pk
10,304'

BRIDGER–TETON
NAT'L. FOREST

To Pinnacle Peak

To Horse Creek

2 MILES

3 KILOMETERS

HIKES 68–73

Snow King Trail Network

CACHE CREEK, GAME CREEK
and WILSON CANYON

68. Cache Creek Canyon Loop
CACHE CREEK TRAILHEAD · SNOW KING AREA

Hiking distance: 4 miles round trip
Hiking time: 2 hours
Configuration: loop
Elevation gain: 350 feet
Difficulty: easy
Exposure: forested hillsides and open meadows
Dogs: allowed
Maps: U.S.G.S. Cache Creek · Adventure Maps: Jackson Hole
　　　 Beartooth Publishing: Grand Teton, Jackson Hole, Teton Valley
　　　 Greater Snow King Area Trail Map

The Greater Snow King Trail Network is adjacent to the town of Jackson to its southeast. The extensive and well-used trail network criss-crosses 8,000-foot Snow King Mountain and connects with trails in the surrounding drainages through Cache Creek, Game Creek, and Flat Creek, all tributaries of the Snake River. Snow King is Jackson's original ski hill and Wyoming's first ski area. From atop Snow King Mountain are great views of Jackson and the Teton Range, all within close proximity to the town.

Hikes 68–73 explore the summit of Snow King, Cache Creek, Wilson Canyon, and Game Creek along the mountain's northeast and southwest flanks. The multi-use trails are open to hikers, bikers, and equestrians. Dogs are allowed.

This trail into Cache Creek Canyon makes a loop around both sides of Cache Creek. The well-used Cache Creek Trailhead is located on the east edge of Jackson and close to downtown. The trail starts at the mouth of the canyon in the Gros Ventre Range and skirts the outer edge of the Gros Ventre Wilderness. This is a popular hiking, biking, and cross-country ski trail that weaves through the forest alongside the creek and connects with other trails deep in the wooded backcountry. The loop hike follows the first 2 miles of the trail on each side of the creek. The hike can be combined with the Game Creek Trail (Hike 73) for a 11.7-mile, one-way shuttle.

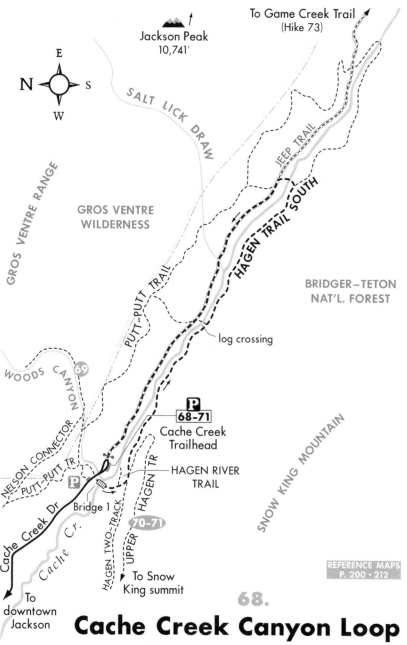

To Game Creek Trail
(Hike 73)

Jackson Peak
10,741'

N E S W

SALT LICK DRAW

JEEP TRAIL

GROS VENTRE RANGE

GROS VENTRE
WILDERNESS

HAGEN TRAIL SOUTH

PUTT-PUTT TRAIL

BRIDGER–TETON
NAT'L. FOREST

log crossing

WOODS CANYON

89

NELSON CONNECTOR

P
68-71
Cache Creek
Trailhead

PUTT-PUTT TR.

P

HAGEN RIVER
TRAIL

HAGEN TR.

Bridge 1

Cache Creek Dr

Cache Cr.

HAGEN TWO-TRACK

UPPER HAGEN

70-71

SNOW KING MOUNTAIN

REFERENCE MAPS
P. 200 • 212

To Snow
King summit

To
downtown
Jackson

68.

Cache Creek Canyon Loop
Cache Creek Trailhead
SNOW KING AREA

To the trailhead

From the town square in downtown Jackson, drive a half mile east on Broadway (the main street through Jackson) to Redmond Street. Turn right and continue 0.4 miles to Cache Creek Drive. Turn left and go 1.2 miles to the parking lot at the end of the access road.

The hike

Walk 50 yards back down the entrance road to the bridge crossing Cache Creek on the left. Cross the bridge (Bridge 1) to a streamside path on the left 40 yards ahead. This narrow side path—the Hagen River Trail—fades out at the south bank of the creek. Continue on the main path another 40 yards to a 3-way split. The two right forks head up the hillside and lead up Snow King Mountain on the Upper Hagen Trail (Hikes 70 and 71). Take the left fork (Hagen Trail South) and traverse the hillside above Cache Creek. The path parallels the southwest side of Cache Creek, heading upstream. At one mile, there is the option to cross the stream at a log crossing and return on the jeep trail for a shorter 2-mile loop.

For a 4-mile loop, continue on the same trail farther into the valley. At two miles, there is a Y-fork in the trail. The right fork continues deeper into the canyon and connects to Goodwin Lake (Hike 66), Game Creek (Hike 73), and Granite Falls (Hike 76). To return to the trailhead, take the left fork and cross the creek. (If you wish to stay dry, there are down logs in both directions of this crossing that can be carefully used as a bridge.) After the stream crossing, follow the trail through a meadow to the jeep trail, which heads gently downhill back to the trailhead.

To combine this hike with the Game Creek Trail for a one-way shuttle, continue up Cache Creek Canyon to the posted junction on the right at 3.8 miles. ▪

69. Woods Canyon
CACHE CREEK TRAILHEAD • SNOW KING AREA

Hiking distance: 2 miles round trip
Hiking time: 1 hour
Configuration: out-and-back
Elevation gain: 580 feet
Difficulty: easy
Exposure: forested hillsides and open meadows
Dogs: allowed
Maps: U.S.G.S. Cache Creek

**map
page 206**

Woods Canyon is a narrow side canyon in the Gros Ventre Range that heads north from the mouth of Cache Creek Canyon into the wilderness. The greater Snow King area is popular for mountain biking, but the Woods Canyon Trail is open to foot and horse traffic only. The trail winds up a narrow, stream-fed canyon in the Gros Ventre Wilderness.

To the trailhead

From the town square in downtown Jackson, drive a half mile east on Broadway (the main street through Jackson) to Redmond Street. Turn right and continue 0.4 miles to Cache Creek Drive. Turn left and go 1.2 miles to the parking lot at the end of the access road.

The hike

From the main parking area, walk 100 yards back down the entrance road to the bridge on the left crossing Cache Creek (Bridge 1). Take the opposite path across the road on the right. Pass through a pole fence, and climb a short knoll to a junction. The left fork returns to a parking area on Cache Creek Road. Bear right and wind through aspen groves and a lush understory of vegetation to a posted junction with the Putt-Putt Trail on the left, a popular mountain biking trail along the base of the Gros Ventre Mountains. Continue 30 yards straight ahead to another junction. The Putt-Putt Trail curves right. Take the footpath left, heading into Woods Canyon to a posted trail split. The left fork is a connector trail to Nelson Drive. Stay to the right into the narrowing canyon, entering the Gros Ventre Wilderness. Continue up the canyon floor. As the trail curves north, the grade gets steep, crossing talus slopes between towering rock formations. This is the turn-around spot. Return by retracing your steps. ▪

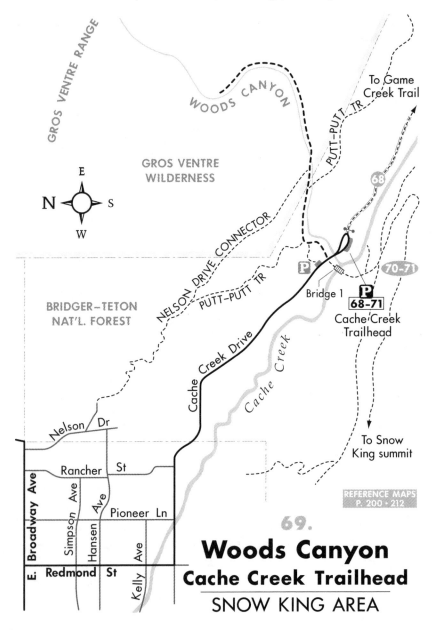

69.

Woods Canyon
Cache Creek Trailhead
SNOW KING AREA

70. Hagen Loop

Upper Hagen Trail • Hagen Two-Track Trail

CACHE CREEK TRAILHEAD • SNOW KING AREA

Hiking distance: 2.7-mile loop
Hiking time: 1.5 hours
Configuration: loop
Elevation gain: 450 feet
Difficulty: easy
Exposure: mix of shade and exposed hillside
Dogs: allowed
Maps: U.S.G.S. Cache Creek and Jackson
  Adventure Maps: Jackson Hole
  Beartooth Publishing: Grand Teton, Jackson Hole, Teton Valley

map
page 208

The Hagen Loop combines the Upper Hagen Trail with the Hagen Two-Track Trail (also known as the Hagen Highway). The undulating trails form a loop that contours the lower northeast slope of Snow King Mountain in Cache Creek Canyon. The trail alternates from shaded forest to open, flower-filled meadows. For a longer loop up to the Snow King summit, continue with Hike 71.

To the trailhead

From the town square in downtown Jackson, drive a half mile east on Broadway (the main street through Jackson) to Redmond Street. Turn right and continue 0.4 miles to Cache Creek Drive. Turn left and go 1.2 miles to the parking lot at the end of the access road.

The hike

Walk 50 yards back down the entrance road to the bridge crossing Cache Creek on the left. Cross the bridge (Bridge 1) and pass the Hagen River Trail on the left after 40 yards. Follow the signposts to the Hagen Trail and Ferrin's Trail. The path alternates from shaded forest to open, flower-covered meadows to a signed junction. To the right is the Hagen Two-Track Trail (also called the Hagen Highway), the return route.

Begin the loop to the left. Pass the Hagen Trail South on the left, which parallels Cache Creek up canyon. Veer to the right on the Upper Hagen Trail. Traverse the north-facing slope, with a view into Woods Canyon and to the majestic Teton Peaks. At 1.2 miles is a posted junction. Ferrin's Trail goes left and climbs the mountain to the Snow King Summit (Hike 71).

For this hike, take the lower loop, bearing right on a downward slope. Follow the contours of the hillside to a signed junction. The left fork leads to the base of Snow King and the chairlifts. Make a sharp switchback to the right on the Hagen Two-Track Trail. Gently descend through the lodgepole pines, passing a neighborhood connector trail on the left. Continue straight, heading up the slope. Traverse the hillside, completing the loop at the junction with the Upper Hagen Trail. Retrace your steps to the trailhead. ■

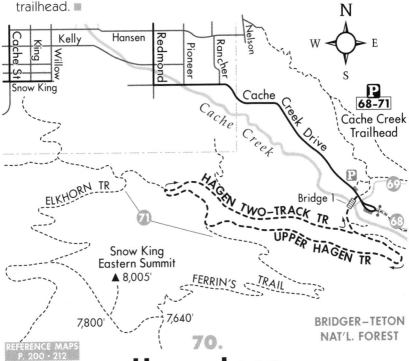

70.
Hagen Loop
Upper Hagen–Hagen Two-Track Trails
Cache Creek Trailhead
SNOW KING AREA

71. Cache Creek Canyon to Snow King Summit

CACHE CREEK TRAILHEAD · SNOW KING AREA

Hiking distance: 6.8-mile loop
Hiking time: 4 hours
Configuration: loop
Elevation gain: 1,400 feet
Difficulty: moderate to strenuous
Exposure: a mix of shaded forest and exposed hillsides
Dogs: allowed
Maps: U.S.G.S. Cache Creek and Jackson · Adventure Maps: Jackson Hole
Beartooth Publishing: Grand Teton, Jackson Hole, Teton Valley
Greater Snow King Area Trail Map

map
page 211

This hike up to the Snow King Summit heads up the northeast slope of Snow King Mountain from Cache Creek Canyon, making a loop along the Hagen Trail and Ferrin's Trail. The Hagen Trail meanders up the lower slope of Snow King Mountain through shaded forest and open, flower-filled meadows. Ferrin's Trail is a partially shaded single-track path that continues up the northeast slope to a saddle at the head of the West Game Creek drainage, just below Snow King's eastern summit. The hike returns on the Elkhorn Trail (also known as the Snow King Mountain Trail), a dirt maintenance road. The road zigzags down the face of the ski mountain, returning to a footpath in Cache Creek Canyon. Throughout the hike are great vistas of the surrounding mountains, the Teton Range, the elk preserve, the Gros Ventre Range, and the town of Jackson.

To the trailhead

From the town square in downtown Jackson, drive a half mile east on Broadway (the main street through Jackson) to Redmond Street. Turn right and continue 0.4 miles to Cache Creek Drive. Turn left and go 1.2 miles to the parking lot at the end of the access road.

The hike

Walk 50 yards back down the entrance road to the bridge

crossing Cache Creek on the left. Cross the bridge (Bridge 1) and pass the Hagen River Trail on the left after 40 yards. Follow the signposts to the Hagen Trail and Ferrin's Trail. The path alternates from shaded forest to open, flower-filled meadows to a signed junction. To the right is the Hagen Two-Track Trail (also called the Hagen Highway), the return route.

Begin the loop to the left. Pass the Hagen Trail South on the left, which parallels Cache Creek up canyon. Veer to the right on the Upper Hagen Trail. Traverse the north-facing slope, with a view into Woods Canyon and to the majestic Teton Peaks. At 1.2 miles is a posted junction. The Upper Hagen Trail continues to the right (Hike 70).

For this hike, take Ferrin's Trail to the left, and wind through the lodgepole pine and Douglas fir forest. Climb at a steady but easy grade with the aid of switchbacks. At 3.3 miles, Ferrin's Trail ends on a 7,640-foot saddle in a flower-filled meadow. Straight ahead, the trail descends to Five-Way Meadow via West Game Creek. The West Game Creek Trail leads to Wilson Canyon (Hike 72) and Game Creek (Hike 73). Bear right, toward the Snow King summit, and cross the sage-covered terrain. Curve around the west side of Snow King's eastern summit to a 7,800-foot saddle. A service road on the right leads to the radio towers atop the east summit. Follow the dirt road straight ahead, descending to a junction just shy of the chairlifts on Snow King's west summit.

Take the Elkhorn Trail—a rocky service road—sharply to the right. Zigzag down the mountain along four switchbacks to a T-junction. The left fork leads to the base of Snow King and the chairlifts. Go to the right, passing another chairlift as the dirt road narrows to a footpath. Curve right, returning to the Cache Creek drainage and a posted Y-fork. The right fork ascends the hillside and returns to the lower end of Ferrin's Trail. Veer left on the Hagen Two-Track Trail. Gently descend through the lodgepole pines, passing a neighborhood connector trail on the left. Continue straight, heading up the slope. Traverse the hillside, completing the loop at the junction with the Upper Hagen Trail. Retrace your steps to the trailhead. ▪

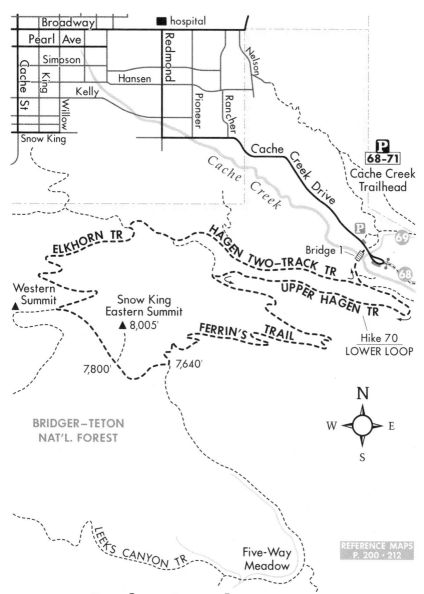

Broadway
hospital
Pearl Ave
Simpson
Cache St
King
Hansen
Redmond
Nelson
Kelly
Willow
Pioneer
Rancher
Snow King
Cache Creek Drive

P 68-71
Cache Creek Trailhead

Cache Creek

ELKHORN TR
HAGEN TWO-TRACK TR
Bridge 1
P
69
68
UPPER HAGEN TR

Western Summit
Snow King Eastern Summit
▲ 8,005'
FERRIN'S TRAIL
Hike 70 LOWER LOOP

7,800'   7,640'

BRIDGER–TETON NAT'L. FOREST

N
W   E
S

LEEKS CANYON TR
Five-Way Meadow

REFERENCE MAPS
P. 200 · 212

71. Cache Creek Canyon to Snow King Summit
Cache Creek Trailhead
SNOW KING AREA

72. Wilson Canyon to Five-Way Meadow
SNOW KING AREA

(Trail closed from 12/1 to 4/30 to protect wintering wildlife)

Hiking distance: 7 miles round trip
Hiking time: 3.5 hours
Configuration: out-and-back
Elevation gain: 1,300 feet
Difficulty: moderate to strenuous
Exposure: mix of shaded forest and exposed meadows
Dogs: allowed
Maps: U.S.G.S. Cache Creek and Jackson · Adventure Maps: Jackson Hole
   Beartooth Publishing: Grand Teton, Jackson Hole, Teton Valley
   Greater Snow King Area Trail Map

Stream-fed Wilson Canyon flows out of the lower southwest side of Snow King Mountain towards South Park and into Flat Creek, a tributary of the Snake River. This hike begins from the mouth of the canyon, across from the South Park flatlands. The trail climbs up to Five-Way Meadow, where Leeks Canyon, West Game Creek Canyon, Wilson Canyon, and two minor drainages converge.

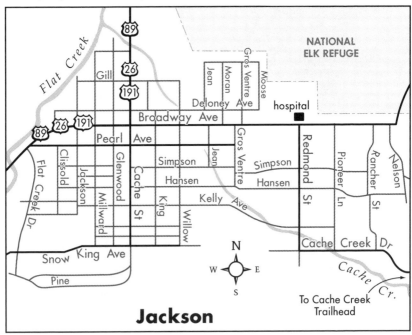

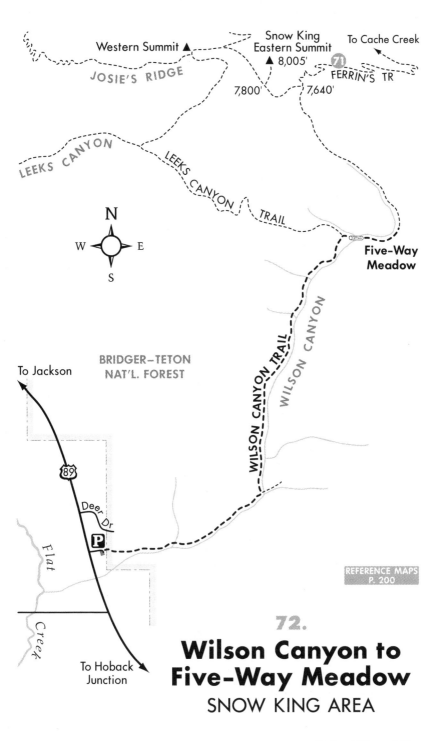

Western Summit ▲

Snow King
Eastern Summit
▲ 8,005'

To Cache Creek

JOSIE'S RIDGE

7,800'

7,640'

FERRIN'S TR

LEEKS CANYON

LEEKS CANYON TRAIL

Five-Way
Meadow

N
W   E
S

WILSON CANYON TRAIL

WILSON CANYON

BRIDGER–TETON
NAT'L. FOREST

To Jackson

89

Deer Dr

P

Flat

Creek

REFERENCE MAPS
P. 200

To Hoback
Junction

72.

Wilson Canyon to
Five-Way Meadow
SNOW KING AREA

The trail winds through the narrow canyon along the waterway through a mixed forest with meadows and weather-carved rock outcroppings in the Gros Ventre Range.

To the trailhead

From the town square in downtown Jackson, drive 5.3 miles south on Highway 89 to 4000 South Highway 89 on the left. The paved parking lot entrance is located just south of Deer Drive between mile markers 150 and 149. Turn left and park at the end of the paved area, straight ahead.

The hike

Pass the posted trailhead and cross the open, rolling meadow to the mouth of Wilson Canyon. Walk up the open draw amid the sagebrush, then bend left as the canyon narrows. Enter a mixed forest with pines, spruce, and aspen. Jagged rock outcrops line the canyon walls. Steadily climb the south flank of the canyon floor at a moderate grade to an unsigned Y-fork. Veer left, following the bend in Wilson Canyon as the rocky path gets steeper. Wind through the deep forest with a lush understory of vegetation. Cross a trickling stream by an old log-cribbed dam, skirting the west edge of a meadow. Stroll through the meadow along the waterway at a near-level grade. Cross another stream and leave the forest to the exposed flower-filled slopes. Traverse the west canyon wall to a posted junction in an open wetland at 3.2 miles. The Leeks Canyon Trail bears left, leading up to Josie's Ridge and connecting with the Snow King Summit (but does not exit on Highway 89 due to private land).

For this hike, bear right and cross logs over the creek. Walk through the southeast edge of the wetland, and continue through the tree-dotted draw surrounded by mountains. At 3.5 miles is another posted junction in Five-Way Meadow, where the five drainages merge. The right fork drops down into West Game Creek. The left fork moderately climbs to Ferrin's Trail and the summit of Snow King Mountain, making connections into the Cache Creek drainage. Choose your own turn-around point, and return along the same trail. ▦

73. Game Creek Loop
SNOW KING AREA

Hiking distance: 7.4 miles round trip
Hiking time: 3.5 hours
Configuration: out-and-back with loop
Elevation gain: 200 feet
Difficulty: easy to moderate
Exposure: mostly open meadows
Dogs: allowed
Maps: U.S.G.S. Cache Creek
       Beartooth Publishing: Grand Teton, Jackson Hole, Teton Valley

map
page 216

Game Creek flows through a beautiful, near-level canyon in the Gros Ventre Mountains south of Jackson. Small streams snake through the lower meadow, marbled with marshes and abundant with wildflowers. This loop hike takes in the first 3.7 miles of the Game Creek Trail in the pastoral mountain valley. The trail winds through the wetland meadow while staying on dry land. The hike can be combined with the Cache Creek Trail (Hike 68) for a 11.7-mile one-way shuttle.

To the trailhead

From the town square in downtown Jackson, drive 7.5 miles south on Highway 89. Between mile markers 146 and 147, turn left on Game Creek Road. Drive one mile to a sharp right bend in the road. Within the bend is the posted trailhead parking area on the left.

The hike

Walk 30 yards back down the road to the gravel road on the right that lies just inside the Teton National Forest. Head east on the gravel road, past the trailhead gate. Follow the old road up the open canyon between the tree-dotted hills with rock outcroppings, parallel to the north bank of Game Creek. The road crosses the creek, then curves north. Cross a cattle guard, steadily gaining elevation to the old trailhead by a buck fence at 2.2 miles. Cross the footbridge over Game Creek, and traverse the base of the hillside on the west edge of the meadow. The path remains raised above the wetland meadow, marbled with meandering streams. When the trail crosses through a tributary stream, use the bridge in the brush to the left. Forty yards after crossing, the road narrows to a footpath and curves right, crossing to the east side of Game Creek at a T-junction. The return route is to the right.

For now, head up canyon to the left. Cross a small bridge over a feeder stream, continuing 0.2 miles to a junction with another bridge on the left. This is the turn-around spot. On the return, the footpath follows the east edge of the valley on a gradual downhill slope. Complete the loop 100 yards below the buck fence at the old trailhead.

To hike farther from the far end of the loop, the left fork crosses the bridge over Game Creek and leads to Five-Way Meadow, Wilson Canyon, Leeks Canyon, and Snow King Mountain above the town of Jackson. The right fork—the Game Creek Trail—continues 2.4 miles to the Cache Creek Trail (Hike 68). ▨

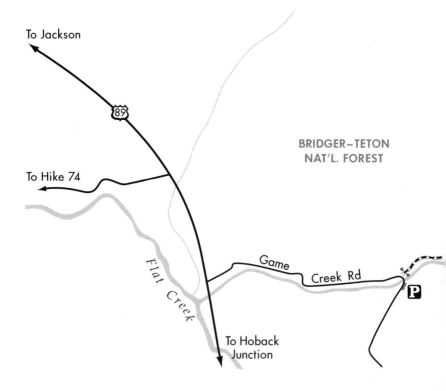

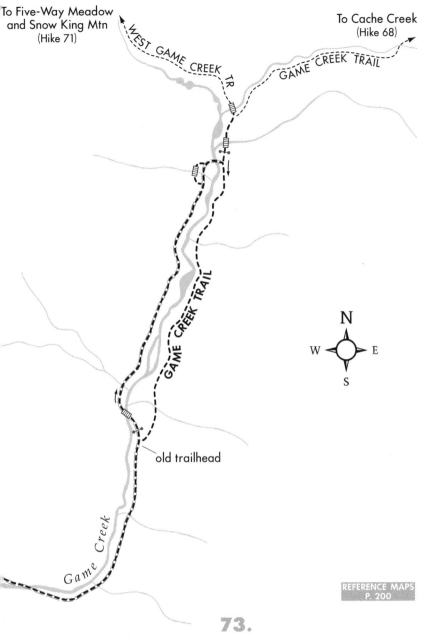

To Five-Way Meadow
and Snow King Mtn
(Hike 71)

To Cache Creek
(Hike 68)

WEST GAME CREEK TR

GAME CREEK TRAIL

GAME CREEK TRAIL

N

W   E

S

old trailhead

Game Creek

REFERENCE MAPS
P. 200

73.

Game Creek Loop
SNOW KING AREA

74. South Park

BIG GAME WINTER RANGE

Hiking distance: 2.5 miles round trip
Hiking time: 1.5 hours
Configuration: loop
Elevation gain: level
Difficulty: easy
Exposure: open meadows and some shaded forest
Dogs: allowed
Maps: U.S.G.S. Jackson

South Park is at the lower end of the Jackson Hole valley in the flatlands south of the town of Jackson. Flat Creek, Spring Creek, and the numerous channels of the Snake River slowly wind through the verdant valley, bordered on the west by the Snake River Range and on the east by the Gros Ventre Range. This gentle hike loops through the riparian wetland valley with mountain views in every direction. The trail crosses streams and strolls along the Snake River through a large stand of cottonwood trees. There are picnic areas along the river.

The area is managed by the Wyoming Game and Fish Department. It provides the elk a winter range and feeding ground. During spring and summer it is a bird habitat for feeding, nesting, and raising young.

To the trailhead

From the town square in downtown Jackson, drive 7 miles south on Highway 89. Turn right by the "South Park" sign. Drive one mile down into the valley, and park at the end of the road by the hay sheds and the bridge.

The hike

Pass the trailhead gate and cross the bridge over Flat Creek. Take the level trail to the left across the meadow and past the log corral towards the cottonwood trees at the Snake River. On the left is the old Davis homestead log cabin, built in 1902. Head right on the trail, following the watercourse alongside the Snake River and through the forest. After exploring the shoreline, take the jeep trail that loops back through the meadow. Recross the bridge at the barns and parking area. ■

To Jackson

BRIDGER–TETON NAT'L. FOREST

N
W—E
S

89

SOUTH

P   hay sheds

Flat Creek

corral   homestead cabin

PARK

To Hike 73

Snake River

To Hoback Jct

Munger Mtn
8,383'

REFERENCE MAPS
P. 200

BRIDGER–TETON
NAT'L. FOREST

74.

South Park
BIG GAME WINTER RANGE

75. Dog Creek Trail

Hiking distance: 4.4 miles round trip
Hiking time: 2.5 hours
Configuration: out-and-back
Elevation gain: 300 feet
Difficulty: easy to slightly moderate
Exposure: a mix of shaded forest and open slopes
Dogs: allowed
Maps: U.S.G.S. Munger Mountain
Beartooth Publishing: Grand Teton, Jackson Hole, Teton Valley

Dog Creek, in the remote Snake River Range, flows down a lush canyon and joins the Snake River southwest of Hoback Junction. The Dog Creek Trail heads up the canyon parallel to the creek through an endless garden of wildflowers. Moose and elk are frequently seen in this quiet, backcountry drainage. The trail continues westward to many connections along the Snake River Range.

To the trailhead

From the town square in Jackson, drive south on Highway 89 for 14 miles to Hoback Junction. Take the right fork, staying on Highway 89. Drive 4.8 miles to an unsigned turnoff on the right, located 0.5 miles past the posted Wilson–Fall Creek Road turnoff. Make a sharp right turn. Follow the narrow dirt road 0.4 miles, crossing a bridge over Pritchard Creek on the south edge of Pritchard Pond, to the posted trailhead and parking area by the old corral.

The hike

From the posted trailhead at the mouth of the canyon, take the forested path uphill. Follow the open slopes on the north side of Dog Creek, with views of Wolf Mountain straight ahead. Cross a couple of feeder streams to a junction at one mile. The left fork leads to Cabin Creek and Wolf Mountain. Stay to the right and continue northwest to a junction at 2.2 miles by the confluence of Dog Creek and Little Dog Creek. This is the turn-around spot.

To hike farther, the left fork continues west up Dog Creek to Red Pass, Wolf Mountain, and Indian Peak along the Snake River

Range. The right fork follows Little Dog Creek a short distance and heads north along Pup Creek. ■

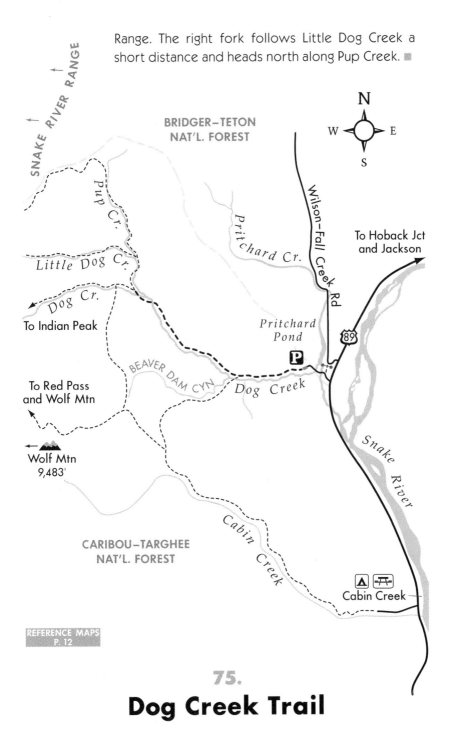

N
W · E
S

SNAKE RIVER RANGE

BRIDGER–TETON
NAT'L. FOREST

Pup Cr.

Pritchard Cr.

Little Dog Cr.

Dog Cr.

To Indian Peak

Wilson–Fall Creek Rd

To Hoback Jct
and Jackson

Pritchard
Pond

P

To Red Pass
and Wolf Mtn

BEAVER DAM CYN

Dog Creek

Snake River

Wolf Mtn
9,483'

Cabin
Creek

CARIBOU–TARGHEE
NAT'L. FOREST

Cabin Creek

REFERENCE MAPS
P. 12

75.
Dog Creek Trail

76. Granite Falls and Hot Springs

Hiking distance: 1 mile round trip
Hiking time: 30 minutes plus soaking time
Configuration: out-and-back
Elevation gain: 300 feet
Difficulty: easy (with a scramble down to base of falls)
Exposure: a mix of shaded forest and meadows
Dogs: allowed
Maps: U.S.G.S. Granite Falls
   Beartooth Publishing: Grand Teton, Jackson Hole, Teton Valley

Granite Falls and Hot Springs are located in the Gros Ventre Mountains east of Hoback Junction. This short hike follows Granite Creek as it cascades over magnificent Granite Falls, a wide, roaring 20-foot cascade. The waterfall was used as a backdrop in the movie *A River Runs Through It*. The trail begins at an elevation of 7,000 feet by Granite Hot Springs, a developed hot springs built in 1933 with changing rooms and a 45x75-foot pool. The hike follows the cascading creek downstream to Granite Falls Hot Springs, a primitive hot springs on the edge of the creek at the base of Granite Falls.

To the trailhead

From the town square in Jackson, drive south 14 miles on Highway 89 to Hoback Junction. Take the left fork—Highway 191/189—towards Pinedale. Drive 11.5 miles to the Granite Recreational Area turnoff. A large sign marks the turn. Turn left and drive 10 miles on a gravel road to Granite Hot Springs. Park in the lot at the end of the road.

The hike

Walk through the gate and across the river towards Granite Hot Springs. To get to Granite Falls, take the right trail along the east side of the creek. From the trail, you will see the powerful Granite Creek swiftly tumbling towards the falls and a view down the Granite Creek valley. Past the falls, take the steep trail to the right, descending down to the creek. At the creek is the hot springs and a primitive soaking pool 50 yards in front of the falls. To return, retrace your steps back to Granite Hot Springs.

Taking the left (north) trail at the beginning of the hike leads through a beautiful forest into the canyon. Moose frequent the meadow that is just 15 minutes from the trailhead. This trail is part of a much longer trail leading northwest to Turquoise Lake (11 miles) and Cache Creek in Jackson (17 miles).

To Turquoise Lake
and Cache Creek

Granite Creek

Antoinette Pk
11,407'

GROS VENTRE RANGE

N
W · E
S

**Granite
Hot Springs**

P

*Granite
Falls*

The Open Door
9,204'

Granite Creek
Campground

BRIDGER–TETON
NAT'L. FOREST

REFERENCE MAPS
P. 12

To Hwy 191/189
and Jackson

76.

Granite Falls
and Hot Springs

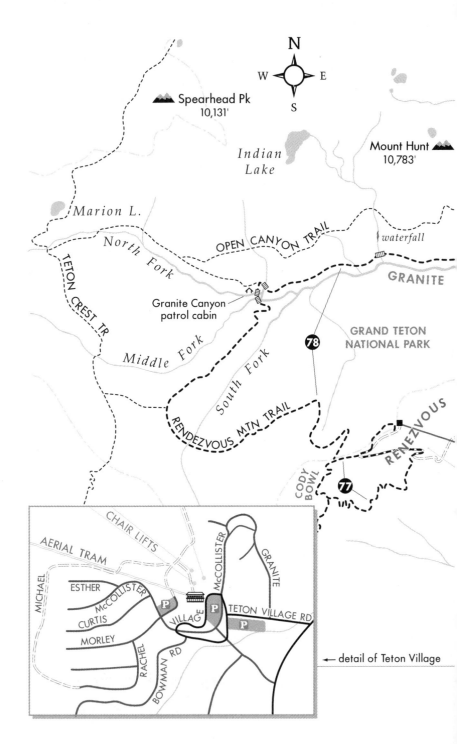

N
W · E
S

▲▲ Spearhead Pk
10,131'

*Indian
Lake*

Mount Hunt ▲▲
10,783'

Marion L.

OPEN CANYON TRAIL

North Fork

▌waterfall

TETON CREST TR

Granite Canyon
patrol cabin

GRANITE

Middle Fork

GRAND TETON
NATIONAL PARK

78

South Fork

RENDEZVOUS MTN TRAIL

RENDEZVOUS

CODY BOWL

77

CHAIR LIFTS

AERIAL TRAM

MICHAEL
ESTHER
McCOLLISTER
CURTIS
MORLEY
RACHEL
BOWMAN RD
VILLAGE
McCOLLISTER
GRANITE

P

P

TETON VILLAGE RD

P

← detail of Teton Village

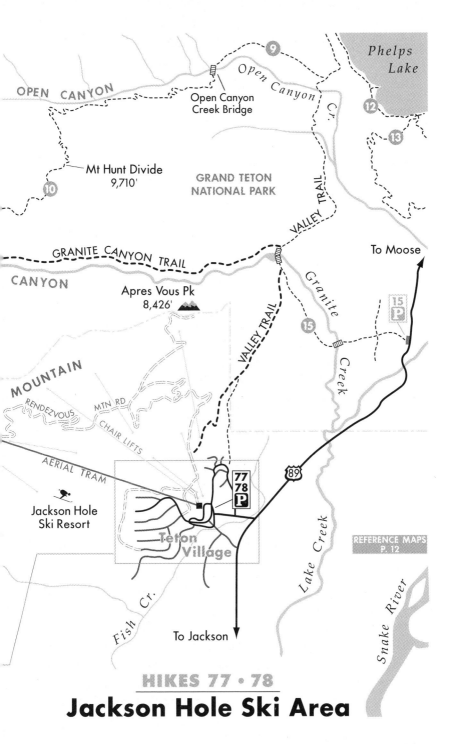

Phelps
Lake

OPEN CANYON

Open Canyon
Creek Bridge

Open Canyon Cr.

Mt Hunt Divide
9,710'

GRAND TETON
NATIONAL PARK

VALLEY TRAIL

To Moose

GRANITE CANYON TRAIL

CANYON

Apres Vous Pk
8,426'

VALLEY TRAIL

Granite Creek

MOUNTAIN

RENDEZVOUS   MTN RD

CHAIR LIFTS

AERIAL TRAM

Jackson Hole
Ski Resort

89

77
78
P

Teton
Village

Fish Cr.

Lake Creek

Snake River

REFERENCE MAPS
P. 12

To Jackson

HIKES 77 · 78
Jackson Hole Ski Area

77. Rock Springs Loop—
Rendezvous Mountain
JACKSON HOLE SKI RESORT

Hiking distance: 4.2-mile loop
Hiking time: 3 hours
Configuration: tram ride to summit, then loop with short spur trail
Elevation gain: 1,100 feet
Difficulty: moderate to strenuous
Exposure: high open meadows and shaded canyon
Dogs: not allowed
Maps: U.S.G.S. Teton Village and Rendezvous Peak
        Rendezvous Mountain Trail Map

The Rock Springs Loop trail begins at an elevation of 10,450 feet at the top of the Jackson Hole Ski Resort. The aerial tram at Teton Village runs year round, taking visitors 2.4 miles to the top of Rendezvous Mountain and gaining 4,139 feet en route to the summit. After the tram ride, the trail traverses across the rugged alpine environment and offers some of the best views of Jackson Hole. Although the weather may be warm down at Teton Village, at this altitude the temperature is cooler and the weather is unpredictable. Bring warm clothing and wear good shoes.

To the trailhead

From the town square in downtown Jackson, drive 1.4 miles south on Highway 89 to Highway 22. Turn right and drive 4 miles to Wyoming Highway 390—the Moose-Wilson Road. Turn right (north) and continue 7 miles to Teton Village. Turn left and park in the parking lot by the tram a short distance ahead.

The hike

Take the aerial tram to the top of Rendezvous Mountain at an elevation of 10,450 feet. Exit the tram and follow the unpaved road west towards Cody Bowl, a glacial cirque. Pass a trail on the left (our return route) to a posted junction on the right near Cody Bowl. The right fork enters Grand Teton National Park and makes a long loop back through Granite Canyon (Hike 78). Continue straight ahead down the switchbacks to the base of Cody Bowl.

Take the Rock Springs footpath uphill to the left to another trail split. To the right is a short, optional detour to the Green River Lookout. After the spur trail, the Rock Springs Trail—the main loop—continues downhill into a large meadow. From the meadow, begin the ascent back up to the tram. At a trail split, take the nature trail, bearing to the right to a junction with the Rendezvous Mountain Road. Take the road to the left, gaining 750 feet as you head back to the tram. ■

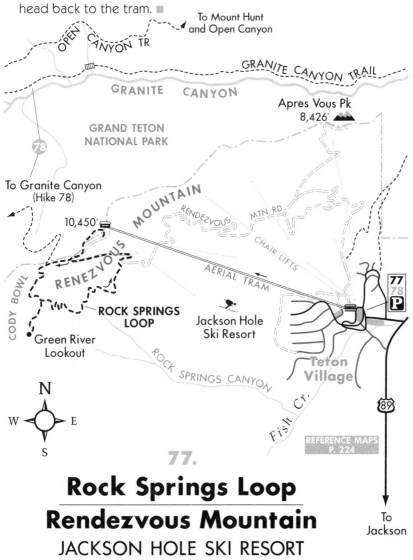

77.

Rock Springs Loop
Rendezvous Mountain
JACKSON HOLE SKI RESORT

78. Rendezvous Mountain— Granite Canyon Loop

JACKSON HOLE SKI RESORT

Hiking distance: 12.4 miles round trip
Hiking time: 6 hours
Configuration: tram ride to summit, then large loop
Elevation loss: 4,100 feet
Difficulty: strenuous
Exposure: high open meadows and shaded canyon
Dogs: not allowed
Maps: U.S.G.S. Rendezvous Peak & Teton Village
Rendezvous Mountain Trail Map · Adventure Maps: Jackson Hole
Beartooth Publishing: Grand Teton, Jackson Hole, Teton Valley
National Geographic Trails Illustrated: Grand Teton Nat'l. Park

map
page 230

This large loop trail in the Bridger-Teton National Forest connects Rendezvous Mountain—at Jackson Hole Ski Resort—with Granite Canyon at the south end of the national park. The hike begins by taking the aerial tram from Teton Village to the top of the mountain. From the summit, the trail enters Grand Teton National Park and, for the most part, follows a downhill course. The Rendezvous Mountain Trail links the summit to Granite Canyon, looping around the upper northwest slope of Rendezvous Mountain. The trail crosses through enormous alpine meadows marbled with small streams and teaming with wildflowers before dropping into Granite Canyon, where there are great views down the rugged creek drainage. The Granite Canyon Trail descends along the cascading creek through a forest between the steep, towering canyon walls.

To the trailhead

From the town square in downtown Jackson, drive 1.4 miles south on Highway 89 to Highway 22. Turn right and drive 4 miles to Wyoming Highway 390—the Moose-Wilson Road. Turn right (north) and continue 7 miles to Teton Village. Turn left and park in the parking lot by the tram a short distance ahead.

The hike

Take the aerial tram to the top of Rendezvous Mountain at an elevation of 10,450 feet. Exit the tram and follow the unpaved road west towards Cody Bowl, a glacial cirque. Pass a trail on the left to a posted junction on the right near Cody Bowl.

Bear right on the footpath towards Marion Lake and Granite Canyon, entering Grand Teton National Park in a high alpine setting. Head down the hillside and cut back on the switchback to the left. The path curves to the right under a towering vertical cirque. Cross a drainage and ascend the mountainside while overlooking Granite Canyon. Top the ridge and descend into a pine forest and then into meadows. Cross over the South Fork Granite Creek to vast open meadows and a posted junction with the Middle Fork Cutoff Trail at 3.5 miles. The left fork leads to Teton Crest and Marion Lake. Stay to the right and descend the open, sloping meadow surrounded by mountains. Pass through pockets of evergreens into forested Granite Canyon. Cross two log footbridges over Granite Creek to the patrol cabin on the left and a posted junction at 5.2 miles. To the left also leads to Marion Lake along the Teton Crest Trail.

Bear right (down canyon) on the Granite Canyon Trail, and cross a bridge over a tributary stream. Head down the south-facing wall of the canyon. Cross another bridge over a stream below a 100-foot waterfall off the north canyon wall. Continue down canyon, passing rocky beaches to a T-junction at 9.9 miles at the base of the canyon. The left fork leads to Phelps Lake.

Bear right (south) and cross two bridges over Granite Creek to a junction a short distance ahead at 10 miles. Take the Valley Trail to the right towards Teton Village. Climb over a small ridge and drop into a valley. Traverse the hillside through aspen groves to a junction at the national park boundary. Leave the park on the right fork, staying on the Valley Trail. Pass the ski maintenance area, and follow the hiking path signs back to the tram. ▨

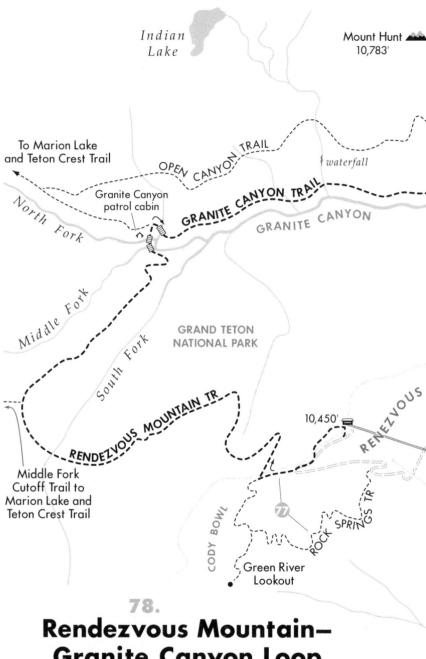

Indian
Lake

Mount Hunt 10,783'

To Marion Lake
and Teton Crest Trail

OPEN CANYON TRAIL

waterfall

Granite Canyon
patrol cabin

GRANITE CANYON TRAIL

North Fork

GRANITE CANYON

Middle Fork

GRAND TETON
NATIONAL PARK

South Fork

RENDEZVOUS MOUNTAIN TR

10,450'

RENDEZVOUS

Middle Fork
Cutoff Trail to
Marion Lake and
Teton Crest Trail

CODY BOWL

77

ROCK SPRINGS TR

Green River
Lookout

78.
Rendezvous Mountain–
Granite Canyon Loop
JACKSON HOLE SKI RESORT

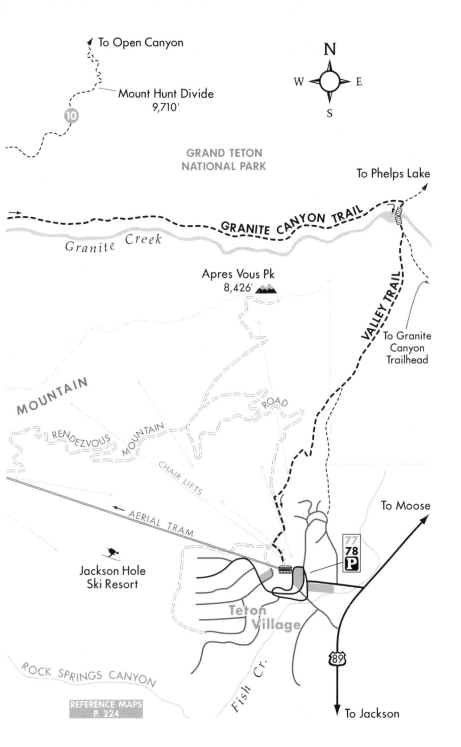

To Open Canyon

Mount Hunt Divide
9,710'

⑩

GRAND TETON
NATIONAL PARK

To Phelps Lake

N
W   E
S

GRANITE CANYON TRAIL

Granite Creek

Apres Vous Pk
8,426'

VALLEY TRAIL

To Granite
Canyon
Trailhead

MOUNTAIN

RENDEZVOUS MOUNTAIN

ROAD

CHAIR LIFTS

AERIAL TRAM

Jackson Hole
Ski Resort

To Moose

77
78
P

Teton
Village

89

ROCK SPRINGS CANYON

REFERENCE MAPS
P. 224

Fish Cr.

To Jackson

79. Snake River Northeast Dike

Hiking distance: 3 miles round trip
Hiking time: 1.5 hours
Configuration: out-and-back with several short spur trails
Elevation gain: level
Difficulty: easy
Exposure: open flat with shaded pockets
Dogs: allowed
Maps: U.S.G.S. Jackson and Teton Village
Beartooth Publishing: Grand Teton, Jackson Hole, Teton Valley

The Snake River Northeast Dike follows the Snake River upstream along a road closed to vehicles. The dikes were built by the Army Corps of Engineers beginning in the 1950s to stop the flooding and erosion of adjacent pasture lands. The man-made rock and dirt berms border both sides of the Snake River, all the way from the Jackson Hole airport to South Park. The levee is a popular year-around hiking, biking, and cross country ski route that is also perfect for dogs, especially those that love the water. The hike begins at Emily's Pond, an eleven-acre public park donated by Emily Stevens as a preserved habitat for moose, deer, and waterfowl.

To the trailhead

From the town square in downtown Jackson, drive 1.4 miles south on Highway 89 to Highway 22. Turn right and drive 3.6 miles towards Wilson. Turn right, just before crossing the bridge over the Snake River. Park on the right in Emily's Pond parking lot.

The hike

Take the paved road past the ponds on the right to the Snake River. Follow the wide gravel road, heading upstream along the dike. The path crosses the lush wetlands. There is no shade along the dike, but side paths lead through the cottonwood and blue spruce forests to the Snake River on the left and the ponds on the right. At 1.5 miles, the trail ends at a locked gate. Return by reversing your route. ▦

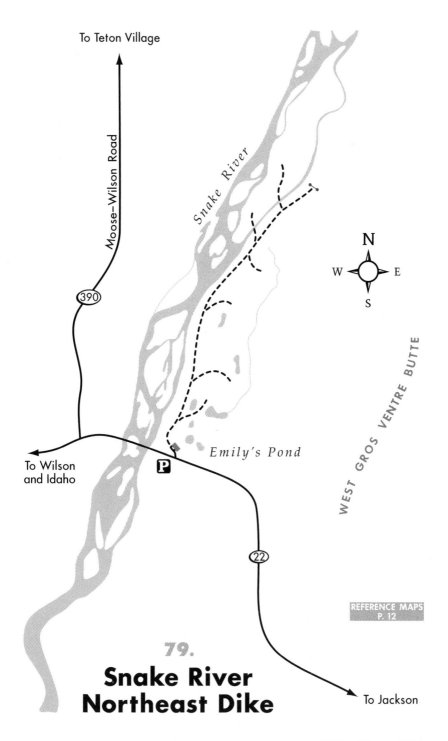

To Teton Village

Moose–Wilson Road

Snake River

390

N
W E
S

WEST GROS VENTRE BUTTE

To Wilson
and Idaho

P

Emily's Pond

22

REFERENCE MAPS
P. 12

79.
Snake River
Northeast Dike

To Jackson

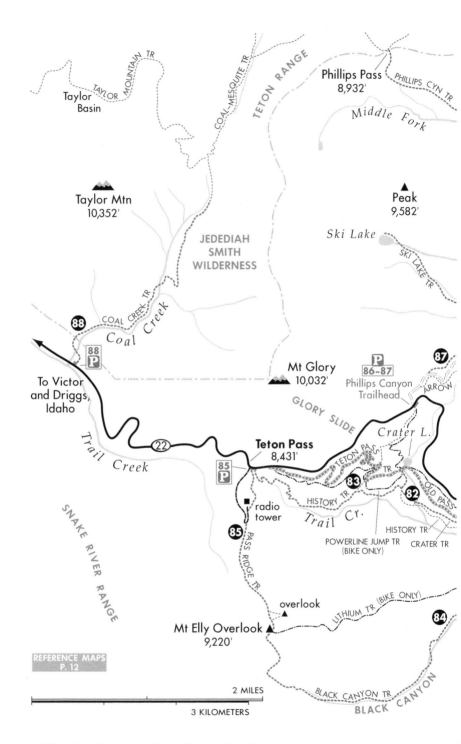

TAYLOR MOUNTAIN TR

Taylor Basin

COAL-MESQUITE TR

TETON RANGE

Phillips Pass
8,932'

PHILLIPS CYN TR

Middle Fork

Taylor Mtn
10,352'

JEDEDIAH
SMITH
WILDERNESS

Peak
9,582'

Ski Lake

SKI LAKE TR

COAL CREEK TR

88

COAL CREEK TR

Coal Creek

Mt Glory
10,032'

86-87
Phillips Canyon
Trailhead

87

ARROW

To Victor
and Driggs,
Idaho

GLORY SLIDE

Crater L.

Trail Creek

22

Teton Pass
8,431'

TETON PASS

83

OLD PASS

82

85

radio
tower

HISTORY TR

Trail Cr.

SNAKE RIVER RANGE

85

PASS RIDGE TR

POWERLINE JUMP TR
(BIKE ONLY)

HISTORY TR

CRATER TR

overlook

LITHIUM TR (BIKE ONLY)

84

Mt Elly Overlook
9,220'

REFERENCE MAPS
P. 12

BLACK CANYON TR

BLACK CANYON

2 MILES

3 KILOMETERS

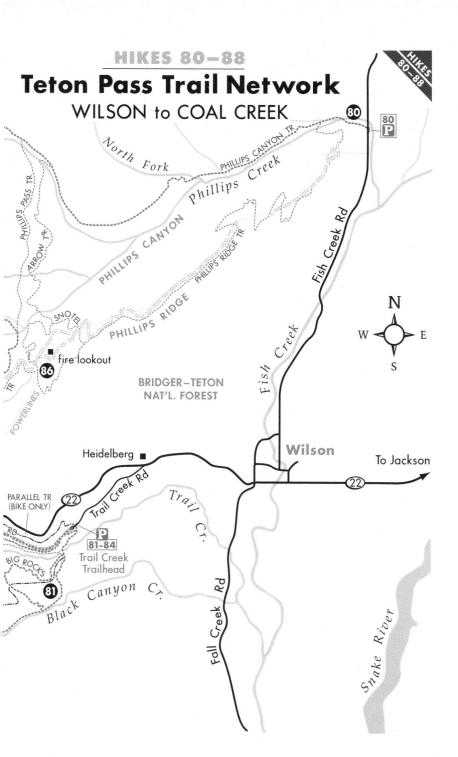

Teton Pass Trail Network
WILSON to COAL CREEK

HIKES 80-88

80
P

North Fork

PHILLIPS CANYON TR.

Phillips Creek

PHILLIPS PASS TR.

ARROW TR.

PHILLIPS CANYON

PHILLIPS RIDGE TR.

PHILLIPS RIDGE

SNOTEL

fire lookout

86

POWERLINES

TR.

Fish Creek Rd

Fish Creek

BRIDGER–TETON
NAT'L. FOREST

N
W · E
S

Heidelberg

Wilson

To Jackson

PARALLEL TR
(BIKE ONLY)

22

Trail Creek Rd

Trail Cr.

RD.

P
81-84

Trail Creek
Trailhead

22

Fall Creek Rd

BIG ROCKS

81

Black Canyon Cr.

Snake River

80. Phillips Canyon Trail to Phillips Pass

TETON PASS TRAIL NETWORK

Hiking distance: 11 miles round trip
Hiking time: 6 hours
Configuration: out-and-back
Elevation gain: 2,600 feet
Difficulty: strenuous
Exposure: a mix of shaded forested and exposed meadows
Dogs: allowed
Maps: U.S.G.S. Teton Village and Rendezvous Peak
Adventure Maps: Jackson Hole
Beartooth Publishing: Grand Teton National Park map

The Teton Pass Trail Network is a system of inter-connected, multi-use trails located between the town of Wilson, Teton Pass, and Phillips Canyon. The trail system is a short drive west of Jackson

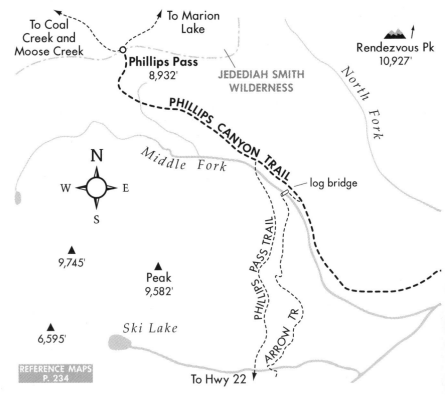

and is a popular destination for day-hiking, biking, and cross-country skiing. Hikes 80—88 explore the Teton Pass Trails. The hikes are easily accessible from Fish Creek Road (heading north from Wilson) or from Highway 22 (heading west from Wilson).

Phillips Canyon is a wide drainage with a year-round creek that tumbles down from Mount Glory and Rendezvous Mountain into Fish Creek, a tributary of the Snake River. This hike begins at the mouth of the canyon near Fish Creek. The trail parallels Phillips Creek up canyon, then curves northwest up the Middle Fork to Phillips Pass at the Jedediah Smith Wilderness boundary. From the wide saddle atop Phillips Pass are spectacular vistas of Taylor Mountain, the Teton Peaks, the Teton Valley, and the Moose Creek and Mesquite Creek drainages. En route, the trail climbs through high alpine meadows and wooded forests with Douglas fir, lodgepole pine, mountain ash, and groves of aspen.

To the trailhead

From the town square in downtown Jackson, drive 1.4 miles south on Highway 89 to Highway 22. Turn right and drive 5.5 miles to the town of Wilson. Turn right (north) on Main Street, and go 0.3 miles to Fish

BRIDGER—TETON
NAT'L. FOREST

PHILLIPS CANYON TR

log bridge

Phillips Creek

PHILLIPS RIDGE TRAIL

Fish Creek Road

Fish Cr.

P

80.

To Wilson

Phillips Canyon Trail
to Phillips Pass
TETON PASS TRAIL NETWORK

Creek Road on the left. Turn left and continue 3.0 miles to a distinct parking pullout on the right, directly across the road from the posted trailhead.

The hike

Cross Fish Creek Road to the trailhead. Head up the rise, gently climbing through the pine forest. Parallel the south side of Phillips Creek, and enter the Bridger–Teton National Forest. Cross a wood bridge over Phillips Creek and another bridge over a tributary stream to a posted trail split. The Phillips Ridge Trail veers left, climbing the mountain to the fire lookout atop the ridge and down to Highway 22.

For this hike, take the right fork on the Phillips Canyon Trail. Climb the north canyon slope along a few dips and rises, then drop down to the canyon floor alongside Phillips Creek. Cross a feeder stream at 1.5 miles. In less than a quarter mile, cross a one-log bridge over the North Fork Phillips Creek. Zigzag up a short, steep section of trail, then traverse the mountainside overlooking Phillips Canyon, Phillips Ridge to the south, and Rendezvous Mountain to the north. As the Middle Fork Phillips Creek nears, pass a high mountain meadow on the left at the base of Peak 9582. At just under 4 miles is the unsigned but distinct Arrow Trail on the left. The Arrow Trail connects with Phillips Ridge. A 0.1-mile detour to the left leads to a flower-filled meadow and a one-log bridge over the Middle Fork Phillips Creek.

Back at the junction, continue 0.4 miles on the mountain slope to the upper end of the meadow and an unsigned fork with the Phillips Pass Trail on the left. The left fork descends 50 yards to a rock-hop crossing of the Middle Fork. (The Phillips Pass Trail connects with Ski Lake—Hike 87—and Highway 22.) From the junction continue straight on the Phillips Canyon Trail, climbing up the meadows among aspens and fir. The last 1.2 miles, from the junction to Phillips Pass, gains over 600 feet through the flower-laden meadows to the signed Jedediah Smith Wilderness atop the divide. From the 8,932-foot summit are views of the Moose Creek and Mesquite Creek drainages, Taylor Mountain, Fossil Mountain, and Housetop Mountain. Return by retracing your steps. ▪

81. Big Rocks—
Lower Black Canyon Loop
TETON PASS TRAIL NETWORK

Hiking distance: 2.7-mile loop
Hiking time: 1.5 hours
Configuration: loop
Elevation gain: 600 feet
Difficulty: easy to moderate
Exposure: shaded forest and exposed meadows
Dogs: allowed
Maps: U.S.G.S. Teton Pass · Adventure Maps: Jackson Hole

**map
page 240**

The hiking-only Big Rocks Trail is a 1.5-mile-long trail at the base of Teton Pass just west of Wilson. The trail forms a loop between the Trail Creek drainage and Black Canyon in a lush forested hillside. The footpath passes glacial erratics—rocks transported down canyon by glacial ice.

To the trailhead

From the town square in downtown Jackson, drive 1.4 miles south on Highway 89 to Highway 22. Turn right and drive 5.5 miles to the town of Wilson. Continue 1.2 miles past Wilson to Trail Creek Road (Old Pass Road) on the left. (It is located directly across from the large "Heidelberg" sign on the right.) Turn left on Trail Creek Road, and drive 0.9 miles to the trailhead parking lot at the end of the road.

The hike

From the south side of the parking lot by the map kiosk, take the signed Black Canyon/Crater/History Trail. At 15 yards, stay left past the Crater Trail on the right (Hike 82). Descend into the open forest, and cross a bridge over Trail Creek at 0.1 mile. Continue 30 yards and veer right on the History Trail, the start of the loop.

Walk 20 yards to a posted trail split. The History Trail goes to the right. Take the Big Rocks Trail to the left. Cross a log bridge over a tributary of Trail Creek, and weave through the lush lodgepole pine forest. Gently but steadily gain elevation, passing a few massive boulders. Make a sweeping left bend, and climb to a

4-way junction with the Lithium Trail (a bike-only path). Carefully cross through the intersection, staying on the Big Rocks Trail. Meander through the forest at a near-level grade, then descend into Black Canyon. Zigzag down to the Black Canyon Trail just above the creek. Bear left and head down canyon, parallel to Black Canyon Creek. Pass the lower junction with the Lithium Trail to the junction with the History Trail, completing the loop. Cross the bridge over Trail Creek and return to the trailhead. ■

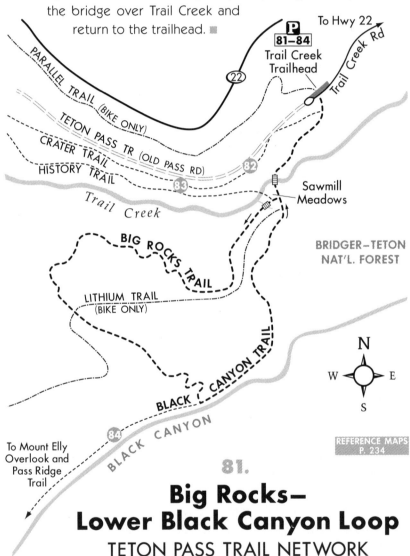

81.
Big Rocks—
Lower Black Canyon Loop
TETON PASS TRAIL NETWORK

82. Trail Creek to Crater Lake Loop
Crater Trail—Teton Pass Trail (Old Pass Road)
TETON PASS TRAIL NETWORK

Hiking distance: 3-mile loop
Hiking time: 1.5 hours
Configuration: loop
Elevation gain: 700 feet
Difficulty: easy
Exposure: mostly exposed with tree-shaded pockets
Dogs: allowed
Maps: U.S.G.S. Teton Pass · Adventure Maps: Jackson Hole

map
page 243

The Teton Pass Trail, also known as Old Pass Road, is the original auto route to Teton Pass before Highway 22 was built in 1970. The old winding road sits on the east side of Teton Pass beneath the towering 10,000-foot twin peaks of Mount Glory. The 4-mile-long road—in the center of the Teton Pass Trail Network—is popular with hikers, bikers, and equestrians. The stretch of former highway leads from west of Wilson to the Teton Pass summit, with connecting trails to Black Canyon (to the south) and Phillips Ridge (to the north).

This hike utilizes the east half of the old road to Crater Lake, a beautiful lake tucked into the mountains below Teton Pass. The lake was naturally formed when an avalanche chute on Mount Glory, named Glory Slide, dammed the North Fork Trail Creek in 1932. The Crater Trail and Teton Pass Trail (Old Pass Road) form a loop to the lake. The hike winds through a pristine area with an array of wildflowers. In the winter, the Old Pass Road is used as a cross-country ski trail.

To the trailhead

From the town square in downtown Jackson, drive 1.4 miles south on Highway 89 to Highway 22. Turn right and drive 5.5 miles to the town of Wilson. Continue 1.2 miles past Wilson to Trail Creek Road (Old Pass Road) on the left. (It is located directly across from the large "Heidelberg" sign on the right.) Turn left on Trail Creek Road, and drive 0.9 miles to the trailhead parking lot at the end of the road.

The hike

From the south side of the parking lot by the map kiosk, take the signed Black Canyon/Crater/History Trail. At 15 yards is a junction with the Crater Trail on the right. Leave the Black Canyon Trail and bear right. Enter the forest and head up the slope. The trail lies just below, and runs parallel to, the Teton Pass Trail (Old Pass Road), which is the return route. A short distance ahead the two trails merge on the paved Teton Pass Trail. Immediately, the Crater Trail footpath veers off to the left again. Veer left and traverse the south-facing hillside above cascading Trail Creek. Pass through a flower-filled meadow beneath Mount Glory, which towers over the trail directly ahead. At one mile, cross a one-log bridge over the North Fork Trail Creek, and pass two junctions with the History Trail. At both signed junctions, stay to the right and join a dirt two-track road. Walk 400 yards to a T-junction with the Teton Pass Trail. Bear right and walk fifty yards downhill on the paved road to Crater Lake on the left.

After enjoying the lake, continue eastward down the Teton Pass Trail. On the left, the Parallel Trail traverses the hillside slope between the Teton Pass Trail and Highway 22. Continue down the old road, completing the loop at the trailhead parking lot. ▨

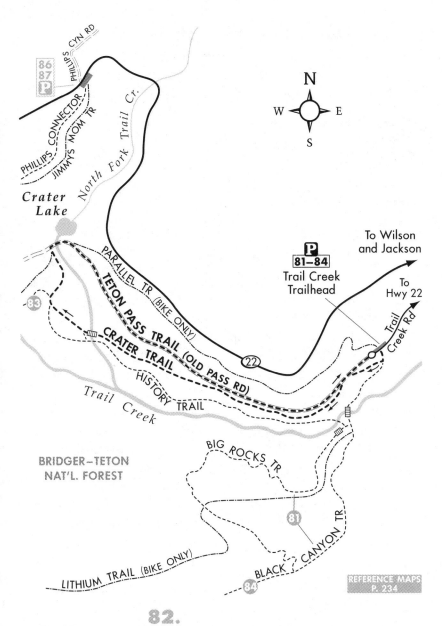

82.
Trail Creek to Crater Lake Loop
Crater Trail–Teton Pass Trail
TETON PASS TRAIL NETWORK

83. Trail Creek to Teton Pass Loop
Crater Trail—History Trail—
Teton Pass Trail (Old Pass Road)

TETON PASS TRAIL NETWORK

Hiking distance: 7.5-mile loop
Hiking time: 4 hours
Configuration: loop
Elevation gain: 1,950 feet
Difficulty: moderate to strenuous
Exposure: exposed hillside and forested pockets
Dogs: allowed
Maps: U.S.G.S. Teton Pass · Adventure Maps: Jackson Hole

map page 246

This hike makes a long, narrow loop up to Teton Pass in the heart of the Teton Pass Trail Network. The loop hike climbs to the pass via the Crater Trail and History Trail, returning on the Teton Pass Trail (also known as the Old Pass Road).

The History Trail follows the historic old wagon route used from the late 1880s until 1918, when the Old Pass Road was built. En route, the trail passes Crater Lake, a pristine, circular lake sitting in a deep depression at the southeast foot of Mount Glory. The lake is fed by the cascading waters of the North Fork Trail Creek, just above its confluence with Trail Creek. The hike then winds up to the 8,431-foot Teton Pass summit, climbing nearly 2,000 feet along eight sweeping switchbacks. After the pass, the hike returns on the Teton Pass Trail. This is the original auto route to Teton Pass before Highway 22 was built in 1970. The old winding road sits on the east side of the pass beneath the towering 10,000-foot twin peaks of Mount Glory.

To the trailhead

From the town square in downtown Jackson, drive 1.4 miles south on Highway 89 to Highway 22. Turn right and drive 5.5 miles to the town of Wilson. Continue 1.2 miles past Wilson to Trail Creek Road (Old Pass Road) on the left. (It is located directly across from the large "Heidelberg" sign on the right.) Turn left on Trail Creek Road, and drive 0.9 miles to the trailhead parking lot at the end of the road.

The hike

From the south side of the parking lot by the map kiosk, take the signed Black Canyon/Crater/History Trail. At 15 yards is a junction with the Crater Trail on the right. Leave the Black Canyon Trail and bear right. Enter the forest and head up the slope. The trail lies just below, and runs parallel to, the Teton Pass Trail (Old Pass Road), which is the return route. A short distance ahead the two trails merge on the paved Teton Pass Trail. Immediately, the Crater Trail footpath veers off to the left again. Veer left and traverse the south-facing hillside above cascading Trail Creek. Pass through a flower-filled meadow beneath Mount Glory, which towers over the trail directly ahead. At one mile, cross a one-log bridge over the North Fork Trail Creek to a Y-fork with the History Trail fifty yards ahead. Stay on the Crater Trail to the second signed junction with the History Trail. Staying to the right on the Crater Trail leads to the Teton Pass Trail and Crater Lake (Hike 82).

For this hike, bear left on the History Trail. Continue uphill through open meadows. The trail closely parallels the Powerline Jump Trail, a popular biking-only trail with mogul-type airborne jumps. Be careful not to accidentally get on this bike path, which is easy to do. If this happens, cautiously climb up to a junction with the Teton Pass Trail. From the paved path, walk 20 yards to the left and pick up the posted History Trail again on a U-shaped road bend. In either event, continue up, traversing the north canyon wall high above Trail Creek. Cross a series of three feeder streams, and begin climbing at a steeper grade with the aid of switchbacks. The History Trail ends at the trailhead parking area atop Teton Pass at the Pass Ridge Trail (Hike 85).

From the 8,431-foot pass, walk to Highway 22. Bear right along the side of the highway and stay to the right onto the Teton Pass Trail (Old Pass Road). Pass the vehicle-restricting boulders, and wind down the north canyon wall below the highway. Pass the bike-only path on the right by the vehicle gate. Head down the Teton Pass Trail on a series of switchbacking bends. At the seventh (right) bend is the Phillips Connector Trail leading up to Highway 22 and the Phillips Pass Trail and Ski Lake (Hike 87). At the next bend are the junctions on the right with the History Trail and Powerline Jump (biking-only) Trail. From here, the old road drops down to Crater Lake on the left. After spending some time at the lake, continue down the Teton Pass Trail. On the left, the Parallel Trail traverses the hillside slope parallel to and between the Teton Pass Trail and Highway 22.

Continue down the road, completing the loop at the trailhead parking lot. ■

To Victor, Idaho

85
P

Teton
Pass

Mt Glory
10,032'

22

(OLD PASS ROAD)

TETON PASS TRAIL

(BIKE ONLY)

POWERLINE

SERVICE ROAD

radio
tower
■

HISTORY TRAIL

85

PASS RIDGE TRAIL

SNAKE RIVER RANGE

▲ overlook

LITHIUM TR (BIKE ONLY)

Mt Elly Overlook ▲
9,220'

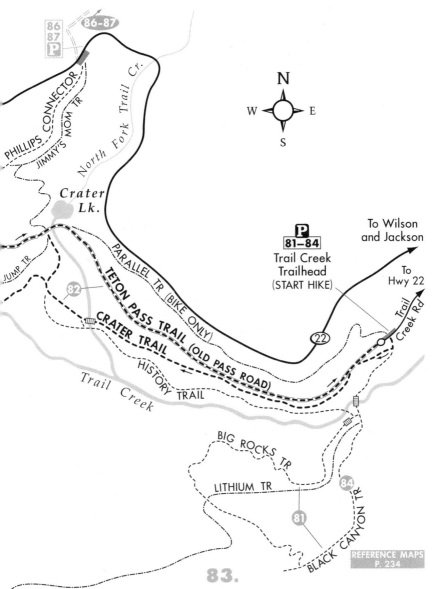

Trail Creek to Teton Pass Loop

Crater Trail–History Trail–
Teton Pass Trail

TETON PASS TRAIL NETWORK

84. Black Canyon Loop
Crater—History—Pass Ridge—Black Canyon Trails
TETON PASS TRAIL NETWORK

Hiking distance: 10.5-mile loop
Hiking time: 5-6 hours
Configuration: loop
Elevation gain: 2,700 feet
Difficulty: strenuous
Exposure: forested canyon and open slopes
Dogs: allowed
Maps: U.S.G.S. Teton Pass · Adventure Maps: Jackson Hole
　　　　Beartooth Publishing: Grand Teton, Jackson Hole, Teton Valley
　　　　National Geographic Trails Illustrated: Grand Teton Nat'l. Park

**map
page 250**

Black Canyon is a stream-fed, forested canyon that resides on the south side of Teton Pass. The canyon is located at the head of the Snake River Range in the Bridger-Teton National Forest. The Black Canyon Trail stretches 4 miles through a lush, towering forest, from the Mount Elly overlook to Sawmill Meadows near the Trail Creek trailhead. The path parallels the waterway through a mix of Douglas fir, limber pine, subalpine fir, and aspen.

This hike utilizes four trails to form a 10.5-mile loop. The hike begins on the Crater Trail and History Trail. The trail skirts Crater Lake, a circular tarn at the base of Mount Glory. The History Trail roughly follows an historic old wagon route, passing the sites of a sawmill, pastures, and old bridges. The Pass Ridge Trail climbs a flower-filled ridge at the head of the Trail Creek drainage, linking Teton Pass to the Mount Elly Overlook at the top of Black Canyon. From the 9,220-foot overlook are views of Jackson Hole, the Snake River, the Gros Ventre Range, and the Snake River Range.

To the trailhead

From the town square in downtown Jackson, drive 1.4 miles south on Highway 89 to Highway 22. Turn right and drive 5.5 miles to the town of Wilson. Continue 1.2 miles past Wilson to Trail Creek Road (Old Pass Road) on the left. (It is located directly across from the large "Heidelberg" sign on the right.) Turn left and drive 0.9 miles to the trailhead parking lot at the end of the road.

The hike

From the south side of the parking lot by the map kiosk, take the signed Black Canyon/Crater/History Trail. At 15 yards is a junction with the Crater Trail on the right. Leave the Black Canyon Trail and bear right. Enter the Engelmann spruce and subalpine fir forest and head up the slope. The trail lies just below, and runs parallel to, the Teton Pass Trail (Old Pass Road). A short distance ahead the two trails merge on the paved Teton Pass Trail. Immediately, the Crater Trail footpath veers off to the left again. Veer left and traverse the south-facing hillside above cascading Trail Creek. Pass through a flower-filled meadow beneath Mount Glory, which towers over the trail directly ahead. At one mile, cross a one-log bridge over the North Fork Trail Creek to a Y-fork with the History Trail fifty yards ahead. Stay on the Crater Trail to the second signed junction with the History Trail. Staying to the right on the Crater Trail leads to the Teton Pass Trail and Crater Lake (Hike 82).

For this hike, bear left on the History Trail. Continue uphill through open meadows. The trail closely parallels the Powerline Jump Trail, a popular biking-only trail with mogul-type airborne jumps. Be careful not to accidentally get on this bike path, which is easy to do. If this happens, cautiously climb up to a junction with the Teton Pass Trail. From the paved path, walk 20 yards to the left, and pick up the posted History Trail again on a U-shaped road bend. In either event, continue up, traversing the north canyon wall high above Trail Creek. Cross a series of three feeder streams. Ascend the open, grassy slope at a steeper grade, overlooking the valley and the Gros Ventre Range. Switchbacks aid in reaching the end of the History Trail atop the 8,431-foot Teton Pass by the trailhead map.

From the kiosk, take the posted Pass Ridge Trail. Head up the hill, traversing the east-facing slope to the radio towers. At the gravel service road, bear left and walk 100 yards to the end of the road. Veer left on the footpath and continue south. Enter an Engelmann spruce and subalpine fir forest. Pass through a series of flower-filled meadows. As you near the ridge, two side paths head off to the left to overlooks of the valley and Jackson.

Continue parallel to the cliffs to the 9,200-foot Mount Elly Overlook at the head of Black Canyon. To the left, the Lithium Trail, a biking-only route, follows the ridge into Black Canyon and returns to the trailhead.

For this hike, go 80 yards to the right at the posted Black Canyon Trail. Weave down the north wall of Black Canyon at an easy grade. Pass through forested pockets and sloping meadows with far-reaching vistas.

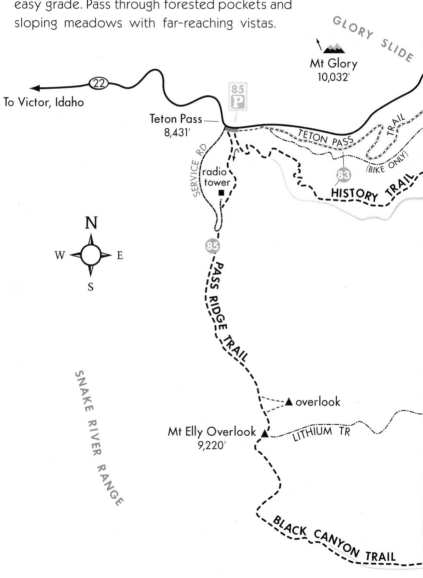

Drop into the lush forest, skirting grassy meadows while slowly winding down to the canyon floor. Follow the canyon bottom, parallel to the stream on the left. Cross the stream and continue down canyon, following the waterway and crossing the creek four more times. Pass the posted Big Rocks Trail, the Lithium Trail, and the History Trail, all on the left. Cross the bridge over Trail Creek, returning to the trailhead.

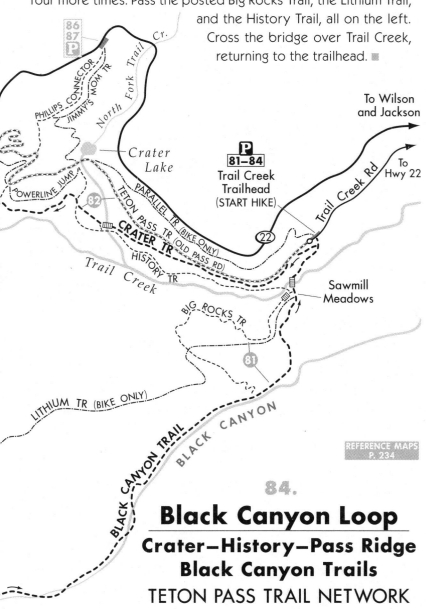

84.
Black Canyon Loop
Crater—History—Pass Ridge
Black Canyon Trails
TETON PASS TRAIL NETWORK

85. Pass Ridge Trail to Mount Elly Overlook

TETON PASS TRAIL NETWORK

Hiking distance: 3.5 miles round trip
Hiking time: 2 hours
Configuration: out-and-back
Elevation gain: 800 feet
Difficulty: moderate
Exposure: mix of open slopes and shaded forest
Dogs: allowed
Maps: U.S.G.S. Teton Pass · Adventure Maps: Jackson Hole
  Beartooth Publishing: Grand Teton National Park map

Teton Pass lies along a divide between two north-south running mountain ranges—the Teton Range to the north and the Snake River Range to the south. The Pass Ridge Trail follows a ridge along the Snake River Range at the head of the Trail Creek drainage. The trail begins atop Teton Pass and climbs the flower-laden ridge to the Mount Elly Overlook at the top of Black Canyon. Along the trail, and from the 9,220-foot overlook, are views of Mount Glory, the Snake River, Jackson Hole, the Gros Ventre Range, and the Snake River Range.

For a longer, 10.5-mile loop hike, continue down into Black Canyon and return on the Old Pass Road—Hike 84.

To the trailhead

From the town square in downtown Jackson, drive 1.4 miles south on Highway 89 to Highway 22. Turn right and drive 5.5 miles to the town of Wilson. Continue 5.6 miles past Wilson to the Teton Pass summit. The trailhead parking area is on the left.

The hike

At the east end of the parking lot is a trail kiosk. From the kiosk, take the posted Pass Ridge Trail south. Head up the hill, traversing the east-facing slope to the radio towers. At the gravel service road, bear left and walk 100 yards to the end of the road. Veer left on the footpath and continue south. Enter an Engelmann spruce and subalpine fir forest. Pass through a series of flower-filled meadows. As the ridge draws near, two side paths head off to the left to overlooks of the valley and Jackson. Continue parallel to the cliffs to the 9,220-foot Mount Elly Overlook at the head of Black Canyon at 2 miles. This is the turn-around point.

To extend the hike, walk 80 yards to the right to the Black Canyon Trail. The trail makes a 4-mile sweep down Black Canyon to the lower trailhead on Trail Creek Road (Hike 84). ■

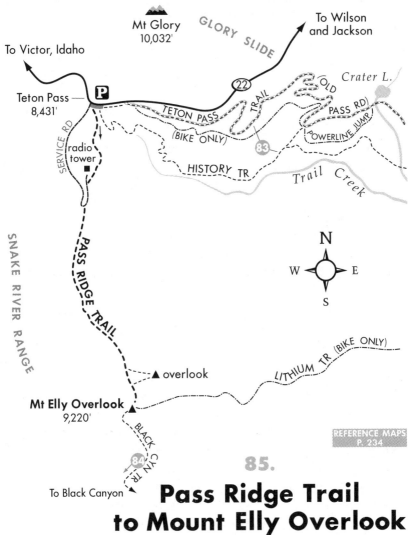

85.
Pass Ridge Trail to Mount Elly Overlook
TETON PASS TRAIL NETWORK

86. Phillips Ridge
TETON PASS TRAIL NETWORK

Hiking distance: 4.4 miles round trip
Hiking time: 2 hours
Configuration: out-and-back with small loop
Elevation gain: 700 feet
Difficulty: easy to moderate
Exposure: forested hillside and open ridge
Dogs: allowed
Maps: U.S.G.S. Rendezvous Peak · Adventure Maps: Jackson Hole

Phillips Ridge lies along the far south end of the Teton Range. The two-mile ridge begins near Teton Pass, west of Jackson, and runs northeast along the southeast wall of Phillips Canyon. The Phillips Ridge Trail follows an unpaved service road through an Engelmann spruce and Douglas fir forest to a fire lookout on the ridge. From the ridge are great views of the valley, the Snake River Range, the Tetons, Rendezvous Peak, and the twin peaks of Mount Glory.

To the trailhead

From the town square in downtown Jackson, drive 1.4 miles south on Highway 89 to Highway 22. Turn right and drive 5.5 miles to the town of Wilson. Continue 4.1 miles past Wilson to the posted Phillips Canyon trailhead on the right side of the road. On the left side is a parking area. Turn left and park.

The hike

Carefully cross the highway to the signed trail and head uphill. Follow the forested road northeast to a signed road fork at 0.4 miles. The left fork, the Phillips Pass Trail, leads to Ski Lake (Hike 87) and Phillips Pass (Hike 80). Stay to the right, continuing up the winding road. For a quarter mile, the road parallels the trail to Ski Lake high above to the left. At one mile, the trail curves right at a Forest Service sign by a buck fence. Disregard the two-track powerline maintenance roads that intersect the main route. A short distance ahead, the road parallels the power lines. At 1.7 miles, the road crosses under the power lines at a road split. At this fork are great views to the west of Mount Glory.

Bear to the right, beginning a loop around the ridge. Head up the ridge through stands of aspens. Short side paths lead to overlooks. Follow the ridge east past a fire lookout at the summit. Continue past the lookout and bear left at a road junction to complete the loop. Return downhill on the same trail. ■

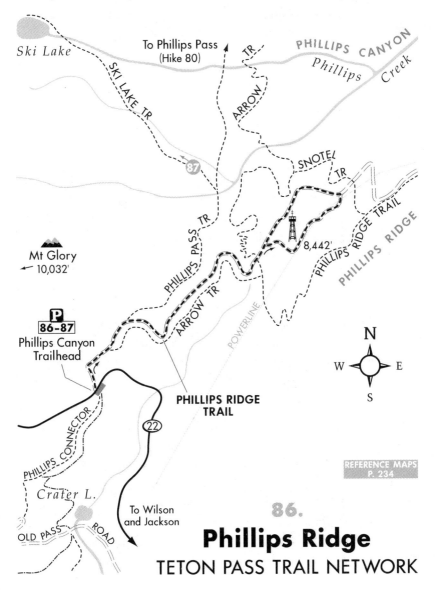

86.
Phillips Ridge
TETON PASS TRAIL NETWORK

87. Phillips Pass Trail to Ski Lake
TETON PASS TRAIL NETWORK

Hiking distance: 4 miles round trip
Hiking time: 2 hours
Configuration: out-and-back
Elevation gain: 900 feet
Difficulty: easy to moderate
Exposure: forested hillside and open meadows
Dogs: allowed
Maps: U.S.G.S. Rendezvous Peak · Adventure Maps: Jackson Hole
   Beartooth Publishing: Grand Teton National Park map

Phillips Canyon lies between Mount Glory and Phillips Ridge near Teton Pass at the far south end of the Teton Range. This hike leads to Ski Lake, a circular, deep blue lake tucked into a mountain cirque on the west end of Phillips Canyon. Along the way, the trail winds through a lodgepole pine forest and an open meadow bursting with wildflowers. Phillips Canyon opens out into this meadow. The trail winds past the canyon, crossing a beautiful stream en route to Ski Lake. From the lake are views of the Gros Ventre Range in the east and the Jackson Hole valley.

To the trailhead

From the town square in downtown Jackson, drive 1.4 miles south on Highway 89 to Highway 22. Turn right and drive 5.5 miles to the town of Wilson. Continue 4.1 miles past Wilson to the posted Phillips Canyon trailhead on the right side of the road. On the left side is a parking area. Turn left and park

The hike

Carefully cross the highway to the signed trail. Hike up the gravel road under a canopy of fir trees for 0.4 miles to a signed junction on the left. There is a Forest Service sign pointing the way to Ski Lake. The trail is a steady, but not steep, uphill climb. At one mile, drop into a beautiful flat meadow with wildflowers and a stream running through it. Continue to a signed trail fork at 1.2 miles. The Phillips Pass Trail continues to the right up to Phillips Pass (Hike 80). Take the left fork beside the creek through the open forest of aspens and fir. Cross the outlet stream of Ski Lake, soon reaching the east shore of the lake. After enjoying the surroundings, retrace the route back to the trailhead. ▪

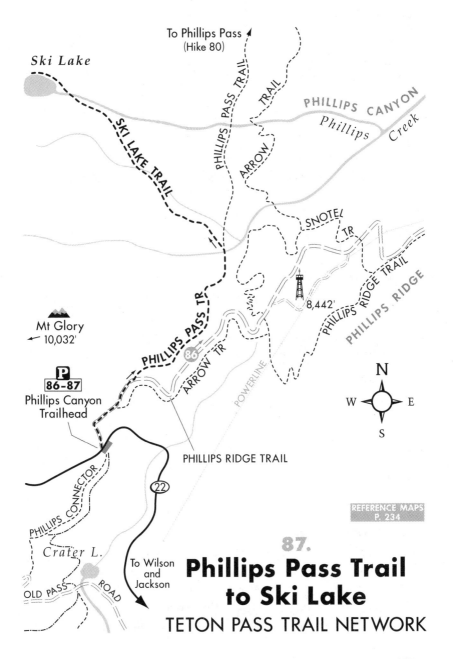

87.
Phillips Pass Trail to Ski Lake
TETON PASS TRAIL NETWORK

88. Coal Creek Trail

Hiking distance: 4.4 miles round trip
Hiking time: 2.5 hours
Configuration: out-and-back
Elevation gain: 700 feet
Difficulty: moderate
Exposure: a mix of shaded forested and exposed meadows
Dogs: allowed
Maps: U.S.G.S. Rendezvous Peak · Adventure Maps: Jackson Hole
Beartooth Publishing: Grand Teton National Park map

The Coal Creek drainage is nestled between Taylor Mountain and Mount Glory in the Jedediah Smith Wilderness. The lightly used Coal Creek Trail parallels the creek along the southern slopes of the Teton Mountains from the Idaho side of Teton Pass. The hike leads through a beautiful backcountry area to Coal Creek Meadows in an open bowl. There is a steady elevation gain all the way to the meadow.

To the trailhead

From the town square in downtown Jackson, drive 1.4 miles south on Highway 89 to Highway 22. Turn right and drive 5.5 miles to the town of Wilson. Continue 8.2 miles past Wilson—over Teton Pass—to the Coal Creek trailhead parking area on the right.

The hike

The trail heads north past the trailhead sign at the mouth of the canyon. Begin hiking through meadows with stands of subalpine fir, and cross a log bridge over Coal Creek. Continue up the draw, entering the Jedediah Smith Wilderness in the shadow of Taylor Mountain. The trail continues along the northwest bank of the cascading creek to another creek crossing at 1.1 mile. After crossing, the trail leaves the creek, curving to the right through an aspen grove on the east slopes. The gradient steepens as the trail curves left, again heading north. Continue uphill to a ridge at 2.2 miles where the trail levels out in Coal Creek Meadows. This tree-lined meadow is the turn-around spot. Return on the same trail.

To hike farther, continue to the north end of the meadow and a junction. The left fork heads west over Taylor Mountain, climbing

1,000 feet in one mile, then drops down to the Moose Creek trailhead. The right fork heads north, climbing to the 9,197-foot Mesquite Creek Divide and Moose Meadows (Hike 89). The trail then follows Mesquite Creek and Moose Creek to the Teton Crest Trail. ▪

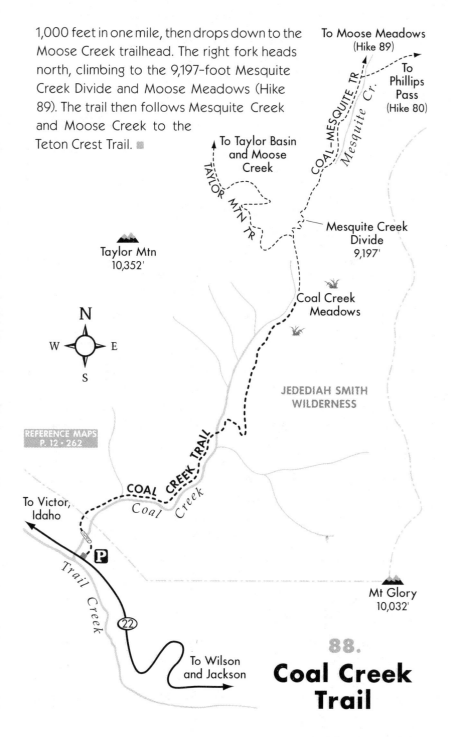

To Moose Meadows
(Hike 89)

To Phillips Pass
(Hike 80)

COAL-MESQUITE TR.

Mesquite Cr.

To Taylor Basin and Moose Creek

TAYLOR MTN TR.

Mesquite Creek Divide
9,197'

Taylor Mtn
10,352'

Coal Creek Meadows

N

W · E

S

JEDEDIAH SMITH WILDERNESS

COAL CREEK TRAIL

REFERENCE MAPS
P. 12 · 262

COAL CREEK TRAIL

Coal Creek

To Victor, Idaho

P

Trail Creek

Mt Glory
10,032'

22

To Wilson and Jackson

88.
Coal Creek Trail

89. Moose Creek Trail to Moose Meadows

JEDEDIAH SMITH WILDERNESS

Hiking distance: 10 miles round trip
Hiking time: 5 to 6 hours
Configuration: out-and-back
Elevation gain: 800 feet
Difficulty: moderate to strenuous
Exposure: forested canyon and exposed hillside and meadows
Dogs: allowed
Maps: U.S.G.S. Victor and Rendezvous Peak
Adventure Maps: Jackson Hole
Beartooth Publishing: Grand Teton, Jackson Hole, Teton Valley

map
page 262

The Jedediah Smith Wilderness encompasses the western slope of the Grand Teton Range, adjacent to Grand Teton National Park. Moose Creek forms on the upper west slope of Rendezvous Mountain within the rugged wilderness. The creek flows ten miles, from Moose Lake through Moose Creek Canyon, where it empties into Trail Creek.

The Moose Creek Trail begins at the mouth of the lush canyon on the Idaho side of Teton Pass. The trail leads into the heart of the Grand Teton Range, connecting with a network of trails. This hike follows the Moose Creek Trail—parallel to the waterway—to Moose Meadows beneath Rendezvous Peak. The high altitude meadow is a wet marshland filled with willows and prolific with wildflowers. The area is prime moose habitat, supporting some of the highest densities of moose in Wyoming. En route, the hike overlooks wetlands and slow-moving water, popular moose feeding grounds. The drainage is also a winter range for elk and mule deer.

To the trailhead

From the town square in downtown Jackson, drive 1.4 miles south on Highway 89 to Highway 22. Turn right and drive 5.5 miles to the town of Wilson. Continue 14 miles past Wilson, crossing over Teton Pass, to the posted Old Jackson Highway on the right. (It is located a quarter mile past the Mike Harris Campground and just after crossing posted Moose Creek.) Turn right on the Old Jackson Highway for 70 yards to a T-junction. Turn left, drive 200 yards, and turn right onto posted Forest Service Road E10800S (also signed for Moose Creek Ranch). Continue 1.4 miles to the trailhead parking area near the end of the road on the right by the information kiosk.

The hike

From the east end of the parking area, head east on the posted trail. Walk along the south (right) side of Moose Creek in a lodgepole pine forest. At 0.3 miles is a Y-fork. The Taylor Mountain Trail veers right and leads up to Taylor Basin and Coal Creek Meadows. Stay left, continuing up Moose Canyon. Gently climb through the mixed forest of firs, pines, and aspens. Follow the south canyon wall and enter the Jedediah Smith Wilderness. Traverse the hillside above Moose Creek, and cross a culvert over Bear Creek at just over one mile. Cross over a series of feeder streams to a junction with a horse crossing. The left fork wades across Moose Creek. Stay to the right and cross a log over a side channel, then cross a wooden bridge over Moose Creek. Follow the north canyon wall, crossing another group of tributary streams. Steadily gain elevation while overlooking the cascading creek and forested canyon. Walk through a flower-filled meadow, then return to the forest. Pass an overlook of a wetland with beaver ponds, which is a great area for spotting moose. Drop down to the meadow and cross a stream. Skirt the north edge of a vast wetland and cross another stream. Bend left and continue through more meadows. Descend to the canyon floor and a posted junction on the southern edge of Moose Meadows at 4.8 miles, where the canyon opens up. This is the turn-around spot.

To extend the hike, the Coal-Mesquite Trail bears right, crossing Moose Creek. The trail leads 2.4 miles, crossing over Mesquite Creek Divide to Coal Creek Meadows (Hike 88). The Moose Creek Trail continues straight ahead, skirting the northwest side of Moose Meadows. It is 1.4 miles to Moose Falls, a two-tier waterfall plunging through a notch in the cliffs, and 2.9 miles to a junction just shy of the Teton Crest Trail. From here, the right fork connects with the Teton Crest Trail and leads into Grand Teton National Park near the head of Granite Canyon (Hike 15). The left fork leads 1.5 miles to Moose Lake, the largest in a group of eight subalpine lakes that lie within a mountain cirque at 9,300 feet. ▦

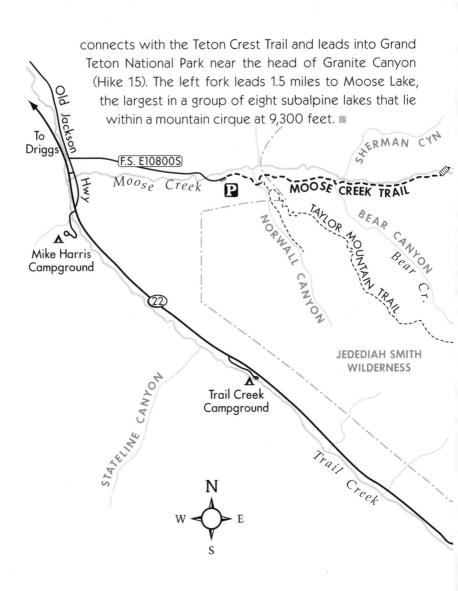

89.

Moose Creek Trail to Moose Meadows
JEDEDIAH SMITH WILDERNESS

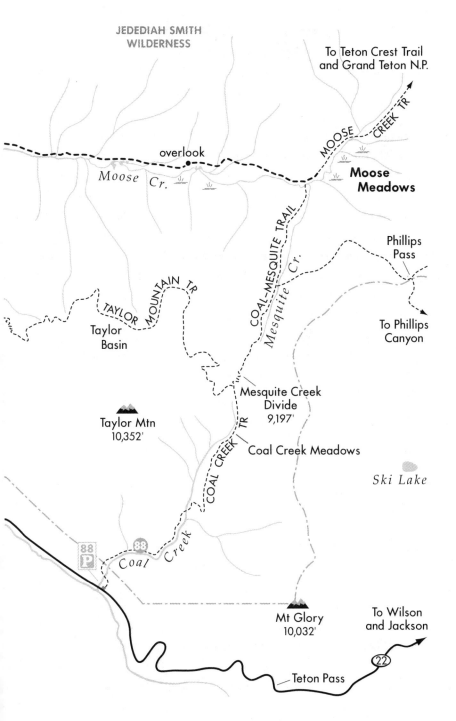

JEDEDIAH SMITH
WILDERNESS

To Teton Crest Trail
and Grand Teton N.P.

overlook

MOOSE CREEK TR

Moose Cr.

Moose
Meadows

COAL-MESQUITE TRAIL

Mesquite Cr.

Phillips
Pass

TAYLOR MOUNTAIN TR

Taylor
Basin

To Phillips
Canyon

Mesquite Creek
Divide
9,197'

Taylor Mtn
10,352'

COAL CREEK TR

Coal Creek Meadows

Ski Lake

88
P

88

Coal Creek

Mt Glory
10,032'

To Wilson
and Jackson

22

Teton Pass

DAY HIKE BOOKS

Day Hikes In Yellowstone National Park ....978-1-57342-048-8...$12.95

Day Hikes In Grand Teton National Park ....978-1-57342-069-3....14.95

Day Hikes In the Beartooth Mountains
Billings to Red Lodge to Yellowstone N.P......978-1-57342-064-8....15.95

Day Hikes Around Bozeman, Montana...........978-1-57342-063-1....15.95

Day Hikes Around Missoula, Montana...........978-1-57342-066-2....15.95

Day Hikes In Sequoia and Kings Canyon N.P. ...978-1-57342-030-3....12.95

Day Hikes In Yosemite National Park ....978-1-57342-059-4 ....13.95

Day Hikes On the California Central Coast ......978-1-57342-058-7.....17.95

Day Hikes On the California Southern Coast ....978-1-57342-045-7 ...14.95

Day Hikes In the Santa Monica Mountains ....978-1-57342-065-5....21.95

Day Hikes Around Sonoma County................978-1-57342-053-2....16.95

Day Hikes Around Napa Valley ....978-1-57342-057-0 ...16.95

Day Hikes Around Monterey and Carmel ....978-1-57342-067-9 ...19.95

Day Hikes Around Big Sur.............................978-1-57342-068-6.....18.95

Day Hikes Around San Luis Obispo................978-1-57342-051-8 ...16.95

Day Hikes Around Santa Barbara ....978-1-57342-060-0 ...17.95

Day Hikes Around Ventura County.................978-1-57342-062-4 ...17.95

Day Hikes Around Los Angeles......................978-1-57342-061-7 ....17.95

Day Hikes Around Orange County ....978-1-57342-047-1....15.95

Day Hikes Around Sedona, Arizona ....978-1-57342-049-5 ...14.95

Day Hikes On Oahu ....978-1-57342-038-9.....11.95

Day Hikes On Maui......................................978-1-57342-039-6.....11.95

Day Hikes On Kauai....................................978-1-57342-040-2 ....11.95

Day Hikes In Hawaii ....978-1-57342-050-1....16.95

These books may be purchased at your local bookstore or outdoor shop. Or, order them direct from the distributor:

The Globe Pequot Press

246 Goose Lane • P.O. Box 480 • Guilford, CT 06437-0480
on the web: www.globe-pequot.com

800-243-0495 DIRECT   **800-820-2329** FAX

DAY HIKES IN
Yellowstone
NATIONAL PARK

82 GREAT HIKES
Robert Stone

DAY HIKES IN
Grand
Teton
NATIONAL PARK

89 GREAT HIKES
Robert Stone

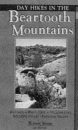

DAY HIKES IN THE
Beartooth
Mountains

Robert Stone

DAY HIKES AROUND
Bozeman
MONTANA

INCLUDING THE GALLATIN
CANYON AND PARADISE VALLEY
Robert Stone

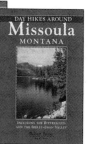

DAY HIKES AROUND
Missoula
MONTANA

INCLUDING THE BITTERROOTS
AND THE SEELEY-SWAN VALLEY
Robert Stone

DAY HIKES IN
Sequoia
&
Kings Canyon
NATIONAL PARKS

Robert Stone

DAY HIKES IN
Yosemite
NATIONAL PARK

80 GREAT HIKES
Robert Stone

DAY HIKES ON THE
California
Central
Coast

125 COASTAL HIKES FROM
SANTA CRUZ TO SANTA BARBARA
Robert Stone

DAY HIKES ON THE
California
Southern
Coast

100 GREAT HIKES
Robert Stone

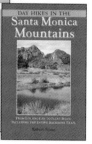

DAY HIKES IN THE
Santa Monica
Mountains

FROM LOS ANGELES TO POINT MUGU
INCLUDING THE ENTIRE BACKBONE TRAIL

DAY HIKES AROUND
Sonoma
County

95 GREAT HIKES
Robert Stone

DAY HIKES AROUND
Napa
Valley

68 GREAT HIKES
Robert Stone

DAY HIKES AROUND
Monterey
& Carmel

128 GREAT HIKES
Robert Stone

DAY HIKES AROUND
Big Sur

99 GREAT HIKES
Robert Stone

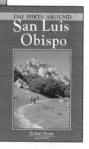

DAY HIKES AROUND
San Luis
Obispo

Robert Stone

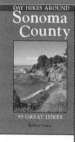

DAY HIKES AROUND
Santa
Barbara

135 GREAT HIKES
Robert Stone

DAY HIKES AROUND
Ventura
County

116 GREAT HIKES
Robert Stone

A LOS ANGELES TIMES BESTSELLER
DAY HIKES AROUND
Los
Angeles

135 GREAT HIKES
Robert Stone

DAY HIKES AROUND
Orange
County

108 GREAT HIKES
Robert Stone

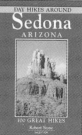

DAY HIKES AROUND
Sedona
ARIZONA

100 GREAT HIKES
Robert Stone

Day Hikes In Yellowstone National Park

Yellowstone National Park is a magnificent area with beautiful, dramatic scenery and incredible hydrothermal features. Within its 2.2-millions acres lies some of the earth's greatest natural treasures.

Day Hikes In Yellowstone National Park includes a thorough cross-section of 82 hikes throughout the park. The guide includes all of the park's most popular hikes as well as a wide assortment of secluded backcountry trails. Highlights include thundering waterfalls, unusual thermal features, expansive meadows, alpine lakes, the Grand Canyon of the Yellowstone, geysers, hot springs, and 360-degree vistas of the park.

184 pages • 82 hikes • 4th Edition 2005 • ISBN 978-1-57342-048-8

Day Hikes In the Beartooth Mountains

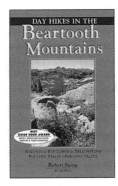

The rugged Beartooth Mountains are Montana's highest mountain range. This beautiful range in the Rocky Mountains rises dramatically from the plains in south-central Montana and stretches to the northern reaches of Yellowstone National Park.

Day Hikes In the Beartooth Mountains includes an extensive collection of hikes within this mountain range and the adjacent foothills and plains. The 123 hikes range from 11,000-foot alpine plateaus to treks along the Yellowstone River as it begins its journey through the arid plains. A wide range of scenery and ecosystems accommodates all levels of hiking, from relaxing creekside strolls to all-day, high-elevation outings. Included are many hikes along the Beartooth Highway and 16 hikes in the Billings area.

336 pages • 123 hikes • 5th Edition 2012 • ISBN 978-1-57342-064-8

INDEX

A

aerial tram, 60, 226, 228

Alaska Basin, 34, 91

Albright Peak, 35

Amphitheater Lake, 70

Antelope Flats, 16, 179

Antelope Peak, 179

A River Runs Through It (movie), 222

Avalanche Canyon, 64

B

Bearpaw Lake, 100

Bechler Meadows, 166

Big Game Winter Range, 218

Big Rocks Trail, 239

Black Canyon, 239, 248

Blacktail Butte, 16, 19

Bradley Lake, 66

Buck Mountain, 36

Buela Lake, 164

C

Cache Creek Canyon, 202

Cache Creek Trailhead, 202

canoeing locations, 100. *See also fishing access*

Cascade Acres, 169

Cascade Canyon, 81, 84, 88, 92, 106

Cascade Creek, 166, 169

Cathedral Group, 10, 92

Cattlemans Bridge, 117

Chapel of the Transfiguration, 22

Christian Pond, 128, 130

Cleft Falls, 73

Climbers' Ranch, 68

Coal Creek, 258

Coal Creek Meadows, 258

Cody Bowl, 226

Colter Bay, 138, 140, 142, 144

Continental Divide, 10

Cottonwood Creek, 68

Craig Thomas Discovery and Visitor Center, 22

Crater Lake, 241, 244, 248

cross-country ski trails, 154, 179, 202, 232, 237, 241

Cunningham Cabin, 172

Curtis Canyon, 193

Curtis Canyon Campground, 193

Curtis Canyon Viewpoint, 190, 193

D

Death Canyon, 31, 34, 37, 91

Death Canyon Shelf, 37

Death Canyon trailhead, 28

Dog Creek, 220

E

Emily's Pond, 232
Emma Matilda Lake, 119, 130
Exum Climbing School, 97

F

Falls River, 164, 166, 169
ferry (replica), 22
fishing access, 110, 117, 146, 177
Five-Way Meadow, 212
Flagg Canyon, 150
Flagg Ranch, 152
Fox Creek Pass, 37

G

Game Creek Trail, 202, 215
Garnet Canyon, 66, 70, 73
Geraldine Lucas, 68
Glacier Gulch, 72, 74
Glade Creek, 156
Glory Slide, 241
Goodwin Lake, 195
Grand Teton, 73, 84, 88
Grand Teton National Park, 10
Grand View Point, 123, 132
Granite Canyon, 44, 60, 228, 262
Granite Falls, 222
Granite Hot Springs, 222
Grassy Lake, 161, 164, 166
Grassy Lake Road, 152

Green River Lookout, 227

Green River Lookout, 227
Grizzly Lake, 187
Gros Ventre Campground, 18
Gros Ventre River, 182
Gros Ventre Slide Interpretive Trail, 182

H

Hagen Highway, 207
Hagen Trail, 207, 209
Hermitage Point, 144
Heron Pond, 142
Hidden Falls, 80, 81
historic sites, 22, 134, 172, 244
Holly Lake, 102, 107
Horsetail Creek, 184
hot springs, 154, 222
Housetop Mountain, 61
Huckleberry Hot Springs, 154
Huckleberry Point, 52
Hurricane Pass, 88

I

Inspiration Point, 81
interpretive trails, 134, 172, 182

J

Jackson (map of town), 212
Jackson Hole, 10
Jackson Hole Ski Area, 225, 226, 228

Jackson Lake, 109, 112, 140, 142, 144, 146

Jackson Lake Lodge, 116, 134, 136, 138

Jackson Peak, 195, 198

Jackson Point Overlook, 114

Jedediah Smith Wilderness, 37, 237, 258, 260

Jenny Lake, 76, 78, 81, 84, 88, 92

Jenny Lake access roads, 103

Jenny Lake boat shuttle, 81

Jenny Lake Loop, 78

John D. Rockefeller Jr. Memorial Parkway, 148, 150

JY Ranch, 54

L

Lakeshore Trail, 140

Lake Solitude, 92

landslide, 182

Laurance S. Rockefeller Preserve, 48, 51, 54, 57

Lavender Hills, 184, 187

Leigh Canyon, 106

Leigh Lake, 76, 100

Lookout Rock, 122, 130

Lower Slide Lake, 182, 184

Lunch Tree Hill, 134

Lupine Meadows, 70, 73, 96

Lupine Meadows trailhead, 70

M

Marion Lake, 60, 229

Menor's Ferry, 22

Mesquite Creek Divide, 259

Middle Teton, 73, 88

Mike Harris Campground, 262

Moose Creek, 260

Moose Falls, 261

moose habitat, 24, 32, 96, 117, 136, 138, 142, 159, 177, 220, 232, 260

Moose Meadows, 260

Moose Ponds, 96

Mormon Row, 16

Mountain Ash Creek, 166

Mount Elly Overlook, 248, 252

Mount Glory, 241

Mount Hunt, 44

Mount Hunt Divide, 44

Mount Meek, 37

Mount St. John, 82

Mount Woodring, 102

museums, 22. *See also visitor centers*

N

National Elk Refuge, 16, 190

Noble Cabin, 22

O

Old Pass Road. *See Teton Pass Trail*

Open Canyon, 41, 44, 60

Open Canyon Creek bridge, 41, 44

Oxbow Bend, 117

P

Pacific Creek, 124

Pacific Creek Road, 119, 126

Paintbrush Canyon, 102, 106

Paintbrush Divide, 93, 106

park headquarters, 22

Pass Ridge Trail, 252

Phelps Lake, 26, 28, 51

Phelps Lake Overlook, 28

Phillips Canyon, 236, 256

Phillips Pass, 236

Phillips Ridge, 254

Pilgrim Creek, 136

Polecat Creek, 152

Powerline Jump Trail, 249

R

Reclamation Road, 156

Red Hills, 187

Rendezvous Mountain, 60, 226, 228

rock climbing locations, 16, 73

Rockefeller Parkway. *See John D. Rockefeller Jr. Memorial Parkway*

Rockefeller Preserve. *See Laurance S. Rockefeller Preserve*

Rockefeller Preserve Center, 48

Rock Springs, 226

S

Sargents Bay, 146

Sawmill Ponds, 24

Schoolroom Glacier, 88

Schwabacher's Landing, 177

Second Creek, 136

Shadow Mountain, 179

Sheep Creek Canyon, 190, 198

Signal Mountain, 114

Signal Mountain Lodge, 114

Ski Lake, 256

Skillet Glacier, 140

Snake River, 110, 117, 150, 177, 218, 232

Snake River Fisherman's Trail, 110

Snake River Northeast Dike, 232

Snowdrift Lake, 91

Snow King Mountain, 202, 207, 209, 212

Snow King Trail Network, 201, 202

South Boundary Lake, 158, 161

South Boundary Trail, 158, 161

South Jenny Lake trailhead, 78

South Landing, 112

South Park, 218

Spalding Falls, 73

Static Peak, 35

Static Peak Divide, 34

String Lake, 98, 106

Surprise Lake, 70

Swan Lake, 142

swimming areas, 98, 100

T

Table Mountain, 89

Taggart Lake, 64, 66

Tanager Lake, 159

Taylor Mountain, 258

Tepee Pillar, 73

Terraced Falls, 169

Teton Crest Trail, 37, 60, 91, 229, 259, 261

Teton Glacier, 72

Teton Pass, 244, 248, 252

Teton Pass Trail, 241, 244

Teton Pass Trail Network, 235, 236

Teton Range, 10

Teton Village, 225

Toppings Lakes, 174

Trail Creek, 241, 244, 248

Trail Creek Campground, 262

Two Ocean Lake, 123, 132

Two Ocean Plateau, 124

U

Union Falls, 166

V

Valhalla Canyon, 85, 89, 93

visitor centers, 22, 48, 78, 134, 152

W

The Wall, 88

waterfalls, 73, 80, 169, 222, 261

Whetstone Creek, 126

The Wigwams, 93

wildlife observation, 16, 24, 96, 117, 124, 128, 136, 138, 142, 152, 159, 177, 218

Willow Flats, 136, 138

Wilson, 235

Wilson Canyon, 212

Woods Canyon, 205

Y

Yellowstone south entrance, 158

LINDA STONE

About the Author

Since 1991, Robert Stone has been writer, photographer, and publisher of Day Hike Books. He is a Los Angeles Times Best Selling Author and an award-winning journalist of Rocky Mountain Outdoor Writers and Photographers, the Outdoor Writers Association of California, the Northwest Outdoor Writers Association, the Outdoor Writers Association of America, and the Bay Area Travel Writers.

Robert has hiked every trail in the Day Hike Book series. With 24 hiking guides in the series, many in their fourth and fifth editions, he has hiked thousands of miles of trails throughout the western United States and Hawaii. When Robert is not hiking, he researches, writes, and maps the hikes before returning to the trails. He spends summers in the Rocky Mountains of Montana and winters on the California Central Coast.